S   ERS

91

Rethinking development

By the same author

Theories of development
New trends in development
Making sense of development

Rethinking development: essays on development and Southeast Asia

P. W. Preston

An Excellent wk, A must! Esp. for ch. 3 onward

1987

Routledge & Kegan Paul

London and New York

First published in 1987 by
Routledge & Kegan Paul Ltd
11 New Fetter Lane, London EC4P 4EE

Published in the USA by
Routledge & Kegan Paul Inc.
in association with Methuen Inc.
29 West 35th Street, New York, NY 10001

Set in 11 on 12 point Ehrhardt
by Pentacor Ltd., High Wycombe, Bucks
and printed in Great Britain
by Richard Clay Ltd., Bungay, Suffolk

Library of Congress Cataloging in Publication Data

Preston, P.W. (Peter Wallace), 1949–
    Rethinking development.

    Bibliography:p.
    Includes index.
    1, Asia, Southeastern-Economic policy. 2. Asia,
Southeastern-Social policy. I. Title.
HC441.P.75 1987 338.959 87–4905

British Library CIP Data also available

ISBN 0–7102–1263–1

Contents

Acknowledgments   vii

Introduction   ix

1 Rethinking development   1

2 The rediscovery of the rationalist tradition   30

3 Boeke and Furnivall's 'Southeast Asian sociology'   82

4 Arguing on behalf of scholarship: Barrington Moore   100

5 Arguing on behalf of 'the planners': Chen, Fisk and Higgins   111

6 A. G. Frank: the mode of engagement of the 'political writer'   129

7 Analysing dependent capitalist development: the Asian NICs   155

8 Constructing nation-states in Southeast Asia   178

   Notes   225

   Bibliography   252

   Index   259

Newton saw an apple fall and deduced gravitation. You and I might have seen millions of apples fall and only deduced pig feeding.

Admiral of the Fleet Lord Fisher, O.M., letter to *The Times* 12 January 1920.

Acknowledgments

This set of essays, which continues earlier work itself flowing from my PhD research, was begun during my time at the National University of Singapore and completed whilst I was at the Cooperative College at Stanford Hall in the UK. My thanks to my colleagues and students of both institutions.

Introduction

In a recent text[1] I suggested that it would be fruitful to consider the exchange between problems of social theory and matters of development theory and I argued that both areas of intellectual/practical enquiry could be reinterpreted by invoking a 'dis-integrated' notion of social theorizing. By this I meant that social theorizing was best seen as a fairly diverse set of ways of making sense of the world – a series of discrete and particular modes of social theoretic engagement. This diversity I proposed be ordered around the concerns of the 'classic' tradition of social theory – intellectually broad, value-based, attempts to render given sets of historical circumstances clear. I spoke of all social theorizing as being, in the end, practical; aiming to produce circumstances sensitive and problem-specific understanding. The present text follows this general orientation and addresses a series of points in respect of development theorizing and Southeast Asia. It is my intention both to illustrate my claims about the diversity of modes of social theoretic engagement by looking at a series of particular strategies of interpreting Southeast Asian development and to advance, a little way, understanding of the wider theoretical issues generated by this 'dis-integrated' conception of social theory.

The text is ordered around a series of issues and these fall roughly into three groups. Thus the essays of the first group offer surveys of, respectively, post-Second World War development theory and current debates about the nature of social theory. The second group of essays comprises more formal discussions of specific ways of doing social theory. And the final set offers two substantive discussions of problems of analysing Southeast Asia. The essays comprise an interrelated set drawing upon a common set of assumptions. It might be helpful if I drew attention to the 'gross assumptions' underlying this text before going on to review in a little more detail the substance of the various essays.

So, first, this book is concerned with 'theory', yet does not attend in any very great detail to the material of the philosophy of science/ social science. The apparent lacuna is easily explained. The debates of the philosophy of science/social science both carry a heavy burden of 'receives positions' and rather tend to the abstract and general. This is not improper of course, as philosophers have their own tasks. Related, closely in recent years it seems, is the disposition amongst philosophically sophisticated social scientists to an inappropriately distanced practicality – to what has been called 'theoreticism'. I hope that by eschewing any very direct engagement with the philosophy of science/social science I will be able to re-present not only the crucial issue of the practicality of social theoretic engagement but also the variety of modes of engagement available. My discussion in chapter 2 of the philosophy of social science is a general 'reminder' of its nature and importance rather than an attempt at detailed work.

My second gross assumption relates to the position of development studies in relation to the wider group of social sciences generally and sociology in particular. Indeed this assumption is more of an, as yet unwritten, manifesto in regard to my estimation of the importance of development studies for sociology. Thus I take the view that the emergence of development studies from its technical social scientific ghetto and movement back into the mainstream of the 'classical tradition' of social theorizing (Marx, Weber, and Durkheim) is now increasingly clear and appropriate. I pursue this matter in chapter 1.

Thirdly, and closely related to my first point, there is my resolute rejection of discussions of natural science as starting points for considering the nature of the social sciences. The familiar supposition – or insistence – by the orthodox that social science must be modelled upon natural science (as it is ordinarily and arguably wrongly understood both in society generally and within the community of social scientists) simply strikes me as utterly foolish: indeed that this claim is still advanced seems to me to be an interesting social scientific problem in itself. To be clear about this I would add that I am content to grant that natural science is the jewel in the crown of our Western European civilization – and thus warrants all the attention that scholarship lavishes upon it – but nonetheless I would insist that there are other jewels in this same crown, and that these (including social science) warrant attention in their own right. So, in sum, I consider it right and proper to consider directly just what has been produced under the general heading of 'social science' and to work from that report to a detailed elucidation of its intellectual and social character.

The body of this text opens with two survey pieces of which the first endeavours to capture the broad pattern of post-Second World War debate in respect of 'development' and relate this to similar discussions about social theorizing *per se*. It seems to me that we can read this career of development studies in a variety of ways. The orthodox (and in a somewhat different way the marxists) have pursued the project of an autonomous disciplinary status for development studies, but I think that this project has failed. My own position embraces two characterizations: the material produced can best be seen as a series of discrete efforts of theorizing; the post-war career I survey by offering a series of sociology-of-knowledge analyses of these 'theories'. More generally, as I have noted, this career can be seen to involve a progressive broadening of attention and deepening of intellectual reflection as the initial narrow technical ghetto of 'growth theory' was left behind. Development studies, I would argue, is now back in the mainstream, which in turn is poised for a shift back into social philosophy. The body of work of forty years or so is of interest insofar as the ideas of earlier generations impinge upon our common sense: I characterize this residue of assumptions around the motif of the assumption of responsibility by optimistic and decent First Worlders for the development of the Third World. In place of this outmoded paternalistic view I propose that students of development attend to the diversity of interests in matters of development.

In the second chapter there is a related survey which attempts both to bridge the gap between, on the one hand, theorists, and practitioners of development and, on the other, the philosophically sophisticated students of social theory and to sketch in the intellectual backdrop of my own notions of social theorizing as diverse, practical and value-based. Using the now-familiar triune formula I review the contributions of the empiricist tradition, the interpretive tradition, and the recently represented critical tradition. The overall movement I take to amount to a rediscovery of the rationalist tradition and this offers the context for my own ideas in respect of the nature of social theorizing.

Moving on from these surveys I present a series of illustrative analyses of particular modes of social theoretic engagement. It seems to me that there is a whole range of ways of actually doing social theory, indeed increasingly I prefer to speak of social theorizing (with its connotation of activity-in-process) rather than social theory (which in comparison has connotations of static reportage – a body of ideas to be cumulatively added to and refined).

In the third essay I look at the suggestion, made by Evers,[2] that the work of Boeke and Furnivall, on respectively dual and plural societies, represents a distinctively Southeast Asian contribution to sociology and thence to development theory. I rather think that Evers's views on the centrality for sociology (and social science) of the problems of change typically addressed by development specialists are close to mine. However, it seems to me to be misleading and wrong to read the work of Boeke and Furnivall in this fashion. If we grant my notion of diverse modes of engagement then we can characterize the work of these two notable thinkers as exemplifying the mode of social theoretic engagement of the colonial administrator-scholar. I think that there is much of interest to discover both from the work of Boeke and Furnivall and in respect of this quite particular way of doing social theory, but I cannot see how their work, or this role, can be taken as the basis for a distinctively Southeast Asian contribution. Evers raises a thoroughly interesting question, but does not advance very far towards a plausible answer.

Following this and by way of a simple reminder of the power of humanistic critical scholarship, I offer a brief discussion of the work of Barrington Moore, in particular his justly famous *Social Origins*. I pursue two matters here: firstly the context and style of his work; and, secondly, the contribution made by the 'revisionist modernisers'.[3] In respect of the first point I note that Moore's 'message' proved to be both un-ignorable, as he actually believed strongly in the virtues of liberal democratic societies and unpalatable in that he stressed the role of violence in establishing these societies. Additionally, at a time of complacent celebration of all things American, he was critical of that society.

Moving on to the second issue, we find in Moore an essentially orthodox reading of the transition to the modern world insofar as it relies on the evolutionist schemes propounded by the more usual (and much less interesting) modernization theorists. Around the issue of evolutionist approaches are ranged a series of, probably familiar, criticisms; in particular, Moore's uncritical regard for the politico-social model of the UK, and his neglect of the broad spread of post-Second World War new nation-states that have been the usual focus of attention for students of development.

In chapter 5 I return to what for me is a familiar issue: the nature of the orthodoxy in social science. Here I consider the habit amongst the orthodox of arguing on behalf of the planners. The interventionist mode of engagement of the post-war orthodox has presented itself in a variety of related guises where all take as a common starting point the pursuit of a knowledge of the social, analogous to that which is evident in the sphere of the natural sciences, that is, technical manipulative knowledge. This goal is clearly wholly laudable – and routinely and impressively attained – in the realm of the natural sciences, but when presented in the sphere of the social it leads to a range of essentially manipulative social theoretic practices. Thus we find social theorists assuming the stance of neutral reporters on how things happen to be in the social world when, as a matter of both simple report and philosophical elucidation, *all* social theoretic enterprises are value-laden. Treating people or groups as things strikes me as wrong both in procedure and ethics. Equally familiar are the roles of policy scientist and, most routine of all, the expert. In the present essay I look to another strategy of manipulative engagement, that of arguing on behalf of the planners. It takes a variety of guises: thus my first example, Chen, uses the 'planner' as a kind of epistemological precept and thereby generates a picture of Singaporean society that is, in my view, so resolutely uncritical as to come close to an apologia for the PAP. Chen's analysis is contrasted with that of two other, explicitly critical, local scholars in order to secure my point about the deformation, or partial nature, of enquiry attendant upon arguing on behalf of the planners.

Following my discussion of Chen's work, I offer two more, rather knockabout, discussions of Western experts. The one offers a series of approving remarks and exhortation to Malaysian planners, whilst the other offers a splendidly foolish apology for some recent failures of planning in that same country: thus the writer in question argues from planning failure to the necessity of *more* power being given to these self-same planners! By way of a concluding note, I suggest that what must be done is to disentangle the threads of social science and policy science, especially in development studies and, thereafter, specify precisely what planning interventions are aimed at achieving because here it is crucial that action be governed by reasonable expectations.

Finally, in this second group of essays I consider the mode of engagement of the political writer and take as my example a theorist usually associated with Latin American matters, that is, A.G. Frank. Here I argue, in sharp contrast to the presently fashionable view of Frank's work as defective by virtue of its polemical content, that if read as that of a political writer his work can readily be seen to be coherent, legitimate and powerful. In order to buttress this claim, I compare his work with that of George Orwell, Noam Chomsky and Peter Worsley. From Orwell I take a series of points in respect of the overall structure of political writing; from Chomsky I take a clue as to the particular style of Frank's writing; and with Peter Worsley I point up the continuities (and discontinuities) of political writing and critically engaged scholarship. Again what I am doing here is urging that social scientific commentary grant the diversity of available modes of social theoretic engagement; in Frank's case this rescues him, so far as I can see, from his usual fate of dismissal by misrepresentation.

The final group of essays in this text offer more substantive discussions of issues relevant to the analysis of development in Southeast Asia. The first of these deals with recent debates in respect of the implications for dependency/neo-marxism of dependent capitalist development in the Asian NICs. In general I argue that the rise of these NICs does not entail the abandonment of recently formulated dependency/neo-marxian work and relatedly, that the material necessary for the presentation of a more intellectually rigorous marxian acount of these phenomena already exists. The first point I pursue via a review of three relevant areas of recent debate: the modernization versus dependency argument in which the former group have claimed the NICs as evidence that the latter were just plain wrong, where I take the view that the problem of this discussion is the confusion of matters of the deployment of delimited-formal ideologies with technical issues; the impossibilism versus inevitabilism debate which is peculiarly fruitless in that both parties are dogged by the mistaken ideal of a perfectly enunciated 'general theory' – it's a wrongheaded commitment;[4] and finally, reformulation and regressive reformulation where the former is an appropriate response and the latter merely a collapse into a policy scientific scheme of dissenting economics. Moving on from this, to my second point, I offer a simple rehearsal of the character of the Asian NICs and suggest that a rigorous marxist analysis, focusing on the key role of the state in these polities, is in process of construction.

In the final essay I turn to the business of the pursuit, by replacement elites, in the wake of the dissolution of formal colonial empires in Southeast Asia, of effective nation-statehood. Ordered around the imputed concern of replacement elites for the establishment, in their sphere of control, of coherence, stability and progress (that is, effective nation-statehood), I look at the issues of firstly, the rise of the very idea of nation-statehood; secondly, Southeast Asian nationalism in pursuit of independence; and, thirdly, the post-independence nationalism aiming at an effective nation-statehood. All of which, with its characterization of the very particular situation of post-colonial 'new nation-states', I take to be a useful comparative perspective to the injunction of the previous essay that we pay attention to the role of the state in securing development: it is clear from this material that the searches for coherence and stability are at least as difficult as the pursuit of development, and by drawing attention to them we can better understand the overall behaviour of post-colonial replacement elites rather than regarding them, as has rather tended to be the case, on the left, as mere puppets of world capitalism or, on the right, as incompetent. By extension, or course, we can enquire more plausibly into the internal dynamics of these 'new nations': neither incompetence nor capitalistic exploitation are the whole of the story.

This, then, comprises the substance of the various and related essays in this text. It is only by attending, in some ordered fashion, to both the diversity of interests which groups might have in the matter of development and to the analogous, but more fundamental, diversity of modes of social theoretic engagement that students of development can move forward from the present situation of confusion and doubt. Similarly, it seems to me, discussions of the nature of social theorizing *per se* could well benefit from looking at the complex debates of post-Second World War development studies as these arguments recall, in my view, in all their intellectual richness, the work of the 'founding fathers' of social scientific enquiry.

1   Rethinking development

1   Introduction

In this essay I will offer an overview of the present status of work on matters of development.[1] This is no simple task because, in addition to familiar problems of survey and evaluation, there are two areas of growing doubt to be taken into account. Confidence in the analytical machineries of development studies is low and there is widespread unease in respect of the precise intellectual status of social theorizing *per se*. It seems to me that there are two complexly interwoven processes of reconsideration in train: *we are rethinking development as we rethink social theorizing.*[2]

This essay aims to contribute to this reworking by attempting to clarify matters in three related areas: the nature of social theorizing *per se*; the character of the post-Second World War career of development studies; and the nature of the 'residual common sense' of studies of development. Given the scope of this task, my remarks should be understood as tentative.[3] I will begin by introducing my theme of 'rethinking' and then look at the three issues noted.

2   Appropriating the past of development studies

Over the last forty years,[4] students of matters of development have produced a very large amount of material: 'development' has been one of the major concerns of governments, international agencies and social scientists. This being so, the presentation of a synthetic survey will, inevitably, involve a large measure of simplification. This is acceptable: we appropriate the past in order to make sense of the present and set tentative agendas for the future. I am going to propose that development studies is presently undertaking a significant 'rethinking' and as a route into the issues raised by this view I will identify three ways of 'appropriating' the past of development studies. I will speak of three – not mutually exclusive – motifs within that history: the attempt to constitute an autonomous discipline; the construction of a series of ideologies; and finally, a progressive movement away from a technical 'ghetto' back into the 'mainstream' of the concerns of social science. I will focus here on the first three readings as it captures, fairly directly, the ethos of the 'intelligent orthodox'. The other readings represent what I think *did happen* and *is happening*.

I have argued elsewhere[5] that the post-Second World War period has seen the attempt to constitute an autonomous discipline of development studies. Autonomous in the intra-social sense of being one distinct social science amongst others; and autonomous in the extra-social sense of the study having its own external object and methods of enquiry appropriate thereto. This, clearly, is a strategy of conceptualization which is informed by the 'received model' of natural scientific explanation – and there are direct links to practical engagement which can now be noted with the familiar term 'policy science'.[6] I further argued that this attempt to constitute an autonomous discipline was identifiable in growth theory and modern-ization theory, where matters of development were conceived (variously) as an extension of positive economic science. I then went on to claim that it was with neo-institutional work, and some dependency work (in particular, 'early' Furtado) that claims to autonomous status were most forcefully and persuasively made. In neo-marxian work – and in the products of some of its 'left' critics – there is an analogous concern: the unreflexive celebration of the idea of 'the one revolutionary mode' and, further, a residually scientistic analytical approach.[7] However this, clearly, is a point that cannot be pressed too far and when I speak of the attempt to constitute an autonomous discipline it will be the orthodox theorists I have in mind.

The attempt to constitute an autonomous discipline of develop-ment studies failed for two general sets of reasons.

The first was the project's own inherent implausibility: the attempt (made by academic theorists, technical experts in government and international agencies, plus a host of miscellaneous commentators) authoritatively to characterize the major elements of the process of transition to the modern world and to lay claim to particular, technical manipulative, expertise in respect of these identified elements was doomed to failure, it seems to me, from the outset. The overall problem area was both too complex and of interest to too many diversely located groups for it to be amenable to the process of reduction of attention and focusing of enquiry which must be necessary to the constitution of a 'discipline'. Failure was built into the project design.

A second area of explanation for this failure is to be found in the success that repeated enquiry had in occasioning refinement of argument. From the narrowly economics-based work of the 'committee of experts'[8] in 1951 there was refinement of argument, in concert with extensive practical experience, along two axes. Firstly we can identify a fairly obvious *spread* of enquiry. The work of a wide range of social sciences was called upon in the efforts to theorize development. Secondly there was a process of increasing *depth* of enquiry. By this I do not mean it was the refinement of technical detail but rather the increasing reflexivity of enquiry that was important.

And when we put together this dual process of refinement, it seems to me, the pattern of concerns which are revealed present us with a second synthetic motif. The career of development studies entails a progressive shift from a narrowly technical enquiry detached from the concerns of the mainstream of the social scientific tradition back into that mainstream. Indeed this motif recalls the claim I have associated with Gellner: the issue of development recalls the work of the 'founding fathers' in terms of the breadth of scope, complexity of elements, and demanding urgency of the problems addressed.[9] The matters which students of 'development' now typically address are those of widespread and pervasive social change and the extent to which it can be comprehended and its direction made subject to human will. The self-consciousness of students of development now coincides with that of other social scientists: it revolves around the continuing effort to render the nature of social theorizing clear. In slightly over three decades the project first enunciated by the 'committee of experts', as a technical matter, has reached a point of being poised to crumble back into social philosophy. The question thus arises: where does all this leave the community of (academic) students of development and the problems they have typically addressed?

At the outset it can be said that it does *not* leave them with a crisis and it is not my intention in this essay to offer any such declamatory announcement. There are two reasons for eschewing such a course of action of which the first is stylistic. More importantly I do not think that a notion of crisis fits into a plausible metatheory of social theorizing. The business of social theorizing presents itself in diverse guises. The generic notion of 'making sense' has to be unpacked in a variety of historical/social/economic/political locations and this view holds for development studies. The range of interests in matters of development is very broad – to speak of a general crisis would be absurd. To speak of a series of crises would be both theatrical and false. Rather I would speak of a *diffuse pattern of re-consideration*. Thus, out of the range of modes of engagement with matters of development I think we can now pick out some impulses to reconsider, in the 'depth' noted above, the familiar assumptions of development studies. These impulses are evidenced in academic commentary – though the extent of reconsideration may, of course, be much broader.

The post-war career of development studies can be read in several ways. I have made reference to the attempt to constitute an autonomous discipline – a project which failed and has issued in a disposition to a thoroughgoing reconsideration. I have also spoken of a shift back towards the social scientific 'mainstream'. I want now to introduce a major motif. This will serve as a corrective to any reading of the post-war career of development studies which is inclined to draw upon the 'received model' and thus be encouraged to look for a spurious coherence. Thus it seems to me that this career can much more plausibly be analysed in terms of the construction of a series of 'schools'. I would argue that it is both possible and useful to identify five such schools. These five schools – which I shall be discussing in section four – can be identified via a fairly simple sociology of knowledge reading of the post-war career of development studies. Each represents a particular exchange between theoretical traditions and practical demands (that is: economic, social and political 'problems'). I think this approach to the history of forty years' work is much preferable to the more usual 'typologies'. Each 'school' is clearly revealed as an exercise in 'ideology construction' – which view I will explain in section three.

My purpose in section five will be to discover whether the subsequent 'decay' of these particular schools has generated any legacy of widely accepted ideas – a *residual common sense* of development studies. If we can identify such a residuum we can then go on to ask whether it is a help or a hinderance to the 'rethinking' process which I have suggested is now taking place.

3   Social theorizing: the construction, critique and comparative ranking of ideologies

Having now presented a simple schema whereby we can 'appropriate' the past of development studies so as to open up the issue of 'rethinking', I want now to turn to the particular business of rethinking social theorizing *per se*. Over recent years there has been much work done on this matter and my remarks here are designed to introduce both my thoughts and the 'line of enquiry' I find most plausible.[10]

The decline and, indeed, eclipse of the dominant post-war orthodoxy has the effect, so far as I am concerned, of freeing us to consider directly the questions of what social theorists have been doing and might, in the future, usefully do.

If we simply look at what has been proposed as 'social theory', then it is clear that we confront no single 'object'; rather we find, to borrow an over-worked metaphor from Wittgenstein, a *family* of activities. This 'insight' is easily gleaned from reviewing either the history of social theorizing generally or the post-war career of development studies. There is, so far as I can presently see, no reason, or intellectual profit to be gained from attempting, to squash this diversity into single mould.[11] Social theorizing encompasses a multiplicity of strategies of making sense of the social world: unity and diversity. A general label might be useful – I am affirming a 'disintegrated' view of social theorizing. The substance of such a view can be *sketched* by offering a characterization of two views of the nature of social theorizing organized around my particular concern with *making sense*. Thus I will distinguish, for my present introductory purposes, between social scientists who adopt some sort of 'naturalist-descriptive' stance, on the one hand, and on the other those who adopt some sort of 'reflexive stance'.[12]

To cast the matter of my interest in social science at a very general level I would say that my concern is with how actors, collectively, make sense of the social world. Now, clearly, the orthodox 'naturalist-descriptive' theorist could also affirm this as their most general interest. It would be understood as the natural science-referring description of structure: Bauman's 'Durksonian' social science.[13] For the orthodox theorists the way in which actors make sense, and the way in which this can be social scientifically appropriated, is conceived in an essentially passive fashion. Thus social science gives a report on how sense has been made, how the world has been patterned: the social world is a reality *sui generis*. Social scientific enquiry is also, itself, cast in passive form: the provision of value-neutral reports on how things are – how the world has been patterned.

The alternative approach is to see the business of making sense as essentially an active process and enquiry itself as active. The given is the process of structuration[14] – the (re)creation of the patterned social world in and through patterned human action. This alternative, 'reflexive' approach also denies the appropriateness of the invocation of natural science made by the orthodox. A passive engagement with the material of enquiry is seen to be unpersuasively and arbitrarily restricted. Thus the alternative seeks to lodge reflexively the community of social scientists (as one group amongst many) within a society which is conceived as an interplay of processes.[15]

It is this second noted scheme which I find the more convincing. I use this general conception within a restricted context: thus my interest in making centres on those (more or less) deliberate or self-conscious efforts at what would ordinarily be recognized as social science-type theorizing. So the paradigm case of my interest is the production of ideologies. Here we find the matter of the effective contribution to structuration of actively produced ideas about structures. Thus the key term for the subsequent discussion and for my own views about the nature of social theorizing – how it is to be characterized, how it embeds in the social world, how it differs from natural science – is ideology.[16]

For the orthodox social scientist the production of knowledge is, essentially, a matter of *reporting how things are*, and problems cluster around *accuracy of reports*. The notions of science and ideology are resolutely divorced and ideology is seen as the repository for all the error to which social science is prey if ever it becomes embroiled in matter of values.

The contrary, 'reflexive', approach takes the production of social scientific knowledge to be less a matter of mimicking the supposed procedures of natural science (i.e. affirming the 'received model') and much more a matter of the construction of argument. And if social science is taken to revolve around argument construction then it is not possible to regard the history of social science as involving the production of ever-improving techniques for the description of an external given reality. It is, on the contrary, a history of particularly located efforts of argument construction. Any progressivity in theorizing will be revealed in the ways in which arguments, appropriate to their circumstances, are constructed. The social scientific (and thus general) measure of progressivity must centre upon the skill with which arguments are crafted so as to uncover the truth. The multiplicity of pragmatic concerns which variously located social actors might have are measured internally and thereafter to the measure central to social science.[17] The concerns, in respect of propriety of explanation, which are typical of this line of thought centre upon the matters of appropriate premises, theoretical frameworks, the role of valuation and the rational judgment of competing claims: upon, that is, the business of the *construction, criticism and comparative ranking* of ideological schemes.[18]

The view of social theorizing, and social science, which I have been adumbrating runs counter to the post-war orthodoxy of social science. I have noted above that there are reasons for seeing this orthodoxy as in decline. However, there are residual elements of that orthodoxy (and the orthodoxy of development studies) which remain powerful. Thus it seems to me that the common-sense image of natural scientific explanation, affirmed as *the* model of a useful and true explanation occasions, quite routinely, a great deal of confusion in social theorizing.

The notion of the 'received model' has been used by Giddens[19] to designate a particular conception of scientific enquiry around which a series of other views cluster as that model is deployed in the context of social scientific concern. In its narrow sense it is a (philosophically unsatisfactory) view about natural science; in its wider sense it becomes an approach to social science. The image of natural scientific explanation and the presumption of the cognitive superiority of that mode of thought can be found both in 'lay' thought, or common sense ordinarily understood, and in the common sense of social science. Consequently, to cast social theorizing in terms of 'discovering how things are in fact', as the orthodox do, is to run with the cultural grain in both a general and a particular way. It seems to me that this coincidence of disciplinary and 'lay' common sense – in respect of this matter – makes it all too easy for social theoretic enquiry to become intellectually deformed.

Now the gist of my own claims in respect of the nature of what is ordinarily labelled 'social science' rests on the view that *social theoretic engagement is about making problem-specific and circumstance-sensitive sense of particular, problematic situations.* The specific role for scholarship seems to be interpretive commentary oriented to the display of the truth. Now this may seem utterly familiar and even banal but the point is that the business, thus conceived, is *not* reducible to the collection and description of facts; scholarship is a particular process: it has its own particular embedding within the generality of processes in the social world. The formulations of scholarly social science have (if they are good, or lucky) their own impacts upon the business of structuration. It seems to me (and here I am short-circuiting an extensive complex of arguments) that (First World) scholarship needs must adopt a Habermas-informed style, so to say. We argue on behalf of 'human kind' in pursuit of a 'reconstructed public'.[20] Let us now look at how theorists of development have argued over the last 40 years.

4 The post-war career of development studies

I want now to look, in a roughly chronological sequence, at the major 'schools' of development theory presented in the post-Second World War period. Each 'school' I will treat as presenting an ideology – in the sense used above – and I will discuss their work in a sociology-of-knowledge fashion. I will ask how they came to constitute their respective 'objects of enquiry' and whether or not their analyses thereafter were adequate to their 'object'. Each of these theoretical and practical departures will be given an 'ideology label' – this will let me sketch the way in which I would rank them. Clearly this is not the usual strategy of commentary: I am following the line of enquiry entailed by my 'dis-integrated' conception of social theorizing. I will conclude with a brief note on how these various approaches to development have *declined*; this will introduce the business of the 'residual common sense' of development studies. The conventional wisdom of development studies, established in the immediate post-war period, is, as we shall see, in its initial presentation quite clearly Keynesian. Thus it is characteristic of the work of this early period that it pursues an interventionist strategy. The notion of development was taken to be essentially technical and, further, it was also assumed that the experts of the presently developed nations had access to the requisite technical expertise. A relationship of super- and sub-ordination was thus legitimated, and responsibility for the future reserved for the technical experts of the developed nations and their agents.

This scheme can be taken to present itself in two broad versions, the first of which I call 'growth theory': *an ideology of authoritative intervention*. And the second, which is characterized by the relative emancipation of the general body of the social sciences from the restrictive domination of economics, I call 'modernization theory': *an ideology of elaborated authoritative intervention*.

I use the term 'growth theory' to specify those schemes treating matters of the development of the Third World. The way these theories of growth in general were used in respect of economic growth in the developed areas is not my concern, though both matters should be seen in the context of the more general *doctrines* of growth which emerge in the wake of the Second World War.

The background to development work has three main elements: the economics of Keynes; the social dislocations of depression and war; and the model provided by the example of Western European recovery in the late 1940s. These elements together determine what can be called the 'structure of the possible' for the post-war theorists.

Initially, of course, these three elements were aspects of a broad pressure for social and economic reform *within* the First World. The history of this period is one of the possibilities opened up by Keynesian work being squeezed between the twin pressures of popular demands for reform and the determination of the USA to make a world fit for (US) business. The pressure for reform is, fairly quickly, defeated and Keynesian economics rendered safe.

This 'structure of the possible' was, however, available for one important grouping – a very diverse grouping, to be sure – the newly established, or aspiring, elites of the new nations constructed from the disintegrating formal colonial empires. The demands of the ideology of nationalist developmentalism provided a crucial impetus to the construction of theories of development. Studies of development were commenced, let us note, at a very particular moment in history; intellectual, social and political.

The theorists of development presented three crucial ideas: the legitimating theorem of development was found in economic growth theory; schemes of organisation were found in ideas of planning; and implementation was to be effected via aid programmes. This trio of ideas forms the heart of the interventionist mode of theorizing development. Clearly they are ideas that remain with us – a matter to which I will return in section five.

The explanatory – and legitimating – core of 'growth theory' revolves around the Keynesian informed scheme now known as the Harrod-Domar model (I will focus on Harrod; Domar reached the same conclusion independently). In a 1939 article[21] written it would seem simply as an academic note on an interesting implication of Keynes's work, Harrod identifies the theoretical possibility of long-term economic growth. Harrod's work is of interest in development studies for several reasons. Not only does the 'Harrod-Domar' model underlie much early discussion[22] – up to and including the (in)famous work of Rostow – but it clearly reveals a particular conception of social theoretic engagement with the social world. In terms which I take from Fay[23] the effort – like that of the early orthodox theorists of development – is essentially 'policy science'.

This term 'policy science' is used, by Fay, to characterize the orthodox self-understanding of social science: it is the pursuit of authoritative and manipulative knowledge – the social science equivalent of natural science. If anyone asks – why have a social science? – the answer can be given that it will aid rational decision-making, or more directly that it '. . . will enable men to control their social environment'.[24] The objective is, so far as Fay is concerned – and I agree with him – illusory: it may also be seen as a part of the pervasive celebration of planning typical of the modern world, a matter to which I will return below.

Harrod's work underlay much of the early post-war period material produced on development. The economist's elaboration of notions of growth rapidly become, as ever, abstruse and technical. The goal, however, was clear and Brookfield notes that: 'That economic planners of the post-war era hoped to find capital investment something like a development vending machine: you put in the money, press the button and get growth.'[25]

I think that it is the pursuit of models (as a basis for authoritative action) and the asumption of the role of expert (the social scientist's version of natural scientific proceedings) that are the most immediately distinct characteristics of this mode of social theoretic engagement and both traits are in evidence in the two works which, arguably, best exemplify growth theory. These are the 1951 United Nations report[26] and Lewis's 1955 text.[27]

Kurihara observes, of the first text, that it was 'an eloquent testimony to the new . . . post-Keynesian hope of raising the living standards of the economically backward countries through deliberate action. . .'[28] This seems to me an apposite judgment.

This orthodox stance is codified in Lewis. Here we have an attempt to invoke the classical nineteenth-century tradition of economics; though it is the perhaps ambiguous figure of J.S.Mill Lewis specifies. In this work Lewis pursues an explanation for 'growth'. Enunciating the three 'basic principles' or 'proximate causes of growth': 'the effort to economise'; 'the increase and application of knowledge'; and 'the dependency of growth on capital'; he then attempts to shift closer to history and to discover why these 'proximate causes' operate in some societies more strongly than in others. Around the Keynesian inspired central role of capital in generating economic growth, matters of the social and cultural character of the underdeveloped are ranged. They are taken as being more or less conducive to growth.

It is my view that the argument strategy adopted by Lewis is seriously deficient. If we look at what he does we find that he begins with assumptions of a superficially formal kind, adds in aggregated empirical notions which characterize 'social types' and builds abstract general models. The return to the practical is effected by removing simplifying assumptions so as to fit the model to the particular 'reality' in question. However it seems clear that there is a great deal of intrinsic 'slack' in this procedure: assumptions can be varied, aggregated notions varied and procedures for stepping down to reality varied. Any claim to scientificity would, I think, be implausible: this sort of procedure allows for the production of a variety of 'answers'. Better, so far as I can see, to forget the strictures of the empiricist-positivist dogma and, instead, *argue an explicit case*.

However, it would be wrong to dismiss the work of Lewis, and the other early theorists. They were alive to the complexity of the task of theorizing development and to the difficulties of re-fashioning established intellectual tools to fit new tasks. That their effort was misconceived is a judgment made easy with the benefit of hindsight. The interesting problem for the present is the extent to which the approach they took continues to be used today. This is not a matter of the particular theorems advanced; rather it is a matter of the way *our thinking* is shaped by *their language*. Why growth theory is worth taking note of today is that it made the first presentation of key elements of the vocabulary of the present – growth, aid, planning, intervention, etc.

When we turn to modernization theory, which for a brief while

Moderngn theory

attained within development studies the status of an (almost) unchallenged orthodoxy, what we find is an extensively worked revision to the legitimating theorem of intervention. In my view modernization theory can be seen as replacing growth theory as the orthodoxy of development studies within the particular context of cold war competition between superpowers for influence in the Third World. I will offer only a brief set of remarks on modernization theory, focusing upon its ideological character, as it seems to me that much of the detailed criticism offered of it is correct.[29]

It is my view that modernization theory can be understood, sociology of knowledge fashion, as the ideological child of the cold war. Thus US theorists operating within the ambit of the notion of containment seek to secure the allies for the US in the Third World. Competition with the USSR necessitates that self-interest be disguised, thus in reply to offers of 'socialism' the US offers 'modernization' and membership of the 'free world'. I do not claim that all, or most, of the theorists who contributed to the elaboration of modernization theory were ideologists in a perjorative sense; rather I point to the general circumstances of theorizing and to the moral code of anti-communism – what Caute has called the 'patriotic impera- tive'[30] – which I take to be the moral core of modernization theory.

The more straightforward intellectual story at this point involves two elements: a denatured Keynesianism and structural-functionalist social science. In the realm of economics a reply is made to Harrod's conclusions about the growth path of an economy, which were typically Keynesian in their pessimism (the growth path was difficult to find and unstable) and recourse to government intervention for regulation. The neo-classical orthodoxy simply struck out the unacceptable parts of Harrod: growth was made simple to achieve, in free market conditions, to those who would have it – an attractive message to the post-war new nations. To this revised economics is added the work of a wide range of structural-functionalist dominated social sciences.

And it is at this point that we can observe the elaboration of the theory of modernization – *essentially a US product*. The approach to theorizing development entailed the deployment of a series of dichotomous constructs purporting to explain the fundamental dichotomy between 'traditional' and 'modern'. These theorists pursued the goal of a descriptive-general science. This, it was supposed, would permit the production of *general models* which descriptively characterized the societies in question in such a way as to permit manipulative, 'corrective', interventions governed by authoritative knowledge. This, so far as I can see, is the effort's strategic error; thereafter it is liable to all the criticisms which attach to the use of evolutionist schemes, ethnocentric ethics, dualistic characterizations, and so on, all of which have – to a cumulatively overwhelming effect – been brought against it.

These two approaches – growth and modernization theory – represent the core of the 'orthodoxy' within studies of development. I want now to turn to two 'radical' approaches – radical in the sense of being *intermediate* between orthodox (bourgeois) and critical marxist approaches. I think this tripartite typology – and I'm not going to concern myself as I said above, with this business of typologies very much – is preferable to the familiar dual typology which simply identifies bourgeois and marxists. It allows a quite distinct grouping to be acknowledged: generally, they could be labelled the 'dissenting economists'.

In 1963 Dudley Seers published an essay[31] which came to be regarded as a 'minor classic'. In it he denies that orthodox economics are helpful when it comes to treating Third World development. Economic analyses have been designed to illuminate the 'special case' (taking a global view) of the rich, industrialized, economies, and their procedures are not transferable. Seers argues that development theorists must forget the received wisdom of orthodox economics and pay attention to the social and institutional contexts of the particular Third World economies which they are dealing with, and to their place within the world economy. This emphasis on 'situating' analysis is typical of the work of Myrdal and his exegetist Paul Streeten. I label this group the neo-institutionalists.

I take the neo-institutionalists to be an interventionist-minded 'school', but in their case the political context, in particular, of calls for intervention has shifted. The period of the elaboration of neo-institutionalism coincides, roughly, with the colonial withdrawal from Black Africa. The neo-institutionalists' theorizing is done in a context which is not concerned with confronting a supposedly expansionist communism, as was the case with modernization theory. Rather they are concerned with the project of re-working long-established colonial relationships. The resources invoked by these theorists include the actual experience of the colonial episode, a distinct European tradition of social thought, and a relationship with government which disposes them to practical policy-making (of a liberal reformist type) rather than to the elaboration of general schemes. Their product is typically problem-centred, piecemeal and sceptical. I label it an ideology of '*co-operative (revised authoritative) interventionism*'. I will now consider the 'schools' argument strategy and elucidate further my label.

So, if we ask after the intellectual roots institutionalism we find an economics associated with the early twentieth-century European social theorist Thorstein Veblen – a stern critic of liberal market societies. In the 1930s neo-institutionalism was closely associated with Roosevelt's 'New Deal' – a program of government planning designed to alleviate the effects of the depression. Myrdal – who was briefly in contact with some of these theorists – works in a very similar fashion (hence my label)[32] but his version is straightforwardly European. He advances the notion of 'World Welfarism' and makes the planner the agent of change. Myrdal advances the idea of 'circular cumulative causation' by which he means that social systems once set on a particular direction tend to adjust, automatically, to reinforce that tendency. It is a notion of *social inertia*. As regards the Third World, these societies are seen as lodged in a debilitating position within the world economy and as crippled by outmoded social forms. The remedy is, as noted, state planning to shift these societies on to a new, upward, track. In terms of argument strategy I think that there are three areas of particular interest.

The first is the business of the use made by the neo-institutionalists of the resources of social science. They deploy what can be called a sociologized economics and pursue *realism* in modelling as a means to order planned social change. The crucial notion here, following Seers, is that concepts have ecologies: that is, concepts only work in particular circumstances. In the case of any Third World economy and society a detailed knowledge of the society is a prerequisite to concept formation and modelling. Essentially this is an empiricist-style epistemology and it rather rapidly disintegrates if questioned. Further than this, not only does social science enable the neo-institutionalists' epistemology to function via its data, but its concepts provide the general conceptual framework for analysing *social systems*.

The second point about their argument strategy concerns their effort to offer a general solution to the problem of 'values'. Myrdal's solution, in addition to reflexive effort to extirpate bias, is to invoke the notion of 'crisis politics' such that in periods of 'crisis' value issues are rendered 'obvious' and therefore unproblematical. This is evidently a simple accommodation with the orthodox distinction between fact/value and is a non-solution to the 'problem of values', but it is typical of this 'school'.

Finally there is the neo-institutionalists' scheme of agency; the mechanism which will effect social change. Here Myrdal presents the view that the state machine run by reasonable men will order and implement programmes of social change. What Myrdal does is to reduce *politics to planning*. Thus he remarks: 'What a state needs, and what politics is about, is precisely a macro-plan for inducing changes. . . . This may, in popular terms, be a definition of what we should mean by planning.'[33]

In the end, it seems to me, neo-institutionalism can be regarded as the most plausible of the policy scientific efforts of the post-war period. The general methodological dictum is the pursuit of *problem-specific formulations* and not general theories. Its analytical machineries are subtle in contrast to modernization and growth theories, and the claim to the 'obviousness' of the stance that the (liberal Western) theorists should take to matters of the development of the Third World may well be a part of the common sense of most of those working in this area – a point to which I will return below.

Turning now to the second of my 'intermediate' group we find the Latin American school of dependency theory. It is Raul Prebisch who makes the first break with the orthodox economic theorums of international specialization – Ricardianism – which had had the effect of (or legitimized) condemning the economies of Latin America to a subordinate position within the world economy, notwithstanding that the area had been politically independent for very many years. Prebisch, and the 'structuralist' economists of ECLA advocated industrialization behind tariff barriers – the pattern, in fact, that had been fostered by wartime dislocations. This new direction in policy/ practice is explained and justified in structuralist analysis. This approach takes the national economy – a smoothly functioning system according to neo-classical schemes – to be a concatenation of 'historical residues', 'enclaves', and 'parasitic' forms.[34] In place of the ideal model of the neo-classicists, we now have an economy characterized by pervasive disarticulation. The gradual failure of ECLA reformism occasions a re-working of their views. In the middle and late 1960s the notions used were 'institutional' and 'structural' economics and, according to Girvan,[35] the revision entailed adding an historical aspect to structural and institutional method, and giving the resulting synthesis the empirical content necessary to generate a full theory of underdevelopment and dependency.

At this point it might be objected that 'dependency' work is *marxist* and I grant that many commentators do argue this. However, once again, if we actually consider the *detail* of argued positions then 'dependency' appears as an *intermediate* position – even though it is true both that dependency does shade into marxian work and that some dependency theorists do indeed come to adopt marxian positions. Given the *amount* of material we are considering under this heading, it would be rather surprising if it were *not* internally diverse.

I will look at the work of Celso Furtado, who is not only a most distinguished Latin American scholar but is, more usefully for my present purpose, a thinker whose *own work* moves steadily from an orthodox to a marxian-influenced position. I will here consider the 'earlier' work of Furtado.[36]

The 'early work' of Furtado (and the Latin American dependency theorists) does bear, I think, considerable resemblances to the work of Myrdal (and the neo-institutionalists). I'll note these resemblances and then note what for me are the crucial differences. Thus we see, in Furtado, a pursuit of realistic models. In his earliest work, indeed, there is a pursuit of a general set of models – a scientistic scheme.[37] There is also similarity in methods of analysis and agreement in granting the centrality of the role of the state: dependency theory offered a complex reform package which was to be carried out by the state.

Reform by the state

The differences are, however, quite clear and I can point them up by looking at the *agent* to whom Furtado appeals for action. It is clear that the natural agent – the vehicle to effect proposed changes – of a stance like that of Furtado, and the other dependency theorists, is the body of 'reasonable men' in control of the state machine. In this dependency resembles neo-institutionalism. However there is a crucial difference: thus where Myrdal *et al.* were dealing with democratic societies, however flawed,[38] the dependency theorists typically have to confront military, usually right-wing, regimes. The 'reasonable men' are not, usually, in control. I think we can see that this apparently politically unfavourable situation has the effect of making Furtado shift this analysis – away from direct argument for reforms and towards more general schemes. His analyses are presented as illuminating the nature of Latin American economies *generally*.

It seems to me that Furtado's political circumstances and intellectual dispositions combine to issue in a quite distinct view of the mode of engagement of the theorist. Throughout this early work there is a tension between the demand for generality of formulation (seen as 'scientific') and the demand for specific, practical analysis. When this is coupled with his awareness of being, so to say, politically blocked, then the whole effect becomes general and *interpretive*. Thus in the Preface to a post-1964 Brazilian coup text[39] we find the thesis of the supra-rationality of the intellectual who is obliged thereby to present analyses free of any particular class loyalties. This non-class-specific theorizing I take to be nationalist, insofar as the entire effort is a reaction to the theoretical and practical dominance of the 'West', and latently populist in that in its developed form it both represents a general non-class-specific recipe for national progress and calls for the removal of present elite groups. I label it an ideology of '*reactive (populist interpretive) interventionism*'.

The work of the neo-institutionalists and the Latin American dependency theorists represent, I have suggested, an 'intermediate' position between the orthodox and the marxist. It is to the work of the marxists that I now turn.

We can usefully begin by taking note that the renaissance of marxian scholarship is recent. In particular it is closely associated with the rise of the New Left. The initial involvement of the renewed line of marxian work with matters of the Third World was, so far as I can see, via cooption of 'liberation struggles' to the efforts of the New Left through the 1960s and early 1970s. The subsequent exchange between this circumstance–specific renewal and the established traditions of theorizing within marxism, coupled with a dawning appreciation of the complexity of the issues raised in connection with 'development', has produced, if not a theoretical babel, then at least a highly complex debate. One centre of this discussion is the matter of the precise nature of a properly marxian analysis of the Third World. This debate can be taken to revolve around the work of Baran, and his notion of dependent capitalism where this denotes the deforming subordinate incorporation of the peripheral areas of the world economy. The complexity of this debate is such as to make any attempt at a simple summary virtually impossible. It should be noted that what follows is inevitably rather cursory.

There are, so far as I can see, three general areas of criticism of Baran-inspired 'neo-marxian' schemes. Thus the effort is taken to be a moralistic, non-marxian, mechanical inversion of the orthodox view.

Baran is taken by several critics to present an essentially *moral critique*. The notion of 'potential surplus' – that which could be generated in a rational, socialist, society – is taken as an idealist, humanist, *standard* against which irrational mature capitalist societies and deformed peripheral societies diverge.[40] This attack is intriguing. It is true that Baran's work – and the key idea of 'surplus' – does have a moral aspect, but it seems to me that the charge of moralism in the hands of Althusserians, who have been the sternest critics of 'neo-marxism', rather misses the point. It is my view that all social theorizing is value-laden – I think this is the wellspring of the whole enterprise. So what is really at issue is *not* whether or not Baran's work is informed by ethical commitments, rather the question must concern the character of the judgments made and the manner of their insertion into social theoretic efforts.

Now Baran's work has been charged with being redolent of Keynesian reformism[41] and it seems to me that this might well be true in terms *both* of the ethics affirmed and the relationship of ethical to other aspects of analysis – that is, potential surplus appears as an ethical *standard* and is thus somehow separate from, rather than intrinsic to his enquiries. So if this reading of the situation is correct then Baran is guilty of surreptitious borrowing from the stances he would attack. However, against his, themselves rather sterile, critics it is fair to invite them to recall the circumstances of production of

Baran's work and to compare it with his contemporary competitors –
1950s modernization theory in the USA. I think Baran's work can be
seen to be hugely sophisticated in comparison!

The second area of attack, related to the first, looks at the key idea
of surplus used by Baran and his followers. Two points are made:
firstly that the idea is in the style of Keynesian aggregative economics;
and, secondly, that whilst the term looks marxist it most definitely is
not. I think both criticisms are correct, but I'm not sure that they are
very interesting. Should we not concern ourselves less with the
exegetical question of whether or not Baran *et al.* have changed the
conceptual machineries of Marx and instead ask whether or not they
have produced *good or bad political economy*? I will pursue this,
following a note on the last typical area of criticism.

This last criticism looks at the concept of capitalism used by the
neo-marxists. It has been cogently argued by Brenner[42] that the *entire*
neo-marxian line in this area of debate reduces to an inversion of
Adam Smith: this is evidenced in their equating, as did Smith,
capitalism with a trade-based division of labour where innovation and
thus expansion is determined by market pressure. Class relations are
taken to just follow on. Brenner speaks of 'historical functionalism'
and 'a classic form of economic determinism' and he thinks this is just
plain wrong: Marx, he argues, reduced economic to social relations.
The upshot of these errors, so far as Brenner is concerned, is that
they present a mirror image of Smith – the peripheries are
incorporated *and* doomed to a subordinate exploited status within a
world capitalist system conceived essentially in terms of exchange
relations.

This line of criticism seems to me to be correct. However, two
points could be made – rather in the style of my comments on the first
two criticisms – by way of a partial defence. Firstly, there is the
business of the diversity of possible modes of social theoretic
engagement: Frank, in particular, is best regarded as a *political writer*
presenting a bold, and richly illustrated idea with a view to effecting
political change. And, let us note, Frank has acted as a very effective
catalyst for much debate and enquiry. The Althusserian critics of
neo-marxism often, it seems to me, make unacknowledged use of the
idea of there being *one* marxian theory and *one* marxian praxis which is
far too mechanical a view. Secondly, and relatedly, there is the
business of the role of *general theories* in social science. I take the work
of the neo-marxist trio, Baran, Frank and Wallerstein, to be offering
general theories whose style, or mode, of theorizing I interpret as the
(preliminary) cashings of moral stances. I think this is a perfectly
legitimate intellectual procedure – the 'general theories' in question
would be the arguments informed by ideas of, respectively, the

winning and using of economic surplus; the linked process of the development of development and the development of underdevelopment; and lastly, the historical and social dynamic of the world capitalist system. Casting these ideas in my own terms (see section 3) these 'general theories' are 'primitive ideologies' – evaluative characterizations of the world which permit the *individual* theorists to order their subsequent enquiries. This is not intended as a denigrating comment, rather, it calls attention to the *cooperative* and *extended* business of ideology construction. Now the trio in question would doubtless not regard their own work in this fashion, talking instead of preliminary research findings needing much further work – 'scientific' work – which is quite different from the business of enhancing the 'power' of an ideological position (it is also intellectually misguided – as I argued in section 3 above). And the Althusserian-inspired critics would be even less pleased. However, it is my view that the trio are closer to the real essence of social theorizing than the scientistic Althusserians are, notwithstanding that the detailed point, made by Brenner, is correct. What we must now do is ask how marxian enquiry can *both* be intellectually revised *and* yet regain the energy and engagement of the trio.

In sum the 'neo-marxian' scheme of Baran, Frank, and Wallerstein is best given the ideology label '*interpretive (initial) critical*'. It is *interpretive* because it aims to illuminate, in a general way, the circumstances of the Third World. It is *critical* because it looks for progressive change. But it is *initial* because it rests content with a relatively simple analytical frame, plus many persuasive examples. It does not produce a fully elaborated political economic analysis which is, arguably, the most appropriate strategy for grasping the dynamic of Third World societies.

Palma[43] advocates that we look at the work of Cardoso, which is presented as being *problem- and situation-specific political economy* in the tradition of Marx. A Cardoso-type enquiry, if it is good political economy, which is directly engaged, might be labelled '*practical-specific (developed) criticism*'. Political economy I take to be broadest and richest intellectual tradition available for those who would treat matters of development. It entails, as a way of constructing an ideology, the deployment of a morally informed categorial frame – as in the case of Marx.[44] The argument strategy differs from the empiricist orthodox: there is no pursuit of abstract-general descriptions. Marx here speaks of 'logical synthesis', the 'intellectual reconstruction of the real', oriented to the display of the possibilities for the future lodged in the present. Two elements are of immediate note: this style of enquiry involves a catholicity of intellectual interest and a thoroughgoing practical intent. The explicit contrast is often drawn with the restricted, partial, institutionalized discourses of the various orthodoxies of social science. Carodos and Faletto speak of 'a comprehensive social science . . . following the 19th century tradition of treating economy as political economy . . . its highest expression in Marx.'[45]

The key to a fruitful enquiry on Palma's exegesis is specificity of engagement: 'It is thus through concrete studies of specific situations, and in particular class relations and class structure . . . that Cardoso formulated the essential aspects of the dependency analysis.'[46] The implications of Palma's critique of 'neo-marxism', if I read him correctly, serve to reinforce my above-noted preferences for seeing social theorizing as essentially practical. If this is true, then we are obliged to grant that what it makes sense for the theorist to say will depend crucially upon the situation he inhabits.

Thus far I have presented a review of the post-war career of development studies in terms of the construction of a series of 'schools' – or, in my terms, ideological positions. This is, I grant, not a usual way of offering analytical surveys of broad areas of work, but I think it is appropriate at the present time – and, in any case, familiar surveys, looking at theories and their policy implications plus notes on performance, are plentiful. The sort of survey I've offered is appropriate, it seems to me, at the present time of rethinking. However, there is one final task to be accomplished before I move on to my next area of concern and that is to review, very briefly, the *pattern of decay* of these various schools. To simplify matters, I will adopt, for present purposes, Ankie Hoogvelt's[47] classification of development theories – bourgeois liberal and marxist.

The bourgeois liberal line, so far as Hoogvelt is concerned, centres upon modernization theory and the path of decay leads into – to simplify – what can be called International Keynesianism. The rationale for the label is clear: where Keynes urged national governments to stimulate demand within their economies during times of depression so as to preserve the system, the International Keynesian line urges the necessity of international agreement on a new international economic order lest the Third World nations collapse into miserable poverty (and, maybe, communism?) and, in doing so, damage the economies of the First World. There are two areas of concern for this position: first the 'rules of the game' which we find in the NIEO program; and, second, the business of reforms in aid and resource transfer, and, crucially, its utilization, which appear in the guise of schemes of basic needs. I do not want to pursue the detail of these debates here: it is enough to note that the NIEO programs are stymied in political disagreement and are likely to remain so, and that the basic needs approach is more of the same neo-institutionalist brew – this time, there is, it's claimed, a *really obvious* crisis in the Fourth World! Streeten has observed, of basic needs, that it is a 'home-coming . . . we are now back where we started in the 1950s . . . But we are back with a deeper understanding . . .'[48] I doubt that Streeten is, but I agree that we now need to 'rethink' matters.

Turning to the marxian line we find a similar situation. There is now, within the marxian camp, much debate as to the precise nature of a properly marxian analysis of development. That this question should exercise marxian theorists is not all that surprising: marxism, both generally and in respect of treatments of development, has only returned to intellectual respectability over the last fifteen years or so. As this process of rediscovery progressed, attention was directed not only to substantive issues but also, reflexively, to the very intellectual machineries being used. There is, of course, a simple contrast to be drawn here between orthodox and marxist theorists: the orthodox theorists had by the post-war period an agreed approach – a consensus – and they supposed that the major problems of social science and methods appropriate thereto were known. Theorizing development simply entailed the application of known intellectual tools to novel situations. For the marxist – emerging from the deserts of 'Marxism-Leninism' – there was no such confidence: the marxian revival was self-conscious from the outset. Amusingly, of course, the consensus of the orthodox has now disintegrated and they face analogous problems to those in the marxian line who, having represented their traditions in neo-marxist guise (Baran, Frank, Wallerstein) now, in the wake of much intense debate,[49] are confronted with the task of securing their approach within the intellectual marxian tradition and deploying it persuasively and to practical political effect.

In sum, I have presented the post-war career of development studies as involving the production of a series of 'schools' or ideologies. I would suggest that there is now, within studies of development, widespread disquiet as to the intellectual status of the enterprise. I think this impulse to 'rethink' coincides with a general impulse to rethink ideas of social theorizing *per se*. I want now to turn to my third area of concern – the 'residual common sense' of development studies.

5   The 'residual common sense' of studies of development

Above I identified a trio of motifs whereby the long and complex history of development theorizing might be grasped in a single synthesizing move. I remarked that this inevitably involved a large measure of simplification. This problem is repeated here. I do not wish to undertake a detailed survey of patterns of decay of schools and identify piece by piece their contribution to a residual common sense. That sort of approach would be, I suspect, disproportionate to the value of the product. Instead I will offer another rather more impressionistic, synthesizing motif and use it as a thread upon which to hang a variety of particular reflections.

The motif which I think runs through much of the work produced in the last forty years is that of the *assumption of responsibility*. This assumption of responsibility is evidenced in the work of academic theorists, agency officials, and by other commentators. Familiarly this 'responsibility' is associated with the presentation of general pro-grammes of development. It is not very hard to fathom the reasons for this approach. A knowledge of circumstances, a supposition of requisite expertise, and an appropriate ethic, logically entail action. Streeten[50] has eloquently reviewed the early days of development studies: in the wake of the Second World War there was a realization of the extent of poverty and, it was thought, its amenability to ameliorative action. Coupled to the reformist ethic of much First World social science the pursuit, once initiated by political needs, of authoritative and interventionist strategies of development flowed automatically. It seems to me that this triune confidence has declined: claims to knowledge, technical expertise and ethical surety are now seen to be deeply problematic.

The first area of concern that I wish to investigate revolves around the idea of intervention. That this idea should figure so crucially in studies of development is not surprising. The idea was available within the historically recent experience of the First World. In the political-intellectual realm there had been the experience of the USSR – successful and influential argues Clairmonte[51] – and the work of Keynes. It is with the name of that great economist that in the First World the legitimacy of planning can be associated: Keynes made it respectable and safe. In the economic realm the requirement of planning was systemic. The nature of the capitalist system had, by the 1930s, clearly entered into a period of change and, whilst the upshot has been variously labelled – monopoly capitalism, advanced capitalism, welfare capitalism – the key to these changes resides in the dual process of economic concentration (private and public sector monopolies dominating a residual, if extensive, market sector) and state direction. So extensive has the role of the state become in monopoly capitalism, so persuasive its involvement in the lives of its citizens, so routinized the pressure to a technocratic politics, that the possibilities of a reconstruction of the public sphere – the key to a politics adequate for modern society – have become a principal concern for the inheritor of the mantle of the Frankfurt School, Jurgen Habermas.[52] This realization of the essential ambiguity of the system-sustaining role of the monopoly capitalist state has not, of course, been restricted to Habermas,[53] nor to the work of those for whom the line he inherits has been influential. However, it seems fair to report that it was with the New Left in Europe and the USA in the late 1960s and early 1970s that consciousness of the manipulative, restricted, competence of the technocratic planning state was first fully enunciated.

Within the context of development studies these doubts have moved in two areas – related but distinct. In the first place doubt has crept in in respect of the claims of the planners – claims have been modified, sights lowered, expectations brought under control – all these in respect of the business of planning development. The related area, and one suspects the place where doubt first arose, centres upon the perceived 'interference' of First World and international agencies – notoriously, IMF and World Bank – in the affairs of putatively sovereign nation-states. Paradoxically it can be, and has been, argued that this sensitivity to outside interference has occassioned responses which only serve to render practical development theorizing (i.e. concrete, circumstance-specific rather than academic or legalistic general) more remote from its context and less effective. Thus the shift of complex patterns of bilateral discussions of aid/development up to the UN level, and the extent to which Third World solidarity actually has, or could, be achieved and what thereafter might be expected, has been subject to much debate.

This post-war celebration of authoritative intervention has been based upon what seems to me to be an eventually untenable conception of the relationship of social scientifically informed experts to their social world. It can also be noted that a belief in the real possibility of a 'science of the social' goes hand in hand – on historical evidence – with a disposition to force recalcitrant social reality into pre-expected forms when plan schemes go awry. Authoritative planning can quickly take on the guise of authoritarian politics.

Alongside ideas of planning (authoritative, central, expert direction) have gone, in the First World at least, schemes of ethics we can label 'liberal good will'. Above I cited growth and modernization theory as authoritative interventionist. In the present context it is probably safe to cite, as 'best example' of liberal good will, the work of the neo-institutionalists. In this tradition what is to count as development or progress is taken as specifiable in terms of the enlightened role of government programmes of reforms. However, this supposition of the general specifiability of what is to count as development must be called into question. It can plausibly be argued that notions of development must, in the light of the rediscovery of the role of specificity in social theoretic engagement, be locally determined. What *is to count as development* in any particular situation will depend precisely upon the future possibilities of that situation – an *a priori* 'liberal' ethic is not helpful.

These two elements (liberal good will and planning) come together in the injunction, expressing the motif of the 'assumption of responsibility', that 'we should so something for them'. Indeed there is evidence that this attitude has been taken on board by Third World thinkers and leaders – the claim that First Worlders *owe* the Third World for past incursions. It seems to me to be an untenable position, and I'll come to it later in the context of a note on 'nationalist developmentalism'. For a moment it is enough to observe that, whilst that attitude was widely shared (by First and Third Worlders) early in the career of development studies, clearly it is of little practical use invoking such an ethic today. Thus we could plausibly claim that continued discussion about 'resource transfers' (etc.) is, at the general level, not much more than ritual.

It might be objected at this point that this discussion is flawed by an apparent contradiction: on the one hand, I am pointing to the way in which capitalism has changed from 'competitive liberal' to 'monopoly', with the associated system-engendered extension of regulative planning, whilst, on the other hand, I am insisting on the extent to which the notion of authoritative intervention, planning, has been overstressed. More strongly, I have said that the idea upon which it rests – a genuine science of the social – is untenable.

Now it is true that the fundamental root of authoritative interventionist schemes of planning is incoherent – there can be no natural science of the social – but the wider debate about just what has been going on in fact under the rubric of planning is less a matter of debate about the nature of social science than a question of how that wrong conception noted has found extension in the social world. Real world planning systems are ambiguous phenomena – more particularly they have, properly, to be regarded as political phenomena. Planning systems are, it seems to me, central to our modern polities – and their usual technocratic ideology is, as Habermas has pointed out, a most subtle false consciousness.[54]

This general issue can be illustratively pursued by asking just how effective has interventionist planning actually been in securing major change? The complex problems of development can here be set aside and we can look instead at change within the DCs, an inherently more simple task, one would think.

If one casually reviews the twentieth-century history of the DCs the striking thing is that major change seems to have been systemic-historical, so as to say, and *not* the result of planning type political initiatives: more particularly change has coalesced around the nexus of war. Thus we see that the dissolution of formal empires flowed from the disintegrating impact of the Second World War (and in not a few cases required a local war to secure). Similarly, associated with the two World Wars is the matter of German liberal democracy – that system was only implanted in (West) Germany as a result of the wars. Or, again, one can call attention to the rise of the modern USSR in the wake of the collapse of Czarist Russia. In the realm of economics – where we start to meet what are routinely taken as systemic matters (or familiar patterns of evidence routinely taken as fairly directly realted thereto) – the shift in the balance of economic power, within the First World, in favour of the USA is clearly related to the disturbances of war. It was the Second World War that enabled Keynesian remedies to the systemic collapse of liberal capitalism to be brought into effect. In the UK for example, the whole edifice of the 'Welfare State' owes its emergence to the social upheaval that attended the war.

The general point seems to be this: social systems, patterns of life, have massive inertia. Myrdal has noted this.[55] So too has Allen[56] who speaks of social change being intermittent – progressive advance is irregular and, in the absence of overriding reasons actually contriving a constituency for a major change within society, seems to be extraordinarily difficult. One role of Myrdal's notion of 'crisis' seems to be to allow the claim that disensus has been temporarily overcome – it is an exhortative appeal to a supposed constituency created by pressure of events.

Returning now to the main point at issue, authoritative planning, it would seem that if the effectiveness of planning initiatives is in doubt in the context of First World economies and societies then there seems to be less reason to rely upon them in the contexts of the Third World where the whole business of 'development' is a hugely complex matter. I would say that it seems as if three difficulties are being compounded: (i) the intrinsic difficulty of theorizing development; (ii) the problems of dubiously effective machineries; (iii) problems of the shift of context between 'forms of life' when it is insisted that 'we ought to do something for them'. In general, then, it seems as if this mental set might well have issued in claims and proposals which are only poorly intellectually grounded, as well as being paternalistic. Perhaps, indeed, we should now regard this interventionist orthodoxy as the product of a particular conjunction of circumstances, politics, and ideas specific to the post-Second World War period. A particular 'historical juncture' has now passed. It does seem that the habit of thought of 'interventionism' engenders a style of enquiry in which the complexity of the process of development is understated and, more crucially, the variety of particular interests in the process is obscured, as is, finally, the variety of ways of making sense of it, or engaging with it.

Closely associated with the interventionist line is a 'spirit of optimism' and my summary slogan can be reworked as follows. To the injunction 'we ought to do something' is added the phrase '*and we can*'. Now all this is going over ground that has been covered already. What I want to bring out is the *optimism* of the orthodox line.[57] This optimism was very strong and Brookfield, writing in the mid-1970s of modernization theory, remarks that in a 'cooler' period the early optimism is difficult to credit.[58] Streeten, writing in 1981, observes: 'It is not easy to convey, in the present atmosphere of gloom, boredom and indifference surrounding discussions of development problems, what an exciting time of ferment these early years were.'[59] The decline of optimism is, at least in part, a result of a dawning appreciation of the ambiguity of planning machineries. The other reasons, of course, derive from the lack of any very obvious success and, relatedly, a nascent appreciation of the complexity of theorizing, and the multiplicity of interests in, development. The unevenness of social advance has been, again, made plain. Social change is slow – Marx observed, famously, that 'men make their own history, but not as they choose': to this we might usefully add – 'nor at the pace they might desire'. In theorizing development areas of effective action and specific (restricted) expectations need to be indicated.

Above I remarked that it seemed to me to be wrong to take for granted the coherence and legitimacy of the ideology of nationalist developmentalism. Now this ideology has been part of the common experience of the new nations of the Third World and it is, arguably, the Third World counterpart to First World planning. Nationalist developmentalism is also an utterly routine element of the common sense of development studies. Clearly, like any element identified as a part of a 'residual common sense', the extent and character of its ready acceptance would vary. Thus (simplifying), for example, the neo-institutionalists would embrace the position as essentially unproblematical, whereas I think the more orthodox, and marxists, would adopt more cautious positions: the former perhaps seeing potential sources of disturbance to free market exchanges and the latter perhaps seeing in the element of 'nationalism' a potential distortion to the historical progress anticipated by the marxian line.

There must also, rather more importantly, be a series of ways in which the general position has been advanced in practice. The understanding of nationalist developmentalism held by, say, Nyerere would have been different from that of his neighbour Kenyatta. Again, one could offer comparisons across continents: Allende (Pinochet), Pol Pot (Heng Samarin), Golda Meir (Begin), etc.

However, for the moment I will set these refinements/complications aside.

The essential claim embodied in the position can be presented by recalling Gellner's work wherein he observes that a society today is legitimate in the eyes of its citizens if it is nationalist and if it is industrial or industrializing.[60] The extent of the ideology's coherence/legitimacy may be approached by noting that the position was as much a product of a particular concatenation of circumstances as was the reformist interventionism discussed above. Now quite evidently merely noting that a particular view of the world was produced at a particular juncture says nothing very much about either the view itself or its continuing relevance. However, taking note of the occasions of presentation does suggest some simple questions in respect of initial conditions and subsequent changes.

If we distinguish between elite and mass then the political programmes presented at the time of the dissolution of formal empires can be analysed in terms of the elements present and the interests of the groups involved. Thus, for example, in the case of the decolonization of Africa south of the Sahara, Davidson[61] offers a jaundiced reading of events which posits, in the majority of cases, a temporary alliance of convenience between the elite, seeking political reform, and the mass, seeking social reform. It is further argued that this alliance, in the main, quickly broke down after formal independence was achieved. Most of the replacement regimes are seen as *neo-colonial*.

Now quite clearly to the extent that this sort of view is correct then the assumption made in studies of development of the coherence/legitimacy of nationalist developmentalism must be undermined. How we actually read the behaviour of particular regimes will be a matter of specific enquiry/judgment. My general point is this: if the 'real world' pattern is more complex than is claimed in nationalist developmentalist ideology, then students of development would surely do well to acknowledge this. Another way of putting this point has been offered above: nationalist developmentalism presents itself in a variety of guises and to proceed in scholarly commentary as if this were not the case, or was irrelevant, is wholly unsatisfactory. Once again, it seems to me, we run into areas of discussion which issue in the conclusion that enquiry/engagement needs must be specific.

In sum, it seems to me that the time has arrived when the 'assumption of responsibility' can be – indeed, has to be – abandoned. The celebration of the efficacy of authoritative planning cannot now continue. Social science does not (never has and never will) deliver the 'knowledge goods' required and, consequently, claims to expertise are intellectually ill-founded and in practice evidently not tenable without sharp reformulation. The paternalism of much development studies work over the last forty years also seems inappropriate: the ethic of reformist liberalism which underpinned this stance is itself a circumstance-specific product and must thus be critically inspected before – to make matters more complex – being deployed in the variety of circumstances in the 'real world'.

The drift to technical characterizations of development; over-general theoretical schemes of development process; the reduction of the multiplicity of possible understanding of and interests in development to a simple notion encompassed by paternalistic reformist liberalism; and the routine habit of playing down or ignoring the world historical scale of matters under discussion, must all be resolutely avoided.

I want now to turn to a brief summary of what, at the present time, I take to be the principal lessons of this career of development studies for our ideas of social theorizing and, by extension, theorizing development. These are the two areas of 'rethinking' I identified at the start of this essay.

6   Rethinking development

I remarked at the outset that I thought it was not unhelpful to 'appropriate' the development studies work of nearly forty years with reference to the motif of reconsideration. Here I will offer a few concluding remarks on the lessons to be drawn from the ongoing, and thoroughly informative, disintegration of orthodox lines (bourgeois and marxist). Two areas can appropriately be noted; firstly there is the matter of the lessons for social theorizing *per se*; and secondly there are the lessons for enquiry into matters of development. Both these areas are hugely complex and the matter of their interrelationships thus far little dealt with within the literature of academic social science: my remarks are, therefore, tentative.

Social theorizing must be understood to be multiple in its guises: the variety of intention/conceptions is large. Making sense of the world – in terms which would be recognizable as in some measure 'social scientific' – is a routine part of the life of human social groups. It seems to me that academic social theorists must acknowledge both this multiplicity of modes of social theorizing and the requirement that they be precise about the character of their own modes of engagement. Mapping the field of modes of engagement and locating ourselves within that field seem to me to be prerequisites of coherent scholarly discourse. The attempt to reduce the multiplicity of modes of engagement to a single model, or a narrowly circumscribed set, seems to me to be a gross error. Thus the naturalist positivist orthodoxy of social science must be rejected: 'policy science' is *not* a plausible social analogue to natural science and it does *not* exhaust the range of possible modes of legitimate social theoretic engagement. Equally unfortunate for enquiry are the *political* 'received models' affirmed by more than a few marxists. It seems to me that we have to acknowledge the diversity and specificity of social theorizing: we confront in our academic role (itself context-specific) a series of situation-sensitive and problem-specific efforts of theorizing. They must be judged, in the first place, in terms of how successfully they achieve their own targets, thereafter, on various specifiable grounds, commentators (including scholars) can decide whether or not the target was clearly seen, or not, and, in the end whether or not it was actually worth aiming at. Human beings are, amongst other things, value-bestowing – and this, I think, is the well-spring of all social theorizing.

Whilst all these debates have been taking place, an analogous review of the post-war career of development studies now seems to have been placed upon the agenda of specialists in development (and, as I have suggested, of social scientists more generally). And with regard to studies of development the burden of my conclusions must, by now, be fairly obvious. Scholarly commentary, concerned at base to 'display the truth', must eschew the pursuit of a general theory or strategy of development – the task is incoherent. Within the post-Second World War career of development studies I think it is fairly clear that this sort of image (of a useful product for the role of scholarship) has been in operation. I have attempted to sketch its outlines in terms of the idea of the 'pursuit of autonomy': and I have argued that the attempt failed, albeit instructively. Presently there is, arguably, a process of reconsideration in train: the 'residual common sense' of development studies centres upon the 'presumption of responsibility'; the view that expert intervention is the key to development theorizing. It should be clear by now that I consider that this is an unhelpful residuum in that it distracts attention from the context-specificity of enquiry and engagement.

My presently formulable conclusion in respect of a concern with development flows from my views about social theorizing. There are, it seems safe to assert, a multiplicity of interests in development – scholarly commentary could usefully begin by acknowledging this. The orthodox bourgeois line of development studies seems to have supposed a common interest in development. But this position is wrong. Even within the narrow area of elaborated theories there have been different ideas about what counted as development. Add to this point an appreciation of the multiplicity of interests in development and the orthodox project collapses as absurd. Arguably, marxian lines have, rather similarly, erred: there has been something of a tendency to oversimplify the business of securing change. Nonetheless, for my part, it is within the ambit of 'post-neo-marxism' that most of the interesting questions are being presented.[62]

To encompass the multiplicity of interests – in a fashion that refers back to social scientific traditions, thus achieving a minimal continuity and coherence for our enquiries/commentaries – it seems that we must focus on the concatenations of socio-historical-economic-political circumstances holding for particular, identifiable, groups in the world system, itself conceived as capitalistic and only slowly changing. This general scale of orienting, an overview, not a sketch of a vast research project conceives in quasi orthodox terms.[63] Particular enquiries, particular modes of engagement – or styles of commentary for scholars – can be lodged within this frame.

2 The rediscovery of the rationalist tradition

The material of this book is addressed, most generally, to the matter of the diversity of modes of social theoretic engagement: in these essays I am offering a series of examples of the ways in which development theorists have approached the particular issue of change in Southeast Asia. In the preceding piece I offered a review of theories of development informed by this notion of the diversity of theorizing and in this chapter I want to sketch in a little of the general epistemological background to my views on the nature of social theorizing (and thus theorizing development).

My aims here are modest and can best be introduced by noting what seems to me to be a fairly radical disjunction between the philosophically sophisticated work of those who address directly matters of the nature of social theorizing *per se* (the philosophers and theorists of social science), on the one hand, and the often philosophically naive yet empirically rich and politically engaged work of theorists of development, on the other. Doubtless this sort of gulf, between the concerns and injunctions of the philosophically minded theorists and the actual procedures of those in pursuit of empirical knowledge of substantive areas of concern, is not to be identified only in the relationship of development theory to the philosophy of social science, but it does seem to me to be particularly acute in this exchange. That the gulf appears very deep here must be a product of several factors. Most obviously one can cite the resolute pursuit of 'recipe knowledge' on the part of the development theorists. In terms of achieving a social scientific understanding of the nature of the contemporary Third World, as opposed to the very different pursuit of policy scientific nostrums, the original errors of conceptualization made by the '1951 committee of experts' were deepened and extended by the construction of modernization theory. In the post-Second World War period development theory has until quite recently been dominated by the pursuit of technical manipulative recipes for development. This withdrawal by development theorists into a narrowly technical ghetto has had two broad consequences relevant to my concerns here: the first being (and this is a simple corollary of my above remarks) that development theorists have, in the main, simply ignored the issues raised by philosophers and theorists of social science and debate within the field has centered on the pursuit of 'better recipes';[1] and the second is that as development theorists withdrew from the mainstream of classical social theorizing, philosophers and theorists of social science disregarded their work, judging, one might suppose, that it had little of interest to offer them. Arguably this was a considerable error and, to address the philosophers and theorists of social science, one has to marvel at their neglect of what has, in the post-Second World War period, been one of the most extensively (if poorly) pursued areas of social science. It seems to me that this mutual unconcern has helped neither group with its own problems and, I would assert, has actually hindered both. This double-aspected claim is easily secured in respect of the work of the development theorists and I have argued for it at length elsewhere.[2] That philosophers and theorists of social science could usefully pay attention to the business of development theorizing is a matter I have not yet fully articulated, much less secured. However, it is my hope that my schema of diversity in modes of social theoretic engagement, illustrated by reference to development theorizing, will eventuate in a plausible claim upon their attention.

The material of this text, and that of an earlier work,[3] is thus addressed both to development theorists and to social theorists more generally. Overall I have argued from the concerns of development theorists towards the interests of social theorists by pursuing Gellner's suggestion that the contemporary attempt to comprehend the business of development recapitulates the concerns of the classical social theorists.[4] In this chapter I wish to argue in a reverse direction, from the material of philosophy and social theory towards the interests of the theorists of development to offer a bridge across the gulf of mutual unconcern which development theorists, presently emerging one hopes from their technical ghetto, can make use of so as to grasp, in rough outline, the patterns of epistemological debate that have progressed within the philosophy and theory of social science in recent years.

What follows is therefore a simple review of those debates in respect of the fundamental nature of social theorizing which have been pursued over recent years by philosophers and theorists of social science. Treading what is by now a familiar path, I will review the debates surrounding empiricist, interpretive and critical theoretic conceptions of social theorizing, arguing that these matters, regarded overall, represent a supersession of the empiricist orthodoxy by a newly refurbished expression of the rationalist tradition.[5] Little of what I say will be novel so far as philosophers and theorists of social science are concerned, but the burden of this review material for development theorists will, I hope, be plain: development theorizing must move sharply away from that practically narrow, and theoretically naive, pursuit of technical manipulative recipes for development which has characterized the enterprise for the greater part of the post-Second World War period.

1   Arguments from natural science

Empiricism

The naturalism of post-Second World War orthodox science, the supposition that social science is of the same intellectual character as natural science, is to be understood as an expression of a very much broader intellectual-cultural movement which drew upon late nineteenth- and early twentieth-century discussions of the natural sciences in order to articulate, in the work of its key figures, an emphatic equation of knowledge with the output of the natural sciences. This key group were the philosophers of the Vienna Circle.

There had been extensive discussions, amongst various theorists, about the nature of the natural sciences ever since the spectacular advances made in the eighteenth and nineteenth centuries.[6] In these discussions there was concern with how, if at all, the success of the natural sciences could be recreated in the sphere of the social. However, for orthodox social science in the post-Second World War period the matter is clear: the understanding of the nature of scientific enquiry which would be affirmed traces back to the Vienna Circle's logical positivism and thence to the slightly broader ideas of logical empiricism of Russell which in turn hark back to Locke, Berkeley and Hume. Orthodox social science is thus the inheritor of the broad philosophical tradition of empiricism.[7]

The doctrines of the logical positivists centered upon its main concern: the desire to clearly divide 'science' and 'metaphysics'. They advanced the notion of the verification principle of meaningfulness which asserted that a statement meant something if it could in principle be verified, or empirically tested. If there was no way, even in principle, to test a statement, then it could not be verified and was thus meaningless. This is a very dramatic position to adopt, for it allows that natural science produces meaningful statement, but denies that ethics, politics, or any other exercise involving judging, are meaningful. The logical positivists thus split discourse: natural scientific and meaningful and the rest, non-meaningful.[8]

As it turned out, it fairly quickly became obvious that the principle of verification not only rules out large areas of scholarly discourse but also large parts of ordinary social language. Most devastatingly, the doctrine ruled itself out for, evidently, the principle of verification itself does not allow of empirical test. However, the logical positivist celebration of natural science and denial of the amenability to reason of matters of value had a profound influence upon social science: it was the logical positivists who gave shape to empiricist thought within the context of recent, post-Second World War debate.[9]

One member of the Vienna Circle, Neurath, did turn his attention directly to matters of social science.[10] Neurath adopted a version of logical positivism called 'physicalism', which advanced the view that statements had meaning if they could be related to observations made of the world by actual observers. The 'physicalist' position was that all 'real problems' were expressible in physicalist terms and any enquiry that could not be reduced to offering and checking 'observation statements' was not scientific. When terms led to non-physicalist questions, then the correct procedure was to stop using them: this, simply, gets rid of the problem. Neurath called this view 'terminological empiricism': it is a programme of making enquiry 'scientific' by getting rid of the 'non-scientific' words people use. Social science was to be purged by terminological empiricists and thereafter pursued by physicalists. So far as I am aware this proposal – which would have produced a radical behavourist social science – was never followed up. Instead different concerns began to be shown for the nature of social science. Thus, as the crack within logical positivism began to show, doubts began to reappear as to whether social science could after all be properly termed 'scientific': thus we find that problems of values and the nature of the role of the investigator were indicated; so too were difficulties of prediction, and the scarcity of 'laws' and paucity of 'hard' facts produced were also noted. In response to these doubts a revised view was advanced, a 'mitigated positivism': it is here that we meet in social science the familiar post-Second World War orthodoxy.

Ernest Nagel[11] offered one such 'mitigated positivist' argument. Holding fast to the empiricist commitment to the unity of scientific method the strategy adopted is twofold: firstly to redefine science away from 'experimentation' towards 'systematic enquiry' and secondly, to eliminate the apparent differences between social and natural scientific enquiry. Both coincide as systematic enquiries and the naturalist position is thus secured. Nagel argues to this position by first contrasting scientific thinking with common-sense thinking.

Nagel talks of human thinking generally as effective and practical, but distinguishes scientific thinking as of a different type altogether. The nature of this specialness is pursued in a series of contrasts with common sense. Thus science is systematic whereas common sense is not; it rests content with the received stock of knowledge plus occasional additions – it is 'folk knowledge'. Science makes limited claims, whereas the claims of common-sense knowledge are never precisely formulated. Science is consistent where common-sense thought is not. Scientific explanation by virtue of its precision is quickly overthrown (by better explanations) whereas common-sense knowledge is vague and thus flexible. Science has a short life, common sense a long life. Science aims for abstract general claims whereas common sense aims at specific, practical, claims. Science tests its claims whilst common sense does not.

Now all of this is both plausible and thoroughly ambiguous. The attempt to elucidate the nature of natural scientific reasoning by contrasting it with 'common sense' is a familiar motif within the empiricist tradition. Theorists committed to the cognitive priority of natural scientific reasoning can, by using this stratagem, offer a plausible sketch of what it is to pursue science. However, one does wonder how much weight to attach to these manoeuvres: they are not even handed investigations of different modes of cognition (the prior commitment to the superiority of natural science rules this out), nor, evidently, are they critical debates with the variety of conceptualiz-ation of natural scientific thought that have been offered by theorists over the years. What it seems to me that we have here are really illustrative distinctions aiming to persuade which are drawn from a position of strong partiality for natural scientific cognition conceived in empiricist fashion. Thus natural science is taken to be evidently better than common sense (check again Nagel's list of oppositions) and, equally evidently, the standard against which all other modes of cognition are to be judged. Nagel in his modest fashion is taking up a position that is suffused with evaluative judgments about knowledge of a most complex kind: this is by no means the 'innocently obvious' starting point that it purports to be. Russell, aiming to elucidate the nature of logical empiricist epistemology, pithily reveals these prejudices by observing that 'What passes for knowledge in ordinary life suffers from three defects: it is cocksure, vague and self-contradictory.'[12] So this strategy, whilst familiar and plausible, is highly dubious and, given the work which the concept of 'systematic enquiry' is going to do, one must doubt the terms usefulness/ plausibility given this method of derivation/elucidation.

Nagel's distinctions can also be challenged directly. Thus, for example, maybe common sense is tested, but over long periods of time: 'folk-medicine' had recently been 'discovered' by orthodox medicine and it turns out that much 'folk medicine' is efficacious even though it has never been subjected to Nagel's systematic enquiry. On the other hand, Nagel acknowledges that the discovery and evidence assessing procedures of science are not codified, they are 'intellectual habits';[13] thus natural science itself is a part of the ordinary world.

Finally, it must be pointed out that Nagel's notion of systematic enquiry does not allow us to distinguish amongst disciplines of learning other than by subject matter; but many people, including I'd guess Nagel, would want to accord natural science a distinct and special place amongst human intellectual efforts. One paradoxical effect of empiricist attempts to naturalistically embrace all areas of cognitive endeavour is that they either brutalize these disciplines (witness Neurath above) or reduce natural science itself to ordinariness by submerging it within an all-embracing scheme of systematic enquiry. Finally, we can assert that it is here that Nagel is really going to have to work: distinguishing natural science from common sense is just too easy, and the real issue is the relations between natural and other sciences.[14]

With this idea of science as systematic enquiry, Nagel then turns to look at the situation of social science and attempts both to blur the familiarly assumed differences between social and natural science and further to argue that if it is not impossible to conceive of a naturalistic social enquiry then present problems are technical only. The argument runs through a review of a series of objections brought to the idea of a naturalistic social science.

Nagel begins with the matter of controlled experiment and the claim that it is impossible in the social sciences. His reply involves distinguishing between 'controlled experiment' and 'controlled investigation'. The latter is what counts, he says, and this is available to social science and, in any case, it's the way natural science really works. Controlled experiment is not so important. Thus does he attempt to bridge the gap and deflect the criticism: I think he fails in both his attempt to demote controlled experiment (it just is the way physio-chemical heartlands of natural science operate), and in his claims for controlled investigations in social science as, to offer a mild comment, their output is (as Nagel admits) feeble when compared to that of natural science.

Next Nagel discusses 'laws': in social science they are history-bound, true only for a specified context whereas in natural science they are absolute. Again Nagel attempts to blur the differences both by arguing that 'laws' in natural science often only have restricted generality and that limited attempts at laws have been made in social science (and here he instances, amongst others, neo-classical economic laws), and then goes on to say that he can see no logical reason why there should not be social scientific 'absolute laws' at some stage when procedural problems are resolved. This strikes me as absurd, but what is interesting is the appeal to 'possibility in logic even if not practically possible'. Upon this fine philosophical thread must hang much of Nagel's argument.

Nagel considers the way social scientific knowledge is social, and thus available to other actors: the output of social scientific research can lead to the original phenomena changing. Here are the empiricists' ideas of 'self-fulfilling prophecy' and 'suicidal predictions'. Again Nagel moves to defuse the issue by (i) blurring distinctions, and (ii) arguing that the absence of logical impossibility means technical difficulty only. Thus he observes that there is 'experimenter effect' in natural science (thus blurring the distinction) and goes on to argue that controlling experimenter effect in social science is essentially the same problem. Thus for social science, in this matter, Nagel thinks there is merely a procedural problem. Again one has to dissent: the position of the social scientist *vis-à-vis* that which he studies is radically different to the position of the natural scientist simply because the 'objects' of social scientific enquiry have their own interpretations of the social world. Giddens on this point speaks of social science's 'double hermeneutic' – the interpretation of that which is already an interpretation.[15]

Relatedly matters of 'subjectivity' are addressed: thus Nagel notes that it has been argued that the natural scientific stance cannot be transferred to the social scientific realm because, typically, this sphere involves human subjective experience. Again Nagel finds no great problems. Matters of 'human subjectivity' correctly presented can be tackled naturalistically. Hermeneutic understanding becomes merely a source of hypotheses which then are treated 'objectively'. To dispute the detail of this claim would not be helpful; at best it can be seen as a curiously restricted engagement with what is, on any view, typically human, and the orientation has in recent years come to be seen as untenable as the philosophical scheme of hermeneutics has been recovered.

On valuation, where it has been argued that social science is inevitably caught up in valuation because social actors are, and because researchers are also social actors, Nagel argues the following. One: valuation can enter in choosing questions, but thereafter study proceeds naturalistically so there is no problem here. Two: ethical valuation can enter social science work, value-bias, but again, with maturity, spotting and extirpating such biases is perfectly possible so there is no problem here. Finally, to meet the attack that fact and value themselves just are fused Nagel distinguishes 'characterizing' and 'appraising' judgments such that the former judge types of phenomena where the latter express approval/disapproval, and if these can be distinguished then a value-free social science survives as a possibility. Again one has to say that this is implausible. Human beings are bestowers of value and they do study society with purposes in mind, and any 'purpose' is going to be embedded in a schedule of values.[16] We might also note here that familiarly social scientific discussions of this issue go beyond Nagel.

In sum then, Nagel attempts to downgrade the role of controlled experiment in natural science and to upgrade the element of systematic empirical enquiry in social science, thus blurring the differences between them. Thereafter he reviews a series of problems for his unified naturalist stance and argues that if a naturalistic social science is not logically impossible then it is only a matter of taking time to sort out the technical and procedural inhibitions to a fully expressed naturalistic social science. Both these elements are set against the unsystemic nature of common sense. Neither element of his argument is persuasive and detailed alternative positions will be dealt with in due course. However, by way of an appreciation of Nagel's efforts in respect of elucidating the detailed procedural nature of natural science, it might be noted that if his position is cut loose from its anchorage in a prior commitment to the cognitive superiority of natural science then his work can be reused. Thus natural science appears as one more variety of human thinking/ acting, which is the strategy of the hermeneutic tradition.[17] For the moment, though, I will turn to the work of Robert Merton who has advanced an equally influential position; one that has less philosophy and rather more sociology in it.[18]

Merton's arguments about the nature of social science reveal clearly how otherwise sophisticated statements of the orthodox position nonetheless collapse back into a simple borrowing from common ideas of natural science when subjected to critical inspection. As in the case of Nagel there is much plausible argument, yet its plausibility, I would argue, flows from its resonances with the common-sense attitude of the modern world rather than from intellectual coherence. The empiricist conception of the nature of natural science – as exemplified in Nagel's work – has been taken into the common discourse of Western culture. Orthodox social scientists thus rest their work on sets of assumptions that are buttressed by common-sense familiarity with these self-same assumptions. The cultural grain of contemporary society runs with empiricist assumptions in respect of science and this must act to support the use of these ideas within social science.

Merton advances the notion of 'theories of the middle range', where these are both intermediate in scope between what C.Wright Mills[19] has called 'grand theory' and 'abstracted empiricism', and comprised of a clearly specified and interlinked set of statements having empirical referents. Merton's notion of 'theories of the middle range' is presented as a realistically modest programme in the light of the extant state of social science. The 'middle range' theory is to be assembled with precision, because 'theory' is a precise set of statements about relations between variables and it is not just an 'orientation' to data. Such 'middle-range' theories will be modest, but demonstrably secure, and over time social science can reasonably expect to accumulate such 'middle range' work and eventually begin to aggregate them. At the heart of this scheme is thus a commitment to the idea that social science is, or ought to become, like the natural sciences, that is, an empirical accumulative enterprise. This will, argues Merton, be the work of a long-time period because social science, as evidenced by its present internal confusion, is an immature discipline.

The commitment to an 'accumulative' view of knowledge-gathering is evidenced in Merton's distinction between the history and the systematics of theory. In the natural sciences, Merton has observed, theory is routinely adjusted and updated. Thus natural scientific texts go through numerous editions fairly quickly, in order to keep pace with the most recent findings of the research workers. This notion of theory – 'most up to date statement of the thoughts of the community of enquirers' – is the one that has to be stressed. In social science theory, consequently, a concern for the history of theory – what various people have successively said – has to be distinguished from the systematics – the presently accepted set of statements of theory. Interestingly, for my subsequent discussions of interpretive social science, Merton explicitly distinguishes this sort of theoretical accumulation (of precise statements of relations between variables) from the 'after the fact' dialogic interpretations offered by some; these last he finds woefully lacking: these are precisely what interpretive social science aims at. Merton then goes on to advocate functional analysis as one such modest theory of the middle range; and we need not follow him into this area, as enough has been said about functionalism.

With Neurath, Nagel and Merton we have taken note of a series of specific arguments which were designed to address particular problems commonly taken to stand in the way of a naturalistic social science. All three texts thus have, to some extent, the character of 'programmatic statements': however, and this is the point I wish to pursue, all these texts also offered complex 'package deals' in respect of epistemology, social scientific research, and social scientific practice.

One philosopher and social theorist whose work has provoked much debate and who operates within the empiricist tradition is Karl Popper. What Popper presents is a complex package which claims to combine the following: a non-positivist philosophy of science; a means of separating science from non-science; and a defence of liberal democratic pluralism and piecemeal social reform as social arrangements appropriate to our knowledge-getting abilities. The whole package is labelled 'critical rationalism'.[20]

In his texts *The Logic of Scientific Discovery* (1959) and *Conjectures and Refutations* (1963), Popper discusses his philosophy of science. It centers on a series of revisions to traditional empiricism. So far as Popper is concerned, orthodox empiricism took the logic of science to be inductive where this involved the observation of many particular instances as the basis for generalized statements (laws). Popper points to a logical asymmetry between the weakness of confirming instances (which never, so far as he is concerned, secure a general claim) and the strength of a disconfirming, or refuting, instance (where one refuting instance is enough to disconfirm any general statement). Thus if a scientific theory claims 'a' it only needs one instance of 'not a' to refute it, or as Popper puts it, to falsify it. Popper declares that logically he is a 'naive falsificationist', but methodologically he is more tolerant as constructing and interpreting empirical tests of theory (so as to attempt to falsify it) is in practice a laborious business.

In place of a logic of enquiry which postulates that science proceeds by collecting many observations of particular instances as the basis for inductive generalization and subsequent confirmation by further observation (a trio of steps Popper regards as, respectively, implausible, untenable, and not credible), Popper proposes a logic of conjecture (a guess, more or less educated) followed by the derivation of specific empirical claims which are then tested. Test leads either to refutation of the conjecture (hypothesis) or provisional support. This conjecture is kept just so long as it is not refuted in tests. Natural scientific knowledge is thus never final. But as a hypothesis survives attempts to refute it it is thereby corroborated (rather than confirmed).

Popper's logic of enquiry is the creative anticipation of nature: he contrasts this explicitly with the image of enquiry that the inductivists conjure up, namely, the slow laborious collection of facts and the conservative and cautious generalization therefrom. Of this comparison we can note two points: firstly, that Popper is recalling the seventeenth-century philosophical stress on scientific method[21] – a stress which carries its own limitations, as I'll note in a moment; and, secondly, that in linking natural scientific effort to the creative deployment of reason *per se* he is advancing the claim that natural science is the 'jewel in the crown' of Western culture, and this, without in any way detracting from the achievements or importance of natural science is a thoroughly questionable[22] and ambiguous[23] claim.

The notion of falsification serves Popper both as a key to the solution of the problem of induction (and thereby the proper reconstitution of the logic of science) and, most importantly, as a criterion of demarcation between science and non-science (not, he insists, sense and non-sense, which is what the logical positivists had attempted with the criterion of verifiability: but nonetheless for Popper natural science is uncontestably the paradigm case of knowledge-getting so in practice his position is not all that far removed from the logical positivists). Scientific theorums can be falsified because the theorem will make restricted and thus empirically testable claims. Non-scientific theorums do not have this crucial quality of testability/falsifiability and Popper explicitly has marxism and psychoanalysis in mind; indeed it was in order to rule these two out as sciences that led him to formulate the criterion of falsifiability in the first place. Clearly on this criterion both fail to be 'scientific'.

The mention of Popper's hostility to marxism brings us to the third element of the critical rationalist package, which is the theory of society and political action affirmed. Popper's position is presented in his texts *The Open Society and its Enemies* (1945) and *The Poverty of Historicism* (1957). In the former we have an examination of the relationship between notions of intellectual enquiry and socio-political principles of organization (or political praxis). Popper tackles Plato and Marx and in both cases claims to find that an early optimistic epistemology conjoined with a liberation politics of emancipation gives way, with the rise of inevitable disenchantment, to a later conjunction of pessimistic epistemologies with authoritarian politics of elite direction of society. Thus where Plato shifts from the early Socratic dialogues to the later schemes of *The Republic*, Marx shifts from the libertarian optimism of his discussions of alienation to the manipulative authoritarianism associated with the political economy-buttressed 'scientific socialism'.

The treatment of Plato we need not pursue. With Marx, however, what we find is a denial that Marx has actually achieved a science of society. In Popper's view this is all false science and this is pursued in the second text noted where it is argued that historicism enjoins the social sciences to aim for large-scale historical prophecy. Repeating the above ideas Popper sees this intellectual procedure as underlying totalitarianism.

So much for Marx. Against this backdrop Popper presents his own position. Critical rationalism advocates the pursuit of restricted, and hence testable, claims to knowledge. In the social sphere all that can safely be done (intellectually and politically) is the pursuit of small monitorable changes in social arrangements. Popper calls this piecemeal social engineering and it is the policy science of a liberal pluralist society (which itself is buttressed by critical rationalism as this 'open society' is, in contrast to totalitarian 'closed systems', itself a sphere of free critical debate). Thus does Popper's epistemology carry over into a favoured politics.

In regard to this package, and its various elements, there have been strong criticisms brought to bear: the status of critical rationalism has been queried; the utility of the notion of falsification has been challenged; and the persuasiveness of the model of politics has also been called into question.

It has been pointed out that the status of the notion of critical rationalism is open to question. On Popper's argument the notion of critical rationalism is ungrounded in the sense that there is no rational basis for our adoption of this stance. We simply decide to use this procedure and this decision is non-rational. Evidently this is a rather odd position for a celebrant of natural science, and an advocate of critical rationalism to adopt. McCarthy[24] argues that Popper rests here because he refuses to follow through the implications in respect of a transcendental grounding of knowledge (pursued, as we'll see, by Habermas) produced by his own stress on reason as critical. This refusal flows, in turn, from Popper's commitment to a classic empiricist correspondence theory of truth. In the end Popper's commitment to critical rationalism turns out to be a version of the seventeenth-century philosophical celebration of scientific method. One cost of this position is that it fails to secure a notion of progress, and many would argue that progress is evident both in natural science and human affairs more generally.[25] Relatedly Greene[26] argues that Popper's scheme actually abolishes learning and substitutes the random accumulation of novelties. In place of any notion of the progressive display of the truth we have merely a collection of theorums which have thus far survived attempts at refutation.

One of the original intentions of Popper was to provide a means whereby science could be clearly demarcated from non-science. The solution to this problem was found in the notion of falsification. Science tests its theories, that is, attempts to falsify theorums via empirical examination of deduced hypotheses, whereas non-science does not do this: and, of course, Popper has marxism and psychoanalysis in mind. The notion of falsification drew much support from its apparent simplicity. But on closer examination it becomes evident that there is a conceptual difficulty (and not just a practical one) in deploying the notion because what is to count as a disconfirming instance (a falsification) is open to debate. Putting natural scientific theorems to the test involves interpreting experimental results, so falsification is not the simple criterion it is presented as being.[27]

The notion of falsification was also taken by Popper to be the key to reformulating the logic of scientific discovery so as to evade the problem of induction. Hume had argued that inductive reasoning, from observed particulars to general statements, was logically broken-backed. Thus, in Popper's example, no matter how many observations we make of white swans (particulars) we cannot logically argue that all swans are white (general). However, we can decisively refute the general claim by making one observation of a black swan. This insight is built into the heart of Popper's scheme of critical rationalism. All our scientific theorems are provisional: we can corroborate (rather than confirm) our theorems by testing empirical hypotheses deduced from them, and we test by attempting to falsify. If a theorem survives attempts to falsify it then it is said to be corroborated. However, we have already seen that what is to count as a falsification is inherently ambiguous and thus Popper's notion of theory corroboration by testing is also undermined.

In a related criticism it has been argued that Popper's scheme of corroboration actually rests itself on induction in that we are enjoined to move from particulars (exercises in empirical testing) to the general (the provisional acceptance of the theory as corroborated).[28] Or, again, Greene[29] suggests that Popper uses both inductive reasoning and its familiar prop of the assumption of regularity in nature, when he assumes that what is refuted today (particular) will be refuted tomorrow and permanently (general).

On the Popperian package generally we can note that the epistemology, the schema of the logic of science and the translation into liberal democratic pluralist politics have, generally, been rejected. The destruction of the critical rationalist underpinning of the liberal democratic pluralism leaves that position open to all the usual attacks made upon it.[30] We might also note that critical rationalism has been deployed in the sphere of development theory by Ernest Gellner: here we find a sophisticated defence of modernization theory and I have criticized this elsewhere.[31] Overall it can be said that Popper's work has been passed by as a result of intellectual and political events.

By way of a summary note, echoing Giddens's remarks about the deployment of the 'received model' of natural science in the sphere of the social[32] what we find here in empiricist social theory is a double commitment: firstly to the idea of 'theory' as some sort of very elaborate, essentially passive, report on how the world actually is; and secondly, to the idea that the role of the 'theorist' is that of a compiler of value-neutral reports on the world. However, this double claim is untenable because, as will be shown below, theory is active and creative, and the role of the theorist is also active. I can illustratively anticipate these claims (and pursue the notion of theories as 'packages') by considering how they apply to the orthodox empiricist position itself.

The orthodox empiricist position in social science takes its business to be the provision of value-neutral reports on how the social system, conceived on the analogy of natural systems, actually works. The sort of knowledge aspired to is the social analogue of the output of natural science, that is, detailed, technically precise causal knowledge. The result is the view that the social system can be understood and manipulated in a technical scientific manner. And the agent who will carry out these manipulations is, again, the social analogue of the natural scientist, the technically competent, knowledgeable, authoritatively placed policy scientist/planner. This figure may be found in commercial corporations, quasi-government bodies, or the state bureaucracy itself. These variously located practitioners have it in common that they stand in the same relationship to the social system as does the natural scientist to his object of study. Orthodox social science typically engages with the social world in this way and, clearly, 'arguing on behalf of the planners' can hardly be called 'value neutral' and nor, given the nature of the interests of the planners, is 'theory' to be seen as 'passively reporting'. Brian Fay has labelled orthodox social science 'policy science'.[33] That this mode of engagement has been routinely affirmed within development theory hardly needs to be pointed out.[34] It is also, we might note, the familiar orientation of neo-classical economics upon which much development theory has drawn.[35]

Over recent years this aspiration on the part of social science to become like natural science has come under increasing attack. It has come under attack from a wide variety of sources: the majority of the sources cited here are usually philosophical or social theoretic in inspiration. However, what can be noted is that often criticisms of the empiricist orthodoxy were linked to, or fuelled by, broader judgments about the extant intellectual-historical situation. The attack on functionalism is an example. In the case of development theory we can see something of the same happening: thus, for example, the rise of dependency theory was occasioned by Third World resistance to both the politico-economic and intellectual hegemony of the First World and presented a sharply different intellectual scheme to that of the First World modernization theory consensus. In terms of my 'ideology labels', presented in the foregoing essay, dependency is interpretive rather than interventionist. It might indeed be the case that the apparent tenacity of empiricist epistemologies within social science, and development theory, owes something to the way in which epistemological issues have been submerged within broader debates which have often had political aspects to them; and in the 1960s, when several of the epistemological issues mentioned here were first (re)raised, political disputes in the West and within social science were particularly sharp. Nonetheless, and notwithstanding the confusions attendant upon political debates, the epistemological issues can be pursued.

The attempt to rework our conception of social theory and the role of the theorist throws up difficult problems. Bernstein observes:

> Once the limiting perspective of mainstream social science has been challenged and the biases at its foundations exposed, new questions and problems emerge. These cluster about the interpretation and understanding of political and social reality. How are we to engage in this activity? What is the relevance of empirical studies of regularities and correlations to the interpretive process? Looming in the background is the central question of how one can rationally adjudicate among competing and conflicting interpretations.[36]

In the subsequent sections a series of answers are offered to these questions.[37]

2   Arguments from human understanding

In the foregoing section I discussed the heartland of orthodox approaches to social science – ideas we have of natural science and the ways in which it has been supposed that social science could reproduce these characteristic procedures and commitments to produce objective knowledge of an equally objective social world. The project of a natural science of the social has been pursued ever since the eighteenth- and nineteenth-century rise of natural science, and most recently this project has been expressed in terms derived from the philosophical movement of logical positivism. At this point I turn away from material which centres itself upon discussions of natural science and introduce the work of a series of 'streams of thought' which have it in common that they both reject the notion that talk about social science must begin with natural science and assert that the social world is a realm of lived human experience and that this is where discussion should begin. The social sciences do not, as do the natural sciences, confront a realm of objects (having physical causes) they confront a realm of persons (having beliefs, intentions, and reasons).

There are three streams of thought to consider. First, phenomenology, an approach to social science, inspired by philosophical argument, which centres enquiry on the 'life world' – the realm of the common-sense experience of the world. Second, the work inspired by philosophers of language which aims to elucidate the patterns of meaning inhabited by actors in the social world, resting, generally, upon the analogy 'linguistic meaning' – 'social meaning'. Third, the work of those looking to the exegetical tradition of hermeneutics: a tradition which goes back, in social scientific guise, to the nineteenth century and which insists that what is central to human life is meaning and consequently the key notion of social science must be understanding.

Phenomenology

Husserl's[38] phenomenology is explicitly constructed in opposition to the cultural pervasiveness of the 'naturalistic attitude', the common-sensical apprehension of the world as a world of objects. This naturalistic attitude, generated over a long period of time alongside the rise of natural science, in Husserl's presentation rather resembles Weber's rationalization, but in Husserl the perception of some sort of loss of humanity was cast in philosophical terms which cut rather deeper than Weber's formulation. Thus Husserl is objecting, most generally, to the substitution of the natural scientific view of the world (as a realm of causes) for a human view of the world (as a realm of meanings). Husserl's philosophical project centered on the affirmation of the primacy of 'being-in-the-world'. Instead of human beings appearing as objects within a wider system of natural causal relations, they are made central. Being-in-the-world is the base of both natural science, social science, and the world of ordinary lived experience – the life-world.

Husserl proceeds to investigate philosophically the nature of human knowing. What he is after is the fundamental way in which the human life world is constituted: in other words, its essence. The strategy of enquiry he uses is that of 'transcendental reduction', whereby the bases upon which claims to knowledge rest are successively uncovered. The procedure, in Husserl's hands, leads us back through all the assumptions/commitments we make (thereby making the life world we inhabit) into a realm of pure subjectivity. Where Descartes reduced human beings to thinking, Husserl, with an analogous procedure, reduces human beings to 'being-in-the-world': this is the 'essence'. From this point of philosophically secured purity Husserl moves forward to reconstitute the ordinary world, which will now be seen straight. The ordinary familiar world is now reconstructible as a series of complex cultural formulations: and natural science would be one such, resting not on an 'objective real world' but on human 'being-in-the-world'.

Shifting our focus to the realm of the social sciences, we find a problem: Husserl's transcendental reduction uncovered pure subjectivity, but in order to pursue social science a notion of intersubjectivity is needed (indeed in order that the ordinary world is reconstructible a notion of intersubjectivity is needed) and it has been argued that there is no room in Husserl's schemes for intersubjectivity.[39] However, Husserl argued that a part of my subjectivity, when unpacked, is the recognition of others. And this intersubjectivity, when unpacked, is the realm of culture or shared meanings: this is the ordinary life-world.

What Husserl has done is offer an epistemological and ontological revision of the naturalistic vision of the world, the vision centered upon natural science's possesive knowledge of its worlds of objects, and has recentered enquiry upon human beings where all knowledge is grounded in creative subjectivity and constitutes a world of lived experience.

The foregoing represents a very simple sketch of a philosophical position that is complex and problematic. It is the background for a phenomenological sociology. However it has been argued that it should all be labelled existentialist sociology and the basis for this claim is that in the work of Heidegger[40] we find the notion of the life-world made central from the outset (in Husserl it appears rather late). Heidegger also differs from Husserl in that where the latter made understanding a consequence of an ascetic purification procedure (the business of the transcendental reduction) the former sees understanding as routinely evidenced in ordinary social life. The whole of Husserl's transcendental reduction is deemed to be an unhelpful episode: what has to be focused on is the life-world, this is what is given, and understanding of it is latent within human experience.[41] Again what we have is the stress on this idea of the realm of lived experience, but to advance beyond this point into social science proper we have to look at Schutz. It is with the work of Schutz that these philosophical discussions are shifted decisively into the realm of social science: however, there are some problems with Schutz's formulations and at the outset it must be noted that he shared with Nagel a commitment to naturalism and thus in Schutz the legacy of Husserl and Heidegger is ambiguously deployed.

Schutz begins neither with Husserl nor Heidegger but with Weber, and in particular with the notion of verstehen. The discussion of verstehen, he suggests, suffers from unclarity and he picks out three senses: verstehen as an aspect of common-sense knowledge; verstehen as an epistemological problem; verstehen as a method. These three are related in the following way. The first reading is that which characterizes human life as meaning bestowing/understanding. In regard to the second sense Schutz argues that a theoretical account of this understanding has been lacking in social theory but that this defect has been remedied by Husserl especially. The third reading, verstehen as a technique, must acknowledge the foregoing. Bernstein, whose work I have drawn on at this point, expounds Schutz's position like this:

> There are three dimensions of the activity of the social scientist. . . . Like every other man, he is a participant in the everyday life-world. . . . As a social scientist . . . he participates in distinctive forms of social interaction. . . . But qua social scientist he is concerned with an objective representation and explanation of the structure and dynamics of the everyday life-world. . . . His stance . . . is theoretical . . . [not] a practical one.[42]

So verstehen, for Schutz, is a technique to deliver up objective (natural science type) knowledge of the life-world: the social theorist is a disinterested observer. Clearly this seems to involve a return to the realm of the naturalistic attitude that Husserl found so unsatisfactory. The phenomenological project is now descriptive of this realm and not critical.

Schutz begins defining some basic concepts: 'subjective meaning', 'action', and so on and then elaborates the frame of analysis. The notion of meaning is characterized as a way of grasping one's own experiences. Action is experience shaped by intention and understood as meaningful. Actions involve projects, the goal that brought the action into being, and projects are envisioned as taking place in a social realm, thus intersubjectivity enters the story.

From this point on Schutz develops a repertoire of concepts designed to show the way in which the life-world is socially constructed: a picture of layers of knowledge, ranges of relevance, and the biographical acquisition/growth of these life-world meaning structures is filled out. The shift from self to society is made by arguing that 'meanings' are a social resource, unevenly distributed.[43] In sum, in all this elaborate repertoire of concepts what we have, to oversimplify, is a mix of phenomenology and US role theory. Where role theory sees the actor drawing on a stock of available social roles, Schutzian phenomenological sociology has the actor drawing on a socially available stock of knowledge/meaning.

A number of criticisms have been made of Schutz and these are detailed by Bernstein. Firstly, the idea of 'structure' which Schutz makes use of, as in, for example, 'structures of the life-world', is never properly spelt out: it is never quite clear whether these structures are basic to humankind or specific to an historical epoch, and of course this is quite important (and at this point one can cite the recent work of the 'structuralists' – Lévi-Strauss, Althusser, Chomsky and so on, who have pursued the notion of structure in the former sense). Secondly, the notion of 'constitution' is not clear: sometimes it seems to be a report on how sense has been made, and at other times it is the business of making sense itself. Thirdly, Schutz fails to adequately resolve the reason/cause problem in respect of the elucidation of human behaviour: a dilemma evidenced in the work of Weber whom Schutz takes as his starting point. Fourthly, Schutz argues for the role of 'disinterested observer' but this, many would say, is simply not plausible. If phenomenology did secure a general appreciation of how meaning was constituted then it would be in a position to interpret diverse life-worlds both to their inhabitants and to inhabitants of other life-worlds. But Schutz offers no standpoint for handling such interpretive forays, and phenomenology at this point collapses back into injunctions to be objective.

To these specific criticisms we can add a series of objections to the phenomenological project itself. Firstly that there remains a commitment to the 'naturalistic attitude' and the objection here is that we can and routinely do judge and consequently any social theory has to say how and from what positions. Husserl's procedures of the transcendental reduction, whereby a clear point from which the world can be properly reconstructed looks implausible (and solipsistic); and Schutz's adoption of a theoretical attitude of disinterested observation is less than satisfactory. The corollary of this objection to the affirmation of the naturalistic attitude is that any social science that refuses to judge is anyway judging thereby fostering its own self-blindness (an argument we will meet in detail with Taylor below).

The second objection focuses on the way in which the phenomenologists actually go about spelling out the webs of meaning which they take to constitute the social world. Here it is suggested that their work is simultaneously plausible, verbose, and mechanical. The plausibility flows from its focus on the social actor. Bernstein talks about the 'Americanization'[44] of Schutz whereby the social psychological terms made familiar by Cooley and Mead are used: and charges of verbosity follow easily. As regards their being mechanical one can speculate that this follows from their concern to be 'scientific': it is difficult to find in phenomenological sociological work the feeling of intellectual subtlety and depth of, say, Winch. The text by Berger and Luckman, *The Social Construction of Reality* (1966), stands as a good example of this mechanical character of explanation.[45]

Thirdly, phenomenological social science is action and interaction centered; and within this frame their work is often hugely illuminating. However, human social life is, inevitably and crucially, embedded in real history. The phenomenological project seems to have no interest in history and this is in stark contrast to the main traditions of social science which have paid considerable attention to matters historical: think of Marx and Weber, for example.

However, to repeat, the phenomenological approach did, most valuably, call attention to the realm of ordinary human meanings and the generic business of making sense. These matters were of concern to the second group of theorists I want to look at in this section: those inspired by philosophies of language.

The discovery of language

Probably the single most influential philosopher of the middle period of this century has been Wittgenstein: it is with his name that we can associate the recent intense interest in the nature of language. (Additionally there has been a wealth of material from linguistics – Saussure and Chomsky, for example, but here I'll focus on the philosophers.) Discussing these issues takes us right into the heartland of technical philosophical discourse and my points will be very much simplified. The particular philosophical context is that of the exchange between an energetic empiricism with the problem of the nature of language (and meaning). An 'early' and a 'late' Wittgenstein can be distinguished.

In the early position, advanced in the *Tractatus Logico-Philosophicus* (1922) Russell's 'logical atomism'[46] is brought to a fine pitch: now language is to be cleaned up in line with the clarity and precision evident in natural science. This was seen to be the key to solving philosophical problems and, by implication, others too. The nature of language is to be displayed and it is argued that our ordinary language derives from, or is analysable down to,[47] a precise base. The base is the picturing in language of atomic facts: sentences have meaning if they work like this. Some of the implications, for ethics, religion and so on, of this vertical model of language I will look at in a little while.

Wittgenstein came to reject this theory of the nature of language (and meaning). In the text *Philosophical Investigations* (1953) the idea that language has one job, that of stating facts, is rejected. So too is the idea that there is only one way that language can have meaning – via picturing. It is also denied that language had a firm base. Language is now seen in a completely different way: as fluid, flexible and diverse in its uses. Wittgenstein uses the ideas of 'families of concepts' clustering together, each cluster being a 'language game' which underpins or constitutes a 'form of life'. Philosophy is now seen to have no systematic method and nor does it have any supra-scientific task. Philosophy now plots the use of language; and the identification of the limits of language is now piecemeal. Here distinguishing what can from what cannot be said does not have the systematic character of the *Tractatus*. Here we have a horizontal model of language.

This matter of the differences/similarities of the view of language of the early and late Wittgenstein can usefully be pursued. Though Wittgenstein did offer two very different philosophies of language, there are similarities and we can note these whilst also noting that it is the second philosophy offered that has been most influential.

Looking first at the differences. We can begin by taking note that the picture theory of language aimed to characterize language (and thus set its limits) and offer a criterion of meaning. Language, it was thought, was determined by how the world was. Any sentence could be analysed down into its simple constituents: this might be a laborious task but eventually would turn up the basic 'atomic propositions'. Meaningful language comprised 'pictures' of the world. Pictures in language correspond to atomic facts. Language, like natural science, was vertically structured. The facts of the world underlay language. Language was simple and precise in its working and to common sense wholly non-obvious. The task of philosophy, reconstituted in line with the claims of this theory, was to sort out meaningful from non-meaningful statements, beginning with the statements of philosophy. By implication the method cum doctrine could, thereafter, be applied broadly. The radical logical positivists – the broader movement of which Wittgenstein's early discussions were a part – urged that non-factual discourse was just plain nonsense, but Wittgenstein was more sympathetic and preferred to say that the truths of ethics and religion, for example, could not be caught in the net of language. He was, in a sense, something of a mystic.

However, Wittgenstein came to reject the idea that language had one task, that of picturing facts: he came to the view that language has many uses and he introduced the metaphor of the tool-box: just as a box of tools provides for the accomplishment of many specific tasks, so too does the stock of concepts of language. These uses, language tasks, cluster in loose patterns and here he introduces the metaphor of games: thus lots of activities count as game and whilst they do not share the same set of rules they do have family resemblances. Wittgenstein rejected the idea that words get their meanings via naming; the business of picturing atomic facts is rejected as fantastic. Now it is insisted that the meaning of a word is its use: if we want to understand a word then we have to be able to see how it is used in discourse. The idea that language has a firm base is also rejected: language is no longer interpreted after the model of the natural sciences, instead it is returned to the realm of the social. We are offered the idea of clusters of concepts constituting a language game where each language game is the vehicle for a form of life.

Language is now horizontal: ethics and religion and so on are language games, so too is natural science. It makes no sense to attempt to order them hierarchically as each has its specific styles of use. One step from here to social science is rather obvious: we can read social theorizing as a language game. This we will come to. The task of philosophy is to plot the limits of language, to distinguish what can be said from what cannot, sense from nonsense, via piecemeal and unsystematic enquiry. Philosophical analysis is the therapeutic dissolution of superstitions – above, recall, it was the checking and correcting of common sense – and these superstitions derive from ordinary language. Ordinary language offers us false trails and philosophical analysis of elements of language games aims, in Wittgenstein's phrase, to 'free our intelligence from the bewitchment of language'. The method is unsystematic: the nature of language is to be grasped from the inside. The world does not structure language, it is the other way around. Language structures the world: language constitutes the facts – the world – it does not ride on top of them.

So much for the differences between early and late Wittgenstein. Now we can note the similarities. The link is the concern to plot the limits of language: his first, rejected, effort was systematic and supposed language too was systematic and precise; the second effort was unsystematic and supposed language was fluid in the extreme. The linkages can be shown to be more obvious by setting Wittgenstein against the backdrop of European philosophy and this concern for 'limits'.

It is possible to distinguish 'pre-critical' and 'critical' philosophy. The former presented philosophy with the task of offering a synoptic vision of the world: supra-science, i.e. most obviously speculative metaphysics, grandiose schemes that 'explained' everything. The later, where Kant is usually credited with the copernican revolution in philosophizing that puts human beings at the center of philosophy, denies that there is any 'point of view' from which such a synoptic vision can be constructed. Kant instead wanted to plot the limits of creative human thought – and thus get rid of speculative metaphysics and safeguard natural science. Wittgenstein too is interested in the limits of thought: Wittgenstein and all the other twentieth-century 'logico-analytical' philosophers were the 'second wave' of this critical philosophy. They focused on language. However, that said, where Kant stressed the creativity of human reason, the logical empiricists and logical positivists (who were both associated with Wittgenstein's early work and hugely influential generally) came to focus on natural scientific reasoning to the virtual exclusion of all other forms. Thus, to anticipate, the critical theorist Habermas reaches back to Kant (and Hegel) to relearn the real idea of 'critical', lost and deformed, he thinks, by the logical positivists in whose hands the original Kantian concern to 'protect' natural science from metaphysics turns into a narrow and untenable affirmation of natural scientific thought as the only meaningful discourse.

As ever in intellectual history stories are not straightforward: but for the moment we can set all this debate, largely internal to philosophy, aside and simply take from Wittgenstein the realization of the centrality for human life, and thus, inevitably, in reflection upon human life, of language. Language is now seen to be the medium of human existence. As with Husserl above, epistemic revisions are intimately bound up with ontological revisions.

The insights of Wittgenstein were introduced into the sphere of the social sciences by Peter Winch in his book *The Idea of a Social Science and Its Relation to Philosophy* (1958). Published at a time of high enthusiasm for a naturalistically conceived structural functionalist analysis of industrialism the book caused considerable controversy. Winch argued, to simplify, two main points: firstly, that philosophy ought properly to be concerned with society, and, conversely, that any study of society must be philosophical (thus sociology, the core social science, is best regarded as misbegotten epistemology); and secondly, that the conceptual framework (language game) of social science is wholly other than that of natural science; Winch argued that it is impossible to construct a science of society modelled on natural science.

Winch begins by considering the nature of philosophy and the notion of the 'under-labourers' role whereby philosophy sets itself the task of clearing conceptual confusions so that the job of substantive enquiry can go ahead.[48] This was a proper reaction to the 'master scientist' role, speculative metaphysics, and the task has been understood by recent positivistic philosophers as clearing the ground for natural science. Winch objects: clearing up conceptual confusions is not simply clearing up terminological problems. If we think of Wittgenstein's notion of language constituting the world then investigations of concepts are investigations of the world. Thus Winch asserts:

> Our idea of what belongs to the realm of reality is given for us in the language that we use. The concepts we have settle for us the form of the experience we have of the world . . . there is no way of getting outside the concepts in terms of which we think of the world. . . . The world is for us what is presented through these concepts. This is not to say our concepts may not change; but when they do our concept of the world has changed too.[49]

Winch's point is this: there is a great deal we can say about the world *a priori* – before we ever go fact-gathering – and it is the proper role of epistemology to concern itself with this matter; that the world is intelligible *a priori*.

Winch then considers, briefly at this juncture, the nature of social life. He observes, quite plausibly, that we typically inhabit worlds that we understand. We inhabit worlds that we find intelligible, and this 'intelligibility' we constitute in ideas. Winch suggests that to understand the way of life of a monastery we would need to have some understanding of the religious ideas which the life of the monastery embodies. If we ask so how does epistemology, the concern with intelligibility, relate to the social world?, Winch answers by invoking Wittgenstein's idea of a 'rule'. If we are following a rule there has to be a check, to see if we are doing it correctly, and this can only be another. We cannot check our own rule-following. Rules of language are social. The epistemological project, of elucidating the nature of intelligibility *per se*, involves analysing instances of rule following. The instances are embedded in language games and these are the vehicles of forms of life.

Winch now turns to the matter of meaningful behaviour and approaches it via a consideration of the relation of philosophy and sociology (all the above began from philosophy and natural science). He observes that there has often been some doubt as to the position of sociology in relation to the other social sciencies: this, according to Winch, can be illuminated by noting that however the question is answered a major role for sociology must be illuminating the 'nature of social phenomena in general'.[50] And then he adds: 'But to understand the nature of social phenomena in general, to elucidate, that is, the concept of a "form of life", has been shown to be precisely the aim of epistemology.'[51] Thus Winch claims, and here he secures the first of the two main points I noted at the outset, that sociology is really misbegotten epistemology; it is misbegotten because it has wrongly supposed its enquiry to be an empirical scientific one.

Winch now turns towards his second broad question and, citing Weber, asks after the nature of 'meaningful behaviour' and argues that, crucially, it has to be understood in terms of 'following rules'. Behaviour is intelligible if it exemplifies rule-following: the mad man follows no rules. Winch argues: 'all behaviour that is meaningful (therefore all specifically human behaviour) is ipso facto rule-governed.'[52] This is discussed further in the context of habit: Winch observes that habit-governed behaviour certainly counts as rule-governed: rule-governedness is exemplified in intelligibility or meaningfulness – it is not necessary that the actor know, or even be able to spell out if asked, what rules are being followed.

From this point we turn to the familiar naturalist view of social theorizing. Winch begins with the view that social science is in its basic logic the same as natural science and differs only in the complexity of the material it handles. Winch disagrees; the issue is not empirical at all, it is conceptual: 'I want to show that the notion of a human society involves a scheme of concepts which is logically incompatible with the kinds of explanation offered in the natural sciences.'[53] The nub of the debate turns on whether one can use the notion of cause, typical and proper in natural science, in the realm of the social. Winch says not: explanations of human behaviour rest first on motives, and motives are not causes. One can only understand a person's motives in terms of the context-dependent set of reasons for action: once again enquiry is drawn back into the web of rule-governed meanings that social actors inhabit. There is a further complication. The language game of sociology has its own rules, and the 'objects' of its enquiries, social actors, also have their own rules. In social sciences there is what Giddens calls a 'double hermeneutic'.[54] In the natural sciences this is not the case. Winch concludes: the social and natural sciences inhabit different conceptual realms, different language games.

Winch then goes on to offer further remarks upon the way in which social practices embody ideas: the way, that is, that language structures the experienced world. The relationship of concepts and action is internal. Winch has been saying this all along: actions embody concepts and the concepts we have present the world to us. Imagine, invites Winch, a biochemist who discovers a new disease-causing germ: the established stock of knowledge has been augmented. Compare this discovery with the first formulation of germ theory: this required new ways of looking at the world and acting in it.

> A doctor who (i) claimed to accept the germ theory of disease, (ii) claimed to aim at reducing the incidence of disease, and (iii) completely ignored the necessity for isolating infectious patients, would be behaving in a self-contradictory and unintelligible manner.[55]

A really new idea 'implies a new set of social relationships'.[56] Winch ends by suggesting that relationships between social actors are better compared to the 'exchanges of ideas in conversation than to the interaction of forces in a physical system'.[57] In my terms human beings inhabit structured webs of meaning and any aspiration to understand must start from this point.

In sum what we have here is a counterposition to the social scientific orthodoxy. Resting upon the work in philosophy of language, Winch offers an anti-naturalist social science whose task is interpretive and, indeed, is best regarded as a variety of philosophy. In the scientistic context of the late 1950s these claims were radically unacceptable: however, as we will see below, Winch's ideas were very influential and issued, to simplify, in a rediscovery of the notion of ideology. For the present we can note some of the contemporary criticism of Winch's formulation; criticisms made from a general perspective which his work helped, in part, to shape.

Bernstein,[58] in his well-regarded commentary on the state of contemporary social theory, attacks what he calls Winch's 'impossibility' argument, that is, Winch's claims to have shown that a natural science of the social was impossible. Bernstein's first attack involves the claim that for Winch's impossibility argument to work he has to be able to distinguish between conceptual and empirical enquiry quite strictly so as to separate philosophy from empirical science. Thus does Winch identify a role for philosophy – elucidating concepts which he then develops in the direction of analysing forms of life. Bernstein apparently takes the view that Winch cannot secure this position. However, he offers us no arguments to support this contention and, in contrast, philosophers do routinely distinguish their own work as 'conceptual'. The second attack is more direct: thus Winch has said that 'cause' cannot be used in social scientific analysis because it does not make sense within the language game of social enquiry and life. Bernstein objects but, again, he does not tell us why. In opposition to Bernstein it does seem to me that Winch's arguments against the use of the notion of 'causes' in the realm of social scientific concerns is convincing. Bernstein relatedly picks up Winch's point which I labelled, following Giddens, the matter of social science's 'double hermeneutic'. Bernstein cannot, he says, see what this establishes. We can answer: (a) that the 'objects' of social science are self-conscious language-users, they are manufacturers of sense and this is what the social scientist (wholly unlike the natural scientist) begins with; (b) social scientists too are manufacturers of sense who must acknowledge this and that their 'objects' are also sense-makers; (c) consequently the 'objects' of social science are not comparable to those of natural science nor do they stand in a subordinate relationship to the enquirer as the objects of natural science do. Thus, evidently, to force social science into the mould of the natural sciences does violence to the enquiry. The only interesting point so far as I can see in this otherwise unpersuasive material is that Bernstein suggests that just as the concepts clustering around meaningfulness are richly elaborated, then perhaps there should be a similar cluster developed around cause: this is an interesting point (and not one that I have discovered pursued) but it is also besides the point, as the notion of cause used in natural science seems both clear enough and manifestly inappropriate to social scientific concerns.

Giddens[59] offers a series of rather more helpful comments. Thus when social scientists came to consider Winch they were both attracted by and simultaneously unhappy with his notion of rule-governed behaviour. Giddens suggests that the notion of rule-governed does too much work and is never properly discussed. Generally, and this comes up below, the objection seems to be that Winch fails to draw drawable distinctions between varieties of rule-governedness. Giddens thus distinguishes 'language rule' from 'social rule'; where Winch sees rule-following as essentially unproblem-atical, in social life we can ask 'whose rule?' Social rule-following is not unproblematical. I think Giddens is getting at the difference between an abstract general realm of application of the notion of rule – in Winch, philosophically considered language rules – and the specific concrete realm of the social application of the notion of rule, which is the more familiarly social scientific sphere. We could say this: Winch recalls attention to the experiential depth of human social life; whereas Giddens, on behalf of social scientists, recalls the matter of concrete historical formations and their processes of change. This seems reasonable and I'll pursue it with MacIntyre below.

The value of interpretive sociologies (hermeneutics, language philosophy and phenomenology) is summarized by Giddens thus:

> First, verstehen should be treated, not as a technique of
> investigation peculiar to the social scientists, but as generic to all
> social interaction. . . . Second . . . a social investigator draws upon
> the same resources as laymen do . . . the 'practical theorizing' of
> laymen cannot merely be dismissed by the observer as an obstacle
> to 'scientific' understanding. . . . Third, the stocks of knowledge
> routinely drawn upon by members of a society . . . [is] . . . of a
> pragmatically oriented kind [and not precisely formulated in
> propositions]. . . . Fourth, the concepts employed by the social
> scientists are linked to, or depend upon a prior understanding of,
> those used by laymen in sustaining a meaningful social world.[60]

The criticism of interpretive sociologies, and we will pursue them when we look at critical theory, centre on the focus upon 'meaning rather than . . . praxis';[61] with, that is, patterns of understanding rather than processes of practical activity. However, in the light of Giddens's remarks, it is clear that the Wittgensteinian infusion (as one of these interpretive schemes) was hugely influential.[62]

Turning now to the business of language and ideology, we move from what, arguably, we can call the articulation of a counterposition to orthodox empiricist philosophy advanced by Wittgenstein, and given preliminary extension into social science by Winch, to explicitly social scientific concerns. The change in conceptions of language/ reality effected by Wittgenstein and given an idealist expression in the sphere of the social sciences by Winch is now aggressively pursued: the theorists we now consider deal directly with matters long familiar to social scientists.

In this work, and I will look at two distinguished representatives, we find a crucial shift taking place in conception of the fundamental character of the social scientific endeavour. It is the shift from the presentation of piecemeal criticisms of an embattled naturalistic orthodoxy in social science to the advancing of claims to the effect that the notions of understanding and reason are the keys to a new replacement conception of the nature of social science. Most obviously the idea of ideology, as that set of structured meanings upon which an actor necessarily draws in routine activity, is rescued from the dust heap of history to which the empiricist ideologues had cast it and represented as a central interpretive/explanatory notion for social science.

Firstly I will look at a discussion of the notion of 'cause'. This follows on from Winch's arguments about the different conceptual realms inhabited by natural and social science. MacIntyre[63] begins by asking about the relationship of beliefs to action; and, in a rather general way, sketches the way sociologists have answered the question with either the stress on belief or upon action followed by talk of two-way interactions. MacIntyre notes that these arguments presuppose two things: that beliefs and actions are separate sorts of things and that they are contingently related by cause. MacIntyre will argue that belief and action are not separate, nor are they contingently related by cause.

MacIntyre considers an example (rather like Winch's doctor confronted by germ theory): a man whose roses have greenfly; and shows that we do in fact understand his behaviour in spraying the roses with insecticide to kill the greenfly in terms of his belief that greenfly are bad for roses. We do not suppose that his belief *caused* his action, rather we say that being a keen gardener and not spraying your roses is so odd as to be unintelligible. Belief and action are logically related and cause does not enter into it. Thus MacIntyre insists 'actions express beliefs. . . . Actions, as much as utterances, belong to the realm of statements, concepts and beliefs; and the relation of belief to action is not external and contingent, but internal and conceptual.'[64] Many sociologists have made this error, thinks MacIntyre, and he cites as an example Max Weber on Calvinism and capitalism. Weber argued that Calvinists who were originally committed to an idea of predestination gave way under psychological pressure (causal) and began saying that doing 'good works' gave a clue to God's intentions. MacIntyre shows that this shift was required by the logic of Calvinism, which asserted contradictory claims (about 'good works') and psychological tension was irrelevant to this revision of doctrine. The role of belief (ideas) is thus shown in the sphere of social action – which, of course, was what Weber wanted anyway.

The relation of belief (ideas) to action is not causal and contingent. We can further illustrate this by comparing 'physical behaviour' with 'human action'. Consider a head movement – is it a nervous tic, in which case its cause is in physical behaviour, or is it a nod, in which case it is a human social action. And to advance the argument, it is only intelligible within the context of social rules that understand a nod as that (and not something else).

MacIntyre now proceeds and makes three points. First, 'for an action to be such it must fall under some description which is socially recognisable as the description of an action',[65] otherwise we have an unintelligible physical movement. Second, that 'if an action is to be my action the description under which it falls must be available to me.'[66] Third, '[whilst] . . . others may recognise what I am doing, fit an apter description to it than I can, it remains true that the agent's honest avowals have final authority.'[67] There is one last extension to this argument: 'The limits of what I can do are set by the limits of the descriptions available to me, not those I possess at any given moment. And the descriptions available to me are those current in the social group to which I belong.'[68] This lets back into social science the notion of ideology: 'If the limits of action are the limits of description, then to analyse the ideas current in a society is also to discern the limits within which action necessarily moves in that society.'[69]

The business of the sociologist is no longer with causes and effects but rather with spelling out the rules according to which sets of ideas shape the social worlds of their inhabitants. The scale can be individual, group or, in MacIntyre's usage of ideology, societal. Human beings inhabit structured realms of meaning and these webs of meaning change through time. Here MacIntyre argues that the key to societal change is rational criticism, and this, he notes, may be deliberately restricted. One final point is added: to explain (individual, group or societal) is not to look for antecendent causes but rather at available choices and ask why one was made rather than another; and this involves us, contra the orthodoxy, talking about the rationality of beliefs, thus valuation enters social scientific enquiry quite centrally.

MacIntyre summarizes the scheme of interpreting he has presented in the following way:

the analysis of ideology must fall into three parts; we have to identify what the ideas and beliefs are which compose it, we have to identify the kinds of limits which they place upon action, and we have to examine what are the consequent means by which it either keeps open the way to rational criticism or attempts to prevent any criticism which does not fall inside the established conceptual framework.[70]

MacIntyre then offers an example of this meaning-interpretive strategy of analysis. The case of Stalinism is discussed. The bolsheviks came to power in a rural country: their notions of marxism saw democracy as growing out of liberal industrial societies. They faced a dilemma: pursue democracy or pursue industrialization. A variety of answers were given, of which Stalin's was 'pursue industrialization and call it democracy'. The only problem was the bolshevik old guard, who knew that there were alternatives. Stalin published a book on 'marxist theory' which presented a 'mechanistic materialism' in which ideas were just parts of causal chains (precisely the view MacIntyre has been at pains to refute), thus he could, and did, argue as follows:

> If actions cause ideas, and Stalinist ideas reflect proletarian class interests, and non-Stalinist ideas reflect hostile class interests, the conclusion follows that to have had non-Stalinist ideas means you must have been performing non-Stalinist actions.[71]

Dissent entails that there has been disloyalty: hence Stalin's 'show trials' where the accused 'confessed', were disposed of, and closed the circle of Stalinist ideology. Once inside the system it all does make sense: the circle of ideas is maintained by circumscribing critical thinking. And the power of this analytic strategy is that it renders intelligible otherwise bizarre behaviour: it also saves social scientific effort as all theories about Stalin's psychology, the need for figureheads, cults of violence amongst Russians and so on are rendered otiose.

The analysis of MacIntyre began from a rejection of the notion of cause as usable within social science. A related line of argument is offered by Taylor who, so to say, begins by rejecting the distinction drawn by the orthodox between matters of fact and matters of value. This can be taken to extend MacIntyre's point about identifying the criteria of choice used by actors/groups/societies: how we judge will depend on the theoretical frameworks which lie behind our interpretive efforts.

Taylor[72] begins by noting how orthodox theory would have its practitioners deal with their own values: declare them, and set them aside; suppress them via calls to scientificity; or make them relevant to the selection of an area of study only. These are familiar strategies and they have it in common that they affirm a split between fact and value. Taylor notes that the orthodox empiricists would have theorists study the facts and leave matters of valuation alone as they belong to some other (usually never specified) realm of discourse.

Taylor is not convinced by this position and he argues that no science can proceed merely by randomly accumulating facts, and if we want to go beyond fact accumulating, we need theories. In social science theories come before the facts and they tell us what sorts of things there are available to look for. Not surprisingly, says Taylor, there are many competing frameworks. Now Taylor advances matters beyond this relatively familiar point by arguing that theoretical frameworks 'secrete values'. Within a given theoretical frame value-positions will be affirmed: this is not evidence of impropriety in theorizing, thinks Taylor, rather it is a consequence of our use of ordinary language. Language, he says, is 'value-sloped'. The argument is further developed by noting that the 'value-slopes', which via ordinary language get built into theory, can be associated with particular models of human beings. Putting this another way we get the claim that when we do social theorizing we depend upon our ideas of how people are, and could become, and thus values get built into the theoretical frameworks which in turn shape our apprehension of the facts. Taylor's moral is that the theorists should pick his or her words carefully. There is a corollary to this: a refusal to grant this inevitable aspect of value commitment in theorizing (with 'obviously' claims to value free work) entails self-blinding and deceit on the part of the theorist concerned – ironical adjuncts to claims to scientificity.

Taylor's essay was concerned primarily with political science. This project of a value-free political science is pursued by MacIntyre[73] who, rather as might be expected now, denies that it is possible. He adds the following sharp comment, having considered the work of political scientists: 'the advice given by political scientists turns out to be simply the advice given by a certain genre of political agent, agents as partial . . . as any other'.[74] It is at this point in the debate that ideas of policy science can be deployed: the mode of engagement of the planners typically involves this sort of bogus claim to neutral expert status. MacIntyre comments, with the political science of the 'industrialism' period in mind: 'This insistance on being value-free thus involves the most extreme of value commitments.'[75]

The hermeneutic tradition

Turning now to the matter of hermeneutics, we find a third stream of thought concerned with the matter of a social scientific understanding of the social world conceived not as a sphere of causes and effects but instead as a realm of lived meanings.

The notion of hermeneutics originally designated the scholarly business of biblical exegesis: the rendering clear of obscure texts to recover the true meaning. Through the period of the rise of the modern world in Europe the notion of hermeneutics slowly broadened: it reached a pinnacle with the work of the philosopher Wilhelm Dilthey who saw all knowledge as history-bound. It is the idea that all knowledge is history-bound, or culturally context-dependent, that has interested those who have, over recent years, taken care to disinter the hermeneutic tradition. Max Weber, with his idea of verstehen, falls within this tradition.[76] This tradition, as Bauman[77] makes clear, stands in opposition to the dominant intellectual tradition of empiricism. The success of the natural sciences in the eighteenth and nineteenth centuries lead, rightly, to many celebrations of that intellectual (as well as social and so on) movement. However, the broad notion of 'understanding', the product of disciplined enquiry, came to be equated with the much more restricted idea of explaining; and explaining centered upon laboratory-controlled experiment. The final resting point of this process of contraction lay in the equation, made in logical positivism, of explanation and prediction. Thus to be able to explain was to be able to predict. Hermeneutics rejected this 'collapse' and, says Bauman,[78] there have been several attempts to meet the hermeneutic challenge and contrive a science of society adequate to the essential character of society – that it is a realm of lived experience, or meanings. The answer Bauman prefers lies in the approach of critical theory, and this we will come to; for the moment, though, we need to review the main tenets of hermeneutics.

Taylor[79] offers a useful sketch of the main claims of hermeneutics and does so in a fashion that shows up the resemblances to the language philosophy-derived claims of Winch and others influenced by Wittgenstein. Taylor's essay is also useful, as he concludes by listing point by point the ways in which hermeneutic interpretive social theorizing differs from orthodox social science.

Taylor argues three main points: first, that empiricist schemes of social science contrive to miss what is characteristic about human life, namely, its 'experiential meaningfulness'; second, that a hermeneutic interpretive science of the social is needed; and third, that hermeneutic understanding is radically different to empiricist notions.

Hermeneutics centers its efforts on the business of interpretation. The attempt to elucidate the nature of the experience of a form of life. The techniques of interpretation have been various, running through textual exegesis (the recovery of meaning from the examination of written material – originally this would have been various translations of religious material but any written, or culturally meaningful, material can be so addressed); to psychological empathetic recovery of intentions of social actors; to a more recent focus on patterns of language in social life. The approach insists that human social life is most appropriately characterized as meaningful and it attempts to recover and display these patterns of meaning. It is thus wholly different to empiricist social science with its stress on objective description of external reality. Taylor, like hermeneuticians generally, takes the view that an empiricist epistemology and ontology which eschews the culturally specific in pusuit of general formulations ends up offering abstract characterizations of society as though they were natural scientific universal truths; and this refusal to close with the culturally specific is taken to issue in a routinely ethnocentric and ahistorical procedure. Truth is not displayed it is rather obscured. Taylor concludes: 'We need to go beyond the bounds of a science based on verification to one which would study the inter-subjective and common meanings embedded in social reality.'[80]

This hermeneutic project will differ from orthodox empiricist social science in a series of important ways. The knowledge generated is characterizable as 'plausible interpretation': there are no hard and fast verification procedures. Evidently, to aim at plausible interpretation opens up all sorts of problems which centre upon the judgment of competing interpretations through dialogue and social practice. The hermeneutic strategy of interpretation may require political judgment or choices to be made as the social world is re-interpreted. Hermeneutics will typically expect that that which was taken for granted (opaque) will be rendered problematic (transparent) and this will require (indeed following Winch and MacIntyre will demand) a response on the part of the 'consumer' of the new interpretation. Institutional patterns of authority, power, wealth, tradition are all key areas of social life and all can be addressed in hermeneutic interpretation.

Hermeneutics is thus typically open-ended: interpretations are made, entered in dialogue, open to counter-challenge and revision. There is no finally correct interpretation to aim at: the social world comprises endlessly diverse forms of life and all are changing.

Scholars have spoken of the 'hermeneutic circle' whereby knowledge of parts depends on knowledge of wholes. This part/whole dilemma is intrinsic to interpretive strategies: we can only understand the detail of, say, relationships of power, by understanding the social whole into which they lodge and conversely we can only understand the social whole via study of the detail that makes it up.

Read broadly,

Understanding means going in circles, rather than a unilinear progress towards better and less vulnerable knowledge, it consists of an endless recapitulation and reassessment of collective memories. . . . It is difficult to see how any of the successive recapitulations can claim to be final and conclusive.[81]

Taylor also usefully observes that hermeneutic social science is understanding after the fact: we interpret what has happened in the hope of illuminating the present and guiding our actions in the future. The interpretive human sciences are thus historical, and prediction, which is the putative goal of the orthodox social scientists, is thus rendered illusory. Prediction is not aspired to in hermeneutics, for it is inappropriate to the task of a genuinely human social science – and in any case it is impossible. In sum, the hermeneutic social sciences are moral sciences.[82]

Reprise

The trio of attacks upon the empiricist orthodoxy (notwithstanding their internal differences) issue in the claim that the lived world of experienced meanings must come to the fore in any study of society that can plausibly claim the title of a social science. This is so because whatever the dispute about the word 'science' it remains true that any science must encompass its declared area of concern in a manner that acknowledges the essential characteristics of that area of concern: human life just is a web of experienced meanings.

I have presented a sketch of all these three streams of thought in such a fashion as to stress the way in which their conception of the nature of their object of enquiry differs from the positions found within the empiricist orthodoxy. Thus in conception their work is hermeneutic (though the 'technical' conception they affirm does vary: from Schutz's disinterested observer, through Winch's confusion dissolver, to Taylor and MacIntyre's ideology critique), and in intention it is interpretive. To advance matters further it will be necessary to pay rather more attention to the purposes of social theorizing than we have thus far. I can most easily do this by looking at the work of Brian Fay, who surveys all these schools from the perspective of critical theory.[83]

Fay is concerned with how theories about society affect our actions within society. In orthodox social science these matters are divorced: there is a distinction drawn between matters of fact and matters of valuation; social science describes and valuation is best left to political philosophers to discuss and moralists, politicians and private citizens to practise. Fay objects that this wholly distorts the nature and role of social theory, because there are necessary logical relations between social theory and political practice. Fay divides the realm of the social sciences into three: positive, interpretive and critical.

Mainstream social science is characterized as affirming the model of the natural sciences and aspiring to produce knowledge of the social of a kind precisely analogous to that of the natural world produced by natural scientists. The orthodox aspire to the production of causally precise knowledge. In the natural sciences, argues Fay, explanation is understood as the ability to control conditions to secure a predicted state of affairs. Thus explanation, prediction and control are linked. So in social sciences, conceived in this fashion, social theory engages with the world, is available for use, in a technical manipulative (expert) fashion. Fay calls this 'policy science': the social theory for the social role of the planner. Fay thinks the position rests on an untenable notion of science (positivism), an untenable notion of social science (positivist) and issues in an incoherent and manipulative politics (one that attempts to reduce politics to planning).

An alternative is to be found in the tradition of interpretive social science. The notion of understanding comes to the fore as the conceptualization of the social is sharply reformulated. No longer seen as the realm of causes and effects amongst objects (with human beings seen as a peculiar variety of object) but rather to be seen as a language-supported realm of meanings. The relation of theory and practice implied similarly alters from technical and manipulative to the enhancement of the possibilities for communication. Interpretive social science offers new possibilities for action by offering new interpretations of the constitution of the social world (within which action is necessarily lodged). Fay presents two objections to this scheme. In the first place, Fay argues, interpretive social science leaves no space for the conditions which surround and give rise to action. In my terms it leaves out the real history in which social practices are embedded. In the second place, says Fay, the notion of the relationship of theory and practice affirmed is unsatisfactory. And this is for two reasons. Firstly, that interpretive social science does not treat resistance to the 'free communication' it posits. Thus people might be systematically dissuaded from listening, and even if they do they might not want to hear what the interpretive theorists are saying: behaviour in society and self-image are linked, so new interpretations may challenge not only vested interests but self-images. Secondly, interpretive social science is conservative in that it tends to explain conflict in terms of breakdown in communication and thus direct attention away from real differences in interests.

The critical social sciences endeavour, on Fay's account, to integrate theory and practice in their notion of social theory. Critical theory acknowledges the usefulness of interpretive categories but, significantly, adds in sets of conditioning circumstances (history), and grounds interpretive efforts in an explicit ethic, and then attempts to link theory and practice by having the theorist enter into dialogue with particular social groups. The notion of dialogue is central to critical theory: it takes active involvement in the world to be a necessary aspect of the pursuit of social science. So much for Fay's trio: it is to critical theory that I now turn.

3 Arguments from the pursuit of freedom

Critical theory

In discussing critical theory we meet one, internally diverse, conception of social theorizing which insists upon the engagement of the theorist with the social world he considers: the unity of theory and practice is affirmed. As we saw above with Fay, this, amongst other things, serves to distinguish critical theory from both naturalistic and interpretive schemes: where these approaches distinguish between the production of theory and its subsequent use, critical theory understands itself as dialogically engaged.

The notion of a critical theory of society can be traced back to the philosophy of Kant and Hegel and it is also found, as might be expected, in the work of Marx. Critical theory, as it is discussed today, certainly derives from the work of Marx, but the intellectual character and status of the most influential present statements of the position, in the work of Jurgen Habermas, are the subject of considerable dispute. In this brief discussion I will work towards present debates by considering the successive phases of critical theory.

The earliest period, which saw the phrase 'a critical theory of society' first used, centres on the work of a group of intellectuals working initially in Weimar Germany known as the Frankfurt School. The Institute for Social Research in which they worked was founded, at the instigation of a young sympathizer named Felix Weil, in 1923.[84] From the outset the institute was avowedly marxist, though is was never associated with any particular political party.[85] Its early work involved political economy and archival work on the German labour movement, as well as the first stirrings of what was later to become its most characteristic preoccupation, that is, with the critique of cultural or superstructural matters.

The intellectual and social circumstances of the early Frankfurt School must be noted, as they both contribute significantly to the nature of the School's final intellectual product and represent one of Germany's, and Europe's, most turbulent periods. The history, put very simply, involves, for Germany, the extensive social dislocation of the post-First World War period where this includes: political upheaval in the form of the removal of the monarchy and, after a failed socialist revolution in 1918, the establishment of the thoroughly fragile Weimar Republic; economic upheaval in the form of a spectacular inflation of the currency with consequent economic damage (to add to the heavy burdens of war reparations); and social upheaval in the form of doubts about the reasons for the failure of the war, doubts about the new Republic, and doubts about the future. Running through the late 1920s to the early 1930s (when the Institute left Germany) there is, finally, the rise of National Socialism. More broadly, for Europe, the period sees a rash of failed socialist agitation and a drift into economic distress and political reaction.

Against this background the Frankfurt School's programme, particularly after Horkheimer became director (taking over from the more orthodox marxist figure of Grunberg) can be seen, as Jay has it, 'as a spirited defence of reason on two fronts'.[86] One line of attack upon reason came from those who reacted against the growing rationalization of the world and celebrated, in a romantic and essentially conservative fashion, the non-rational: the realms of subjectivity, moral striving, aesthetic experience and the like. In the hands of the National Socialists this became a full-blown irrationalist celebration of 'fatherland', 'culture', and 'race'.[87] This celebration of the non-rational can also be seen as an unlooked-for legacy of the world of the 'philosophers of life', Nietzsche, Bergson and Dilthey.[88] The other line of attack upon reason came from the broad late nineteenth and early twentieth-century stream of thought which celebrated natural science, logical empiricism and logical positivism.

Within this double defence of reason there is a particular marxist aspect to note: a rejection of positivistic marxism; and a concern for the failure of the 1918 socialist revolutions in Germany and Hungary. The story of marxism after Marx is still being told, but so far as the Frankfurt School were concerned it was essential to note the intellectual degeneration of marxist ideas in the hands of Engels, The Second (and later Third) International, and the German Social Democratic Party. In brief, they saw the substitution of an economic, scientific and deterministic scheme of the inevitable victory of socialism for the dialectical, processual, critical theory of Marx. Related to this was the experience of the 1918 revolution – and this harked back to the demise of the Second International when, with the outbreak of the Great War in 1914, the proletariat flocked to join their respective national armies – when the proletariat more often rallied to the defence of the status quo than to the revolutionaries. The marxian project, at least in Europe, seemed both politically exhausted and intellectually moribund.

The reply of the Frankfurt school theorists is complex: in essence it involves an affirmation (or re-affirmation) of the notion of reason as investigatory, or critical, rather than, as had happened under the impact of the model of the natural sciences, descriptive, or positive. Simultaneously they shift their attention, especially after Horkheimer becomes Director, to the sphere of the cultural. The 'lesson' of the failure of 1914 and 1918 was that revolution without revolutionary consciousness was not feasible and thus the sphere of culture – of consciousness about how the world was – became a crucial area of enquiry.

What we have, put simply, is a double shift of conception and intention. In this new work political economic analyses of the economic sphere are largely taken for granted, though it is true that some work on political economy was accomplished. The new work set in motion by the Frankfurt School involves adding to the pursuit of political economy the critique of the cultural superstructure. Subsequently, to anticipate matters, this double shift comes to allow critical theory to drift, so to say, into a form of culture-critique seemingly bereft of any very obvious links either to the marxian intellectual tradition or socialist political practice. In its contemporary guise – presented by Habermas – critical theory seems to have become subsumed in a general restructuring of social and political theory.

However, in the pre-Second World War period Horkheimer, Adorno and Marcuse, the key trio of the School, pursued a variety of superstructural enquiries. There was considerable effort made to integrate the insights of Freudian psychoanalysis into the marxian tradition; and beyond that two problems preoccupied them: the nature of authority and the nature of mass society. Under the heading of the former the institute attended to the changed nature of capitalism: now monopoly capitalism, a system whose self-regulation (via the state and corporate planning) demanded ever more social regulation, especially, of course, given the interest in culture and psychoanalysis, internalized or self-regulation. This work eventually came to address the nature of fascism – an authoritarian monopoly capitalism coupled to racist and militarist irrationalism. On the other hand, under the heading of mass society, the Institute looked at the art of monopoly capitalism and, in the USA especially, found that artistic endeavour, both elite and folk, had been effectively marginalized by the rise of the culture industries: an apposite paradigm would be Hollywood which, indeed, styled itself the 'dream machine'.

Eventually Marcuse was to coin the phrase, denoting this and other social processes, 'repressive tolerance': dreaming is allowed, but thinking is not encouraged.

The later work of the Frankfurt School became increasingly less politically engaged – with the very significant exception of Marcuse who retained a clear marxian commitment and who became an important figure for the New Left in the 1960s – and Horkheimer and Adorno's work became increasingly academic, philosophical and conservative. Yet the crucial legacy of the Frankfurt School was already in place: the representation of the idea of critique. Reason could now be understood not as focused on the description of the world and the utilitarian or technical weighing of alternative, but instead as concerned to display the inherent dynamics of the world.[89]

Turning to the work of Habermas,[90] who is generally taken to be the inheritor of the mantle of the Frankfurt School, we find, at the outset, continuities and discontinuities. As Habermas's work achieves a fully articulated form, the discontinuities become ever more obvious. I will discuss the earlier work of Habermas: here we find, following the Institute's work, a concern for the nature of monopoly capitalism and the spread of technical-instrumental rationality within the social world; and these matters are set within a preliminary systematization of the notion of critical theory.

Habermas's political and intellectual project involves the present-ation of politics adequate to the present. This must both recover the ancient philosophical sense of political thought as a 'prudent understanding' of the social world, and at the same time maintain the rigour of thought associated with the newly established natural sciences. We can begin a sketch of this project by looking at Habermas's discussions of contemporary ideas about politics.

Thus Habermas distinguishes between the original idea of political thinking as the pursuit of 'prudent understanding' and the contemp-orary ideal of 'rational decision-making'. The period that links these rather historically, if not intellectually, remote epochs is the Enlightenment. It is in the Enlightenment that we find the modern world's celebration of human kind as rational beings able to understand and shape their world. This Enlightenment optimism saw, through the nineteenth century, both expression (in the rise of natural science, in the development of social science, in the rise of the bourgeoisie and the promulgation of doctrines of republican democ-racy) and denial (in the beginnings of the subjection of natural scientific enquiry to state and commercial discipline, in the collapse of early nineteenth-century social science into orthodox economics and sociology, in the denaturing of the democratic tendency as the bourgeoisie fixed themselves in place in the new society). By the end

the Notion
of Reason
↓
empiricist
positivism

of the century the Enlightenment's notion of reason was largely lost to view and in its place were notions of empiricist positivism. The political thinking of the time, of the whole of the twentieth century indeed, centered its self-understanding (in all its ethically substantive guises, liberalism, socialism and so on) upon a narrow means-end rationality. As the capitalist system matured into monopoly capitalism this means-ends rationality became ever-more pervasive and was buttressed by ever-more sophisticated empirical techniques. Habermas sees the present upshot of all this as a technocratic politics. Thus the political, socially practical, sphere has become absorbed by an essentially incoherent, manipulative reason.[91] Habermas's task is to reassert the social autonomy of the practical political sphere (he talks of a 'reconstructed public') and to provide an intellectual rationale for it. The rationale of this critical theory must both specify how it stands in relation to other areas of social thought and action, the technical scientific (and vulgar bureaucratic especially) and the social scientific, and indicate its own internal logic. This dual project thus generates a characterization of a politics adequate to the present: intellectually disciplined, and radically democratic.

Habermas begins by separating out three strands of human thinking in his 'theory of cognitive interests'. There are, argues Habermas,[92] via a problematical critique of Marx, three deep-seated human cognitive interests and these correspond to fundamental aspects of human life. Reading this as philosophical anthropology, these aspects are: work, interaction and power. From 'work' arises a technical interest and this informs the empirical analytic sciences. From 'interaction' arises a practical interest and this informs the historio-hermeneutic sciences. From 'power' arises an emancipatory interest and this informs the critical sciences.

Of the technical cognitive interest underpinning the empirical analytic sciences McCarthy[93] points out that Habermas's notion of the natural sciences is drawn not from orthodox empiricism which conceives the business of natural science as centering on the pursuit of truth, but instead from the philosophical tradition of pragmatism which sees science as interested in usefulness. The form of life science, is sustained by continually recreating technical instrumental knowledge.

Practical interest flows from the need to maintain a coherent social world, one that 'works' and is 'intelligible' to its members. So this practical interest underpins efforts in the realm of communication: in formally constituted enquiry this is the business of the historical and hermeneutic sciences, those concerned with understanding and interpretation. Comments McCarthy: 'In consequence of the different interest structures of hermeneutic inquiry, the logic of inquiry in the cultural disciplines is, Habermas maintains, fundamentally different from that which obtains in the empirical-analytic sciences.'[94]

When we turn to the third cognitive interest, the emancipatory interest associated with a concern for power, we find a rather different situation to that noted above: thus there is no extant critical theory expressing emancipatory interest as the natural sciences and hermeneutics expressed their interest bases. Habermas must construct critical theory, and it will be based upon this emancipatory interest.

The emancipatory interest that Habermas postulates is associated with the human interest in power. Power understood as power-to-do rather than power-over. It is, so to say, the base of the human individual's will to autonomous being: this implies both an absence of restrictions and the opportunity to act in this self-moving way. It is this aspect of human reason, as Habermas has divided it, that the thinkers of the Enlightenment seized upon: human beings as rational and reason as the key to the future. It is this notion of reason that the early Frankfurt School theorists had in mind when they urged that reason should recover the dynamics of situations and not rest content with describing. It is the idea of critique which eventually traces back to German Idealistic philosophy. The emancipatory interest of human beings has inherent within it a demand for free communication: the pursuit of autonomy via the deployment of reason requires it. Internal to the notion of reason is the requirement of open discussion. This creates the stepping stone to a critical theory: based upon the nature of the emancipatory interest, critical theory will concern itself with the securing of the institutional conditions of open discussion – an open society.

The notion of critical theory characterizes social communication as distorted. Communication suffers from myriad ideologically occasioned confusions and distorted communication blocks rational behaviour and thereby contributes to the maintainance of the status quo. The critical theoretic fracturing of the ideologically functional social common sense will contribute to free debate and help usher in the social changes necessary to fashion a reconstructed public. The technocratic politics of the present irrational monopoly capitalist system will be replaced by an extensive participatory societal decision-making procedure, that is, a democratic system.[95]

For critical theory the key procedure is thus the critique of ideology; and, as this so evidently recalls earlier Frankfurt School work, it would be appropriate to ask, before we consider any more of the detail of these schemes, just how does Habermas's notion of political engagement compare with the earlier ideas? An initial answer, which we can pursue later as this is one point for which

Habermas has been criticized, would be that we seem to have the class-specific theorizing of the Frankfurt School (and marxian tradition) – arguing in the expectation of eventual movement by the proletariat – giving way to a more general characterization of political activity.

From this position I will proceed by borrowing a couple of questions from Bernstein: first, how does critical theory work; and second, how is it grounded. I will end with a sketch of critical theory's general notion of the relation of theory and practice.

Habermas has drawn upon psychoanalysis to provide a metaphor for the nature of the critical theoretic enterprise: indeed he takes psychoanalytic work to be critical in his sense. Thus the relationship of analyst and analysand mirrors the relationship of critical theorist and his chosen social audience. Critical theory is thus essentially dialogic in nature. The critical theorist presents exercises in the critique of ideology (which involve, themselves, hermeneutic understanding of forms of life, analysis of the sets of social circumstances – social systems – within which forms of life rest, and historical analysis which looks to tendential possibilities) to his chosen audience. This interpretation can then be accepted or rejected. In the latter case the critical theorist begins again. In the former case the question to be asked is how do we know if the interpretation is properly understood by its recipients, indeed how do we know if it is a good interpretation in the first place. The answers that Habermas offers centre upon, so far as I can see, the transmitting of the method of critique; if the critical theorist's interpretation is seen to be plausible, given the audience's cicumstances, then it will be listened to; if the audience then proceed to put the interpretations to work, in a critical fashion, then the interpretation was a good one. Evidently this is an open-ended procedure; one can recall Taylor's remarks on hermeneutic understanding at this point.

However, Habermas offers a way of grounding these enquiries: a way of judging between proferred alternative interpretations. This is also the point at which Habermas's arguments start to become very general. What he does is to consider the notion of dialogue and look for a theory of 'communicative competence'. What Habermas is going to claim is that every act of communication, which necessarily uses language, entails affirming the notion of truth and the ideal of undistorted communication. Habermas is saying that language just works this way – transmitting truth – and thus communication acts just are, inevitably, impregnated with commitment to transmitting the truth. This is a very powerful philosophical argument: individual humans may lie, cheat, deceive and so on but they do so resting upon this fundamental character of language. A language which did not act to transmit the truth is simply unimaginable. Habermas links up these claims to an evolutionary schema in which progress in the sphere of technical interest (natural science) is repeated in the sphere of communication (where this embraces both practical and emancipatory interests). Critical theory is thus grounded in human communicative interaction (language) and its emancipatory programme is secured via the evolutionary expectation of progress.

Returning to the level of critical theoretic dialogue, we can now see that this dialogue rests, in the end, on the notion that reason and truth inhere in language and communication. The procedure of dialogue also allows reference to these notions of language: thus within dialogue Habermas distinguishes between 'action' and 'discourse'. Thus communicative action rests on a background consensus and if this consensus is disturbed we get discourse. The objective of discourse is to substitute for their now-challenged taken-for-granted consensus a rational consensus: and this is achieved via argument. The interpretations of the critical theorist, once proferred, are liable to challenge; thereafter the matter must be argued out. Equally, the claim of the audience may be challenged by the theorist. Again, one sees that critical theory is open-textured and open-ended.

This can perhaps be made a little clearer by drawing on Bernstein. Thus the critical theoretic intervention can be seen to have three elements or stages. The first is debate within the social scientific discipline; here we have the pursuit of truth by an unconstrained community of enquirers, and the upshot is a social scientific theory. Next, there is the episode of discipline/audience dialogue and this comprises the process of the transmission of the method and proffered substantive ideology critique. Finally, there is emancipatory action within society initiated by the agent group.

In Habermas's hands this has produced, by way of a substantive analysis, the notion of a depoliticized society liable to legitimation crises. So Habermas attacks the prevalent 'technocratic ideology' of the controlling organs of monopoly capitalism and charges that the system is liable to crises of legitimation precisely because the state has now embroiled itself openly in securing economic success. The critique of the technocratic ideology is the prerequisite of the establishment of a broader democratic strategy of setting social goals and priorities. To date this seems to be the extent to which Habermas's pursuit of a politics adequate to the present has borne direct substantive fruit. Evidently as a substantive political stance it is barely developed. Both the ideas of 'technocratic politics' and 'legitimation crises' are hugely suggestive, but they are hardly the stuff of party manifestoes. This is all we have and, whilst others have pursued these ideas, Habermas has turned more and more to theoretical matters.

Habermas has concerned himself with pursuing the details of the methodology and grounding of his notion of critical theory. This has become the task of presenting a general philosophical theory of human communications. So where above, referring to the earlier work of Habermas, we have his project both sketched out, and moreover sketched out in such a way as to appear as a continuation of the work of the Frankfurt School, with the later work – which I will not pursue – the project is further developed in all its ambitious theoretical ramifications. Any contact with the earlier work of the Frankfurt School becomes not at all obvious and, indeed, many commentators have suggested that as the project adumbrated in the early material comes to be fully expressed so Habermas is seen to have broken both with the Frankfurt School and the marxian tradition.[96] This is one criticism: we can now note some of the other main points made against both the Frankfurt School generally and Habermas in particular.

Held[97] identifies what he terms four complexes of criticism. First, the charge that the Frankfurt School's critical theory does not advance beyond Marx and that rather the reverse is the case because what the theory actually does is return to the sorts of German Idealist philosophical critique that Marx was at such pains to leave behind. In reply it could be argued that this is not obviously true of the earlier work of the Frankfurt School, when they not only took political economy as given but also had members producing new political economic work. However, with the later material it may well be easier to sustain the charge. MacIntyre[98] claims this is true of Marcuse – an interesting attack because Marcuse, of all the School, stayed most closely involved with political action and he certainly took himself to be a marxist (and the agent's honest avowals are final, says MacIntyre). Finally, with respect to Habermas the attack arguably makes little sense, for in his case there is, if anything, a shift from a marxian to a neo-Weberian position.

A second objection is that critical theory is overly preoccupied with matters of philosophy to the exclusion of more recognizably marxian work. To this it may be replied that as the work of the tradition has involved, more or less directly, a concern for the correct apprehension of the presently relevant aspects of the marxian tradition then this objection is rather besides the point: what is at issue is precisely the understanding of Marx affirmed.

The third objection is that critical theory is too preoccupied with the superstructure of capitalism. And here we can say that whilst this is an unreasonable criticism of the earlier work when this was, on the face of it, a pressing issue, it is a charge that looks more damaging as we shift down to the present day. The later work of the Frankfurt School and the work of Habermas shows little concern for, or apparent connection with, the material of political economy which Marx himself made a central concern.

The final point calls attention to the relationship of critical theory to the life of its putative consumers, the proletariat. It is suggested that critical theory is wholly remote from the life of such people. To this we may say that this is only obviously true if an entirely orthodox model of revolutionary change is affirmed. The efforts at deciphering the social world made by critical theorists can be of interest to proletarian and other groups: thus the idea of a technocratic politics has proved hugely influential within sections of the bourgeoisie. Further than this we can reasonably speculate that patterns of change in monopoly capitalism are likely to be removed from the expectations Marx had of the more routinely exploitative system of the nineteenth century.

Turning now to the work of Habermas, we find a similar set of criticisms. Of his overall project it has been said that it is an eclectic, overgeneral, implausible scheme with no obvious agent in sight. These points we have touched on at various places above: it is true that Habermas draws on a wide range of sources for his theories; it is also true that these theories are very elaborate; his notion of legitimation crisis is intriguing rather than compelling; and, finally, it is not clear who his agents are. More specifically there have been objections to Habermas's idea of critical theory. The revisions to Marx – splitting work and interaction – are thoroughly problematical (and certainly leave little of Marx intact). The division of human thought into three areas of interest, each with a corresponding science, has been found dubious: in the Anglo-Saxon empiricist tradition reason is seen as unitary; and in any case, it is objected, just what is the status of these knowledge-constitutive interests. The reformulations that Habermas has made in his later work, where this epistemological starting point is set aside for a 'reconstructive scientific' (quasi-Kantian) approach, which entails offering a general theory of human communicative competence, are taken by many to be just as problematic. Finally, we may note – because there are many other objections – that Habermas's use of psychoanalysis has been found curious: thus individual therapy shifted to the social level might just be a metaphor pushed too far; again, are the goals of analysis really analogous to ideological demystification?

Debate about the work of Habermas – and the Frankfurt School – is presently in full swing and I am not going to attempt to offer any summary judgment. However, it is clear that the massive project upon which Habermas has embarked has had the effect, as Beiner has put it, of 'Rescuing the rationalist heritage'[99] and, given that the business of reconstruction had as its starting point the positivism of Nagel, Merton *et al.*, this is no mean feat.

4   And now where are we?

Giddens[100] has identified three responses to the reawakening of debate about social theory consequent upon the attacks made on the positivistic orthodoxy: the despairing, the dogmatic, the celebratory and his own, the will to a systematic reconstruction of social theory.

The despairing response is a familiar one. The argument goes that if specialists in social theory cannot agree amongst themselves then ordinary practising social scientists would do well to leave them to it and get on with some useful practical work. This is the appeal to usefulness: reasonable men and women, it is claimed, can agree on a whole range of problems that need tackling and it is precisely these problems that ought to be addressed.[101] Some have argued that if social scientists do resolve to act in this fashion then many of the strained and peculiar sceptical doubts of those preoccupied with theory will disappear anyway, and intellectual productivity will be restored.[102] Unfortunately, this neither settles the issues outstanding and nor is a stance of usefulness theory-free.

The dogmatic response is equally familiar. In the face of the confusion there is an appeal to an authority, a figure whose work can be taken to have either settled or perspicaciously anticipated all the outstanding issues. Giddens cites those who have 'turned back towards orthodox Marxist positions'.[103] There is some truth in this example. Many others could be offered: the enthusiasm for Max Weber's work is a rather obvious one.[104] There must be many ways of invoking authority and, as Giddens says, they avoid rather than solve the issues.

The celebratory response embraces present debate as offering both freedom from intellectual dogma of all varieties and evidence of the inherent creative diversity of human thinking. This is an essentially optimistic response and, as such, Giddens approves. However, he is concerned, as I would express it, to order this diversity rather than simply acknowledge it or enthusiastically add to it. I think Giddens's point about retaining a significant measure of coherence in our severally developed enquiries is a good one. Yet I am not too happy with his expression of this point; he looks for a systematic reconstruction. The result of a systematic reconstruction rather seems to me to look like step number one in the direction of a new orthodoxy.[105] Having just escaped from one straitjacket, I cannot see the benefit of acquiring another. I would rather put the matter in this way: we can usefully begin by acknowledging the diversity of social theoretic attempts to make sense of the social world and thereafter we can characterize them and relate them to the broad historical tradition we inhabit. This both orders enquiry, lodges it in society and history, and does not tend to foreclose future options for social theoretic engagements. I label it a 'dis-integrated' conception of social theorizing. In this schema, which I have sketched elsewhere,[106] the prime case of social theoretic engagement is to be found in those broad, interpretive and critical attempts to make sense (promulgate ideologies) of complex patterns of historical change. In Gellner's terms these are attempts to render the essential nature of societies clear and development theory represents one key contemporary area of such enquiry.[107] Around this prime case of social theoretic engagement all the other varieties of engagement with the social world can be ranged.

Turning to the direct implications for development theory of all these epistemological revisions to the naturalism of the social scientific orthodoxy of the post-Second World War period, we find, in brief, the formal demand that we move sharply away from the pursuit of technical manipulative knowledge towards patterns of enquiry that are centered on schemes of interpretive and critical engagement. Substantively the upshot would seem to be a revision to the position centered on recapitulation in favour of a complex tale of economic, political and cultural adjustment in the face of an expansionary world capitalist system.

These revisions, formal and substantive, are already in evidence within development theory work. Here I wish only to call attention to them. Thus I conclude with a schematic overview which stresses these epistemological changes: in any substantive enquiry proferred theorems will, of course, be shaped by many other considerations. In post-Second World War development theory it is not difficult to find evidence of empiricist and interpretive epistemologies: critical theoretic work is rather less obviously present.

The naturalism of the orthodoxy of post-Second World War social science has been linked directly to the functionalist analysis of industrial (as opposed to capitalist) society in the 1950s and 1960s by Giddens.[108] This analysis of industrial society was in turn a part of the broader package of ideas expressed in the trio of 'modernization-industrialism-convergence'.[109] Linked to this package, revealingly, were ideas of the 'end of ideology'.[110] The orthodoxy within development theory at this time was modernization theory and, whilst that approach has been routinely criticized for its ethnocentric evolutionism (and functionalism), in the present context we can add that its philosophical naturalism was also a defect.[111] Modernization theory, in sum, aspired to produce policy science.

The approach is now in eclipse but the descendant of modernization theory – both formally and substantively – is with us in the conservative ideology of supply side economics coupled to concerns for public order and administration.[112] I would argue that whilst this delimited-formal ideology is presently fashionable (and in practice powerful) it is not to be taken seriously intellectually. It remains retrogressive in terms of development theory work and continues in naturalist style, indeed one of its gurus, Friedman, has argued for a positive economics.[113] For development theorists it is arguably the pervasive-informal residuum of this approach that has to be attended to – a point I urged in the foregoing chapter.

New work in development theory has grown up outside the intellectual sphere of modernization theory. Much of this work, for whatever detailed reasons, has also stepped outside the framework of philosophical naturalism. Thus Latin American dependency theory, perhaps most obviously in its structuralist phase, has both rejected neo-classical economics and insisted upon a problem specific approach that, *inter alia*, necessitated the acknowledgment of indigenous cultural patterns. Relatedly, there were nationalist writings available for contemporary theorists to draw on and any assertion of a distinctive Latin American culture must entail a move towards interpretive work.[114] In Southeast Asia, of course, we have the analogous examples of Boeke and Furnivall. Thus the philosophical and social theoretic concern for interpretation is evidenced in development theory work and, whilst to date this has been, given the nature of the orthodox, somewhat marginalized, it does seem that this marginal position is quickly breaking down.[115]

It is also clear that some interpretive work has always been done. Thus, most obviously, anthropologists have been concerned, in various ways, with the elucidation of forms of life. Hitherto it is arguably the case that anthropology has acted as some sort of handmaiden to colonialism – the provision of reports on how people lived which subsequently were taken up by manipulatively oriented colonial administrations.[116] But one can now point to a wealth of material that both interprets the form of life of Third World groups and cuts directly against the familiar intervention-serving assumptions of the eclipsed orthodoxy of development theory. Thus for example, the rise of 'peasant studies'.

In the modernization theory scheme the peasantry of the Third World were characterized in terms of their economies, polities, societies and cultures as 'traditional', which is to say, recalling all the analysis of this particular term, as defectively Western. Recent work on peasant forms of life has shattered this view and substituted an interpretive reading of peasant forms of life as coherent and vigorous. These societies are, it is now appreciated, culturally autonomous. What is then said about the situation of the peasantry in the contemporary world capitalist system is very different to the observations of the modernization theorists: in place of a limping process of movement from traditionalism to modernity (characterized naturalistically) we now see a complex process of active adjustment to the demands of expansionary capitalism. The ways in which the peasants themselves view the pressures on their extant forms of life, and how they severally respond, are now opened up as legitimate and broad areas of concern. This concern is no longer technical-manipulative but interpretive.

The views offered by anthropologically informed First World theorists may of course differ. They can range from the optimism of Scott[117] to the pessimism of Worsley.[118] However, what is important to note, for present purposes, is that adherence to an interpretive epistemology offers a distinct view of all these matters. It should also be noted that interpretive work has not been the sole province of the anthropologists; many historians have contributed to extant stocks of interpretive knowledge. A recent text by Thorne tackles the business of war as a forcing agent for thoroughly tangled pressures for change in Southeast Asia.[119] Anderson, in a slightly different fashion has much illuminated the processes.[120] Nor, finally, should it be thought that the mere adoption of an interpretive strategy is proof against erroneous formulations: of late many have objected to the procedures and conclusions of the orientalists.

It is also the case that the intellectual traffic, so to say, is not all one way. A key implication of interpretive philosophy and social theory is that taken-for-granted categories of analysis must be inspected: Husserl's transcendental reduction, Schutz's analyses of common sense, or Wittgenstein's confusion-dissolving all have it in common that the naturalistic habit of 'looking outwards' to the world is challenged in favour of a view which asserts the value of the critical examination of received cognitive structures and familiar strategies of making sense of the world. If, as these theorists all variously argue, the world is given in our concepts then a routine inspection of these concepts is clearly indicated.

The results of such examinations are not all of a piece in terms of the depth of reconsideration at which they are aimed. Thus, for example, one school within development theory has routinely insisted upon a reflexive approach to theorizing (both concept building and empirical enquiry) and this reflexivity has been oriented largely to the provision of a more subtly articulated naturalism in enquiry. The neo-institutionalists[121] have offered by far the most plausible expression of the orthodoxy of development theory but their work remains firmly within the naturalistically conceived project of an interventionist social science. In contrast we can associate with Winch a much more radical examination of received categories insofar as the theorists' use of Wittgensteinian notions has been taken to issue in a challenge to our notion of rationality itself.[122]

At a more macro-scale an insistence upon an interpretive approach allows what seems to me to be a more adequate strategy of commentary in respect of the development strategies pursued by particular nation-states. In place of the modernization theorists' supposition that the goal of any development policy has to be the world of the 'modern' – by which they meant pluralistic capitalism – we can now use the notion of ideology, after the fashion sketched by MacIntyre, to interpret the choices made by ruling elites. Development programmes can now be read as embodying the moral-political visions of elites. These 'visions' will, of course, be shaped by the historical junctures they inhabit. What is taken to count as 'development' is thus to be seen as locally determined, and this sort of an approach to interpretation generates a much richer view of what is actually going on in the Third World than the modernization theorists' blanket assumption of the pursuit of the recapitulation of the West's experience.[123]

In regard to the theorems offered by First World theorists, a similar interpretive strategy reveals the complexities of intra-First World debate: the modernization theory position, for all its orthodox status, is but one of (at least) five clearly identifiable theories.[124]

Most generally the burden for development theory of the philosophical and social theoretic interpretive line is a general concern for the relationship between First World theorists and the Third World. In the naturalistic perspective of modernization theory this relationship was conceived as one of super/sub-ordination. The orthodox assumption of cognitive superiority (possession of positive science) when deployed in the particular historical/cultural contexts of the post-Second World War period issued in a theory of development which placed responsibility for the whole business largely in the hands of the First Worlders (and their local 'agents'). The realization, in interpretive work, that attention has to be paid both to the autonomy of Third World forms of life and the analytical categories deployed in First World theorizing issues in a sharp movement away from this super/sub-ordinate schema in favour of a focus on the relationship between First and Third World: the formal epistemological revisions have substantive implications for enquiry. The technical expert stance of the modernization theorists which issued in their production of purportedly authoritative recipies of development for consumption in the Third World, now gives way to the tentative proferring of interpretations: such interpretations will acknowledge the cultural autonomy of the Third World forms of life, their embeddedness within the world capitalist system, and the interdependence of First and Third Worlds.

Moving finally, in this schematic review, to critical theory it is probably unsurprising, given the novelty of critical theory within First World social scientific discourse, that a self-consciously 'critical development theory' has not yet been produced. Critical theory as exemplified by the entirety of the Frankfurt School tradition has been preoccupied, firstly, with reformulating the marxian legacy such that the received scientistic political economy of Marx is displaced in favour of a recovery of the method of critique, and secondly, with analysing the cultural superstructure of monopoly capitalism. In the particular hands of Habermas these concerns have broadened into the pursuit of a grounded hermeneutics in his theory of universal pragmatics. The only obvious concern shown by critical theory comes with Marcuse's arguments for the revolutionary role of 'marginal figures' where the dispossessed of the Third World are read as marginal in this sense. This typically 1960s view has subsequently been dismissed as Third Worldism.[125] We must perforce look to the implications of critical theory in a rather more tentative fashion than we did with interpretive schemes.

Critical theory enjoins pursuing a grounded hermeneutic dialogue of theorist and subject. Where interpretive approaches rest content with the implicit emancipatory implications of the business of proffering new interpretations to subjects, critical theory advocates a dialogic exchange, with the theorist explicitly wedded to a radical democratic ethic, between theorist and subject with a view to dissolving ideological confusions and thus aiding human emancipatory action. However, given that critical theory can only get its programme going in a polity which in some fashion resembles Western liberal democracy (that is, having a developed and politically important civil society), the occasions on which critical theoretic material could be deployed in the Third World must be limited as, typically, spheres of civil society are limited or restricted in Third World nation-states by extant social and political forms (including repressive state machines).

One area in which one could envision the deployment of critical theoretic material would be the realm of First World understandings of the Third World: my critique of the residual common sense of development theory is one such preliminary effort.[126]

However it must be granted that the nature of the direct

implications of critical theory for development theory are as yet unclear. In Habermas's work there seem to be major difficulties militating against its use in development theory. Firstly, the reintroduction of evolutionist concepts, the heavy borrowings from systems theory, and the very abstract plane of concern for 'communication', all make the approach look a dubious prospect analytically. Secondly, the radical break with Marx's philosophical anthropology (whereby the stress on human labour, which leads to a concern for political economy, is replaced with a stress on communicative competence, which leads instead to a concern for the sphere of civil society) makes the approach look analytically unhelpful. Thirdly, the political stress on reconstructing a vigorous democratic civil society seems both utterly Western as a preoccupation and, again, less than obviously transferable to the Third World.

Nonetheless, to all this we should add that critical theory has usually taken itself to lodge within the marxian tradition and it is clear, notwithstanding Habermas's strictures on political economy, that this line of approach has had considerable impact on development theory, and a part of this legacy must of necessity be that aspect of critique that Frankfurt School theorists have been at pains to stress.

So, finally, how do all these various thoughts relate to the business of theorizing development? The answer is fairly clear in outline at least. If we want to make sense of development then we have to decisively reject the naturalistically conceived orthodoxy of post-Second World War development theory. Discussions of development, amongst First World commentators, will now have to accomplish the following: (i) the recovery of the usable ideas of nearly forty years' work; (ii) the establishment of an approach that centrally acknowledges the diversity of interests in the general business of 'development' and this implies an interpretive and critical approach; (iii) begin routinely to acknowledge the central role in our severally expressed efforts to 'make sense' of theoretical frameworks, and the requirement that they be routinely examined. All these are matters I presented in the preceding chapter and will illustrate further below.

3   Boeke and Furnivall's 'Southeast Asian sociology'[1]

1   Introduction

In this chapter I will look at the work of J.H. Boeke, who wrote about dual societies, and J.S. Furnivall, who wrote about plural societies. In respect of both these theorists it can be said that there has been, over many years, considerable debate about the plausibility, coherence and usefulness of their theories. I think it would be useful if I made clear what my particular interest is in their work.

We can note that Boeke and Furnivall have been associated – together and separately (and of course with Geertz, whom I don't treat here) – with a series of contemporary debates. Both are taken as anticipators of recent discussions in respect of the application of 'Western' social scientific ideas to 'eastern' cultures. Boeke has been linked to modernization theory's 'dualism'[2] and invoked in debates about the scope of orthodox economics.[3] I have two areas of interest in their work, of which the major one has been signalled in the title of this essay – I'll come to it in a moment. The second – here minor – interest lies in the mode of social theoretic engagement exemplified in their work. I think we can fairly label their efforts as the mode of engagement of the colonial administrator-scholar. I think this mode of engagement is of considerable interest in its own right – more practically, so to say, it evidently has links to the neo-institutionalism of Myrdal *et al.* However, in this essay, I'll focus on the business of a 'Southeast Asian sociology'.

Thus there is a thoroughly interesting question to put to this body of work which I can best present by first recalling that I have argued that social theorizing should not be seen as a mechanically technical discipline treating matters of social life after the presumed style of the natural sciences but rather as essentially concerned with ideology making. I also argued that what was to count as development – read as an ethico-political term – could only, so as to say, be locally determined. There are no *a priori* recipes; only ethico-politically based judgments of what might usefully be done in particular circumstances to move towards specified ends.[4] Thus if we ask whether or not there is a *Southeast Asian version of development theory* – distinct from 'the Western view' – then we find that it has been argued that the work of Boeke and Furnivall offers a preliminary statement of such an 'independent theoretical position'.

Now, Evers apparently makes this claim. First, dismissing recent enthusiasm amongt students of Southeast Asia for empirical social science research as a 'regression'[5] he goes on to say:

> South-East Asia can look back to a long tradition of social science research based on typical South-East Asian social problems. Some scholars have, indeed, followed this tradition and have continued a debate that goes back to the beginning of the century. A continuation of this debate and the raising of new issues based on problems of social change and development of South-East Asia will provide a new impetus for the further development of sociology in South-East Asia, that is both relevant to local problems and of use to the development of sociology throughout the world.[6]

Now, Evers's language is not mine; he speaks of a locally based contribution to sociology in general, a way of conceiving the matter which is apparently essentially orthodox empiricist style. In my case I would rather speak in more particular and ethico-politically based terms: of, that is, the attempt to constitute a non-Western European, or Southeast Asian, theory of development. Evers, to my mind, slurs over some crucial issues of social theoretic *roles* and *interests* when he elects to cast his discussion in these general sociological terms. However, setting that aside, it is quite clear that a most ambitious claim is being made here; but it is worth looking at precisely what *is* said and what is *not* said.

In an introductory essay to a collection dealing with Boeke, Furnivall, Geertz and Embree, Evers follows the above argument (from the Preface) by saying: 'There is hardly any study on South-East Asia that fails to allude to the extreme social, cultural and political diversity of the area.'[7] This, thinks Evers, is apposite and should be the starting point for enquiry: 'this diversity of culture, social structure, economic and political history in the region as a whole as well as within individual countries, should be recognised and analysed.'[8] He continues, recalling my note on his ambitions:

> Confronted by the diversity of South-East Asia and the startling differences between South-East Asian societies and their well known neighbours, particularly India, China and Japan, social scientists had to develop new concepts and new theories to tackle the empirical problems posed by their objects of research.[9]

Evers then cites the quartet of names I noted above, and the concepts for which they are noted, and remarks that: 'All these terms, originally developed in the context of South-East Asian studies, have found wide acceptions in social research elsewhere and have become standard concepts of text book social science.'[10]

From these lengthy quotations it is clear that a series of positive claims are being made: first, the claim that Southeast Asia is diverse (claim to fact); second, that social scientists studying Southeast Asia have developed concepts adequate to the data (claim to intellectual adequacy); and, third, that these concepts have been widely accepted and used elsewhere by social scientists (claim to intellectual status).

Evers then briefly reviews the work of his quartet and concludes by saying (first) that the four: 'represent in a certain way South-East Asia's indigenous contribution to the development of social Science.'[11] He goes on (second) to note that as the ideas developed in Southeast Asia have been 'exported', so too have other ideas been 'imported'. Thus dependency theory 'is of interest to South-East Asian studies as it is concerned with some of the major issues debated already under the heading of "dual society" or "involution" as discussed above.'[12] To the above-noted positive claims Evers is adding that the quartet offer a sort of indigeneous contribution to social science and that they anticipate dependency work insofar as they tackle the same range of issues. Evers then concludes, assuming that the 'regression' noted at the outset is avoided, that:

> a rethinking of basic theoretical issues is certainly necessary to enable a thorough analysis of long term trends in social change and development in South-East Asia. A greater knowledge of and awareness of theories that have emerged out of South-East Asian research in the past as well as appreciation of theories dealing with developmental and macro-sociological problems in other areas of Asia, Africa and Latin America will certainly help to achieve this end.[13]

In sum, Evers, is looking for and indeed is claiming, I think it's fair to say, to discern the outlines of a theory of social change and development that is (a) securely grounded in extensive, subtle, well-regarded empirical research in Southeast Asia – this is the first set of positive claims noted above; (b) in some sense independent, thus his favoured quartet are taken to have presented some sort of indigeneous contribution to the problem; (c) non-dependency whilst anticipating many of the typical dependency type issues anyway.

What Evers does not quite say is that he has actually found it – hence the quote about 'rethinking'. Nor does he cast his enquiries/proposals in politically sensitive terms, as do the dependency theorists. Rather, he argues in a general sociological style. However, Evers is advancing the work of his quartet as presenting a sketch, a preliminary statement, of a Southeast Asian theory of development. This is the route through the materials that I will take: I'll proceed as follows: (i) a presentation and comparison of Boeke and Furnivall's theories;[14] (ii) a review of the collection of essays deployed by Evers to secure his claims, and (iii) a discussion of Boeke and Furnivall as 'colonial administrator-scholars' and the implications of this role, as expressed in their work, for Evers's claims.

2 Boeke and Furnivall

2.1 J.H. Boeke

Boeke (1884–1956) was both a scholar and a colonial administrator in the Dutch East Indies. His first work on the economies and societies of the Dutch East Indies was his 1910 doctoral dissertation and it is here that the notion of dualistic economy was first presented. In his final book, *Economics and Economic Policy of Dual Societies* published in 1953, he is concerned with the same interests. I will offer a brief exposition of Boeke's 'dualism' from this 1953 text.

The method adopted by Boeke can be characterized as 'social economics', and the name of Werner Sombart is cited as a source for Boeke.[15] Boeke, at the outset of his text, claims that:

> It is possible to characterize a society, in the economic sense, by the social spirit, the organizational forms and the technique dominating it. These three are interdependent . . . in their interrelation they may be called the social system, the social style or the social atmosphere of that society.[16]

Evidently this bears little resemblance to the orthodoxies of neo-classicism and, indeed, just as Boeke argued for a new economics for the underdeveloped so, inevitably, he criticized the claims to scientific generality of the orthodox.

Boeke thinks a society can have more than one social system. He distinguishes between homogeneous societies and dual or plural societies. The term dual society is reserved for

> societies showing a distinct cleavage of two synchronic and full grown social styles which in the normal, historical evolution of homogeneous societies are separated from each other by transitional forms as, for instance, precapitalism and high capitalism by early capitalism . . .[17]

In the normal evolutionary run of things, evidenced in the history of the West, social styles evolve and at any one time one style predominates. Dual societies are therefore somewhat aberrant phenomena. Boeke observes:

> In a dual society . . . one of the two prevailing social systems as a matter of fact always the most advanced, will have been *imported from abroad* and have gained its existence in the new environment without being able to oust or to assimilate the divergent social system that has grown up there, with the result that neither of them becomes general and characteristic for that society as a whole.[18]

This is the general model being used. More specifically, historically, the story is of Western capitalism impacting upon the agrarian societies of the East. The Dutch East Indies case is presented as the best example of more general phenomena.

Boeke offers a definition:

> social dualism is the clashing of an imported social system with an indigenous social system of another style. Most frequently the imported social system is high capitalism. But it may be socialism or communism just as well, or a blending of them. Nevertheless even in that case it remains advisable to keep the term social dualism because this emphasizes the fact that the essence of social dualism is the clash between an imported and indigenous social system of divergent character.[19]

Thus far Boeke, with his work informed by a European scheme of dissenting economics and sociology[20] and a long exposure to the colonial experience of the Indies, has invited us to *look at what is the case*. He *points* to the 'reality' he would have us consider *directly* rather than, as is more usual, inviting us to treat it with reference to established theorems. Yamada takes Boeke to be a Don Quixote figure – deciding early that the orthodoxy was nonsensical, and thereafter arguing his case against the odds.[21]

Boeke presents his stance *vis-à-vis* the orthodoxy thus:

> Every social system has its own economic theory. A social economic theory is always the theory of a social system. Even if it announces itself as a general theory it is still historically determined. Therefore the economic theory of a dualistic, heterogeneous, society is itself dualistic. It has to describe and to explain the economic interactions of two clashing social systems. Indeed it will be realistic and not pure theory in so far as it has to be based on historical facts, generalizing them in an 'ideal-typical' (Max Weber) way. In so far it even will have to be three economic theories combined into one: the economic theory of a precapitalist

society, usually called primitive economics, the economic theory of a developed capitalistic or socialistic society, usually termed general economic theory or summarily social economic theory, and the economic theory of the interactions of two distinct social systems within the borders of one society which might be called dualistic economics if this term had not better been reserved for the combined economic theory of a dual society as a whole.[22]

Boeke then laments the lack of such a theory. The work of Indian economists is reviewed and found lacking: the younger economists look to stress the *similarities* of India and the West and amongst the older school – of nationalist politicians – only a handful, in Boeke's view, came close to an *Indian* economics centering on rural life. Gandhi is approved of, not because he's a dualist, rather he rejects capitalism. In Indonesia things are different.

The fact, that in contrast to India, it was mostly Europeans who occupied themselves with the economy of Indonesia in a theoretical sense, wakes expectations of greater objectiveness in stating differences between East and West, but at the same time less familiarity with the eastern conception of life.[23]

This is, evidently, a remarkable passage on several grounds: we are given an insight into the thought of an administrator-scholar of the colonial era. The backward-looking *celebration* of the 'east' (thus the mention of Gandhi is apposite) in contrast to the brash work of the young Indian economists plus, simultaneously, the allocation of indigenes to an *inferior intellectual status* – thus in Indonesia it was *European* scholars that did the job. The mode of being 'colonial administrator-scholar' would be intriguing to explore but that task is beyond my present scope. For the moment let us just compare the tone of the above passage with the objectives set out by Evers, which we noted above. Hardly an obvious fit!

Boeke traces the germ of the idea of dualism back to an anonymous essay of 1850. It was not until 1908 we are told that the idea reappeared to be picked up by Boeke and used in his doctoral dissertation of 1910. The 1953 text continues in this line. Thus Boeke invites us to consider the 'raw empirical data' of Southeast Asia and accept that a dualistic economics is needed. This dualistic economics is sharply different to the orthodox and this is a self-conscious position taken by Boeke, and it is a matter that he pursues.

Boeke argues that orthodox economics rests upon three principles: (a) the existence of unlimited personal wants; (b) the existence of a money economy; (c) the existence of the social institutions of a sophisticated economy. These three principles are then unpacked in a simple economic/sociological/psychological characterization of the 'social style' of western capitalist society. Boeke then notes:

> In all the above respects eastern economics is essentially different from western economics and hence western economic doctrines are not, or are only partly, applicable in the East: money, capital, markets, price formulation, division of labour, competition, the growth of trades and enterprises of trade cycles and so forth – in short all the important problems of western economic theory – do not present themselves, or at most do so only partly and imperfectly to eastern society.[24]

Boeke takes this to be a matter of simple observation: thus his claims can only be confirmed by the 'facts': 'This is why comparative cultural anthropology, primitive economics and sociology are so significant for the student of dualistic economics.'[25] This matter of the difference between orthodox and dualistic economics is further stressed when Boeke goes on to argue that dualistic economics is an intrinsically more difficult study than orthodox market economy economics. The student of eastern society is dealing with 'two social systems, one of which answers to western economic premises, while the other does not.'[26]

Boeke thinks that dualism is a widespread phenomenon: Australia and North America are cited where indigenous peoples have simply been overrun. However, it is in Southeast Asia that the circumstance of dualism is most evident. Boeke rejects the labels 'colonial' and 'tropical' economics: the latter on the obvious ground that dual economics are (have been) found outside the tropics; the former on the ground that the economies and societies of Southeast Asia are not primarily the creation of colonialism but are rather the creation of two incompatible systems, brought together, to be sure, by the arrival of the colonial powers – the bearers of Western capitalism. Boeke prefers the term Eastern economics (as, I assume, a synonym of dualistic economics – often his terminology is a little difficult to keep in clear focus). The basis for this choice is the judgment that the *cultures* of East and West are different and the West's capitalism has not destroyed the local culture – what we have is a dualistic situation. Again the terminology is slippery and Boeke acknowledges that 'Eastern' can mean dualistic (thus, both cultures plus patterns of exchange) or Eastern as opposed to Western. When we come to take note of the criticisms that have been brought against Boeke, we'll find that confusion in terminology is one of them!

The two elements in his dualistic scheme he labels capitalist and non- or pre-capitalist and it is the impact of an historically novel capitalism upon Eastern cultures that has set them 'adrift'[27] and created dualism. The basic evolutionary sequence, found in the West, has been disturbed – East and West are clashing *cultures*, clashing *economies* and (even represent) clashing *evolutionary periods*.

Boeke speaks of an 'antithesis ... between two social-economic periods in touch with one another ...'[28] The antithesis is further elucidated in terms of the antithesis of town and village; the antithesis of Eastern and Western ideas; and the antithesis of native and foreign – and this last antithesis Boeke says is to be rejected: it may be politically important but not analytically. The problem of dualism is economic, he urges, and if this is remembered 'both the dustbin term "colonialism" and the antithesis native-foreign become equally objectionable ...'[29] He adds, 'Hitherto economic dualism and colonialism have been confused by identifying capitalistic interests with foreign domination.'[30]

Evidently there is much in Boeke's theory to debate. First I will summarize what we have so far:

(a) a sociologized economics designed to be adequate to a dual society.
(b) where this involves two (imperfectly) interacting cultures,
(c) where this interaction was occasioned by the irruption of Western capitalism into a traditional agrarian society thereby creating a novel evolutionary path,
(d) and thus novel problems of policy-making,
(e) which cannot be reduced to the antithesis foreign capital – native victim (the nationalists' view),
(f) or tackled using orthodox economics (the view of the economic establishment),
(g) the only solution for the future is the encouraging of *recovery* and this recovery will flow from the now damaged/deformed rural, traditional, Eastern sector – recovery is envisioned in Gandhian 'spiritual' terms rather than narrowly economic.

When we come to present objections to Boeke's theory it is important to be clear about the precise understanding we have of Boeke's objectives and the precise grounds and nature of our own criticisms.

The clue to Boeke's objectives is, I think, fairly clear, but has not been pursued here, as my present interest is restricted to the claims of Evers. Boeke was a colonial administrator-scholar and his interest in Indonesia was shaped by that circumstance. This is a simple sociology-of-knowledge-deprived observation – *all* social theorizing is shaped by its context. Now, having said this, it is also quite clear that Boeke argues a case on behalf of those for whom he assumes a responsibility: he steers a middle course between the, rather indifferent we can plausibly suppose, metropolitan authorities (plus their economists) and the equally unsatisfactory nationalists (with their concerns with political changes).

Now if that is what Boeke was attempting what are we to say about the material produced?[31] Here my comments will be both narrowly academic and shaped by my views about theorizing as propounded above.

Boeke's economics have the great merit of adopting a broad socio-economic approach. The inability of orthodox economics to grasp the dynamics of Third World societies (and First World, come to that) is something that has been repeatedly said over recent years. More specifically, Boeke anticipated the *general approach* to these problems which I have associated above with the neo-institutionalists – the rejection of formalism in pursuit of realism.[32] However, the theoretical stance established by Boeke does have flaws. The terminology he uses is imprecise, as we noted above. Sometimes these imprecisions look important: Thus he tends to speak of the *capitalist economic system* impacting upon the *eastern social system* and, apart from the evident maldistribution of intellectual attention revealed, it can be seen as evidence of stereotypical thinking on Boeke's part (rational materialist West versus religious-minded East although, to be fair, others have said much the same.)[33] This suspicion crops up when we consider that at the outset he called for three economics – of pre-capitalism, of capitalism, and of the interaction between the two. Boeke does not provide these three; rather he continually stresses the differences between 'East' and 'West', and does so by focusing upon the 'East'. The relationship of East and West is also one-sidedly presented: the East is seen as a passive recipient of outside impulses to change: there is no mention of internal forces to change and the destruction or radical deformation of these forces.

Moving on to Boeke's sociology – to oversimplify the mix – we find an extensive celebration of the 'traditional' society and culture of the East. Many critics have said that Boeke's view of rural communities in Indonesia is distinctly romantic – and certainly overestimates the static, timeless and religious qualities, whilst understanding the rational economic. This leads us on to the business of the dualistic conception: Boeke has two separate cultures within the borders of one society. This dualistic presentation he then discusses in familiar ways – I noted two of his antitheses. It is not a satisfactory analytical procedure.

Finally, what are we to say about his practical (political) proposals. Rejecting the (unspelt out) arguments of the (unspecified) national-ists, he proposes a policy of benign neglect: the damaged Eastern sector of agriculturalists must be left to regenerate, Gandhi style, the dualistic society as a whole. I noted above that Boeke dismissed the notion of a 'colonial economy' and here we see a further instance of his neglect (like the other dualists we discussed above) of realities of the extension of Western capitalism into the Third World.

Finally, what are we to say about the project of Evers? As an interim comment – before we return to the matter in section 4 – we can say that Evers, like Boeke, endeavours to cast his arguments in general terms and in so doing obscures the crucial point that social theorizing is *specific* – to times, places and persons. I cannot see how the work of a colonial administrator-scholar, *for all its interest*, can serve as a key part of the foundation of an independent, locally produced theory of change and development in Southeast Asia.

2.2 J.S. Furnivall

Now I turn to J.S. Furnivall. Where Boeke approaches Southeast Asia with a 'sociologized economics', to use my anachronistic label, Furnivall, in the Preface to his *Netherlands India: A Study of a Plural Economy* (1939), reports that 'this book is . . . intended as a contribution towards comparative political science.'[34] Furnivall then speaks of the European colonialists having

> come to recognize a moral responsibility for the welfare of the people; the central problem of political endeavour is . . . to build up a new order of society in which all sections of the community may live together in harmonious relations, and all the people fully realize their privileges as citizens of the modern world.[35]

So, here we have both a rather different approach and goal to contend with: Furnivall's focus is on the *politico*-economics of the territories (where Boeke's was on the culture economics) and aims to identify a progressive route to the future (where Boeke tended to be somewhat backward-looking). It is appropriate to keep these differences in conception and intention clear, because in their discussions there are many resemblances in the detail.

Furnivall's text is a massive and authoritative review of the history, culture and development of the Dutch Indies. The theoretical underpinnings and practical implications of his review are drawn together in a concluding chapter entitled 'Plural Economy'. Furnivall begins with a definition of a plural society, it is 'a society . . . comprising two or more social orders which live side by side, yet without mingling, in one political unit'.[36] This pluralism is a familiar phenomenon, he suggests, and cites the US and South Africa by way of examples. However, 'Netherlands India is ... an extreme type...'[37]

Turning to economics, Furnivall characterizes a plural economy as one where there is no 'common will';[38] and by 'common will' he means a taken-for-granted idea of how society ought to be – a common culture. The implications of such a lack of 'common will' is that there is no taken-for-granted schedule of economic wants: no 'common social demands'.[39] Furnivall thinks that this idea has been neglected by political economists since Adam Smith's day. Political economists have assumed a common schedule of wants and have looked at the issue of production: that is, how to secure those wants. Furnivall insists that 'common social demand' is built up through time and that it is this set of taken-for-granteds that orientate and discipline the behaviour of individuals in their economic pursuits. Now here is the problem: 'in a plural society, social demand is disorganized; social wants are sectional, and there is no social demand common to all the several elements'.[40] This, observes Furnivall, has very considerable implications, indeed 'it is the root cause of all those properties which differentiate plural economy, the political economy of a plural society, from unitary economy, the political economy of a homogeneous society.'[41] The common meeting place – as Furnivall unpacks his analysis – of the elements of a plural society is the *market place*. In a plural society the market place is more rigorously economic than exchange in any other, homogeneous society, *precisely* because the discipline of 'accepted social demands' is missing. A further consequence of this unfettered stress on economic exchange[42] is the sectionalizing of economic production along ethnic lines. This aggravates the original disintegration of societal pluralism. The economic aspect, to introduce a further consequence, comes to dominate even the separate sectors which are comparatively culturally impoverished thereby. All in all, Furnivall is painting a picture of societal degradation.[43] He sums up as follows:

> In a plural society, then, the community tends to be organized for production rather than for social life; social demand is sectionalized and within each section of the community the social demand becomes disorganized and ineffective, so that in each section the members are debarred from leading the full life of a citizen in a homogeneous community, finally the reaction against these abnormal conditions, taking in each section the form of Nationalism, sets one community against the other so as to emphasize the plural character of the society and to aggravate its instability, thereby enhancing the need for it to be held together by some force exerted from the outside.[44]

Now here Furnivall's analysis has shifted from looking at the system itself, to the key issue, in his view, of holding the system together. This is a matter to which Furnivall returns, after having first looked at the issue of the relationship of plural and orthodox economics.

On this issue we find that Furnivall agrees with Boeke that orthodox economics are of little use. However, he does so for slightly different reasons. The problem of strategy of analysis is presented thus:

> Western economic theory is but of limited application in a tropical
> dependency. The reason lies in the political constitution of a
> tropical dependency as a plural society . . . there is no community
> as a whole, and problems of political and economic science differ
> fundamentally from those of homogeneous societies.[45]

Thus, in a plural society, the basic political problem is not securing adequate 'expression of social will',[46] it is rather the 'integration of society'.[47] This, thinks Furnivall, is a much more 'elemental'[48] task. Likewise with economics: in an homogeneous society the problem is of satisfying an 'historically agreed' schedule of wants (that is, there is a 'common social demand'), whereas in a plural society the problem is the 'integration or organization of demand'.[49] Furnivall summarizes these lines of argument thus:

> It would seem then that in homogeneous and plural societies the
> practical ends served by political and economic science are quite
> distinct: in the former the end of political science is to provide
> most adequately for the expression of social will, and the end of
> political economy is to provide most adequately for the satisfaction
> of social and individual demand; whereas in a plural society the
> ends are respectively to integrate society and to organise social
> demand.[50]

Furnivall then returns to the issue of effective political control. Around his view that integration/organization are the crucial problems he looks for policy implications. Here he speaks of 'Resolution of Plural Economy' and identifies four: (a) castes; (b) law; (c) nationalism; and (d) federalism.

Caste is discussed in the light of the observation that 'the outstanding instance of a stable plural society may be found in British India where caste has given a religious basis to inequality.'[51] Caste systems, notes Furnivall, have certainly assisted economic exploitation, but such a relationship of colonizers to colonized is no longer in favour. New justifications, and expectations for the future, rest – as we saw at the very outset of these notes – upon a mission to draw the dispossessed into the mainstream of 'progress'. Furnivall observes that whilst caste does ensure a stability,

> caste and social progress are conflicting principles, and a European cannot accept a social order built on caste without renouncing his heritage and acquiescing in stagnation; neither will Orientals acquiesce in a position of permanent inferiority. For European and Oriental alike caste affords no prospect of a final resolution of the strain inherent in a plural society.[52]

The law will not serve either. The notions of 'equality before the law' and 'the rule of law' are the products of particular concatenations of circumstances: the law, Furnivall is saying, is *made* in society and can only *work* with the acceptance or acquiescence of society. In a plural society there is no general basis for law – the law is reduced to one more set of problems to be viewed pragmatically in the light of a main commitment to economic exchange. If, in addition, the legal code in question is that of liberal market society (which it is – this being the character of Western capitalism), then the law as a source of social integration/organization looks doubly unsatisfactory.

Nationalism is treated in two steps. First, nationalism is linked to democracy (which linkage Furnivall notes has taken place in India). This linkage also advances the claims of social life in general as opposed to narrow economic exchange. It is thus both progressive and tends to the unification rather than disintegration of society. But there is a problem, and here is Furnivall's second step: 'difficulties have already been experienced in applying the doctrine of National-ism where there is no nation'.[53] And Furnivall goes on to argue that in a plural society the relationship between the constituent parts are much more like inter-national than intra-national relations. The principle of democracy – rule of majority – will give power to *one* 'nation' out of the group. Furnivall concludes therefore that: 'The principle of Nationalism provides no solution in itself, for, in a plural society, nationalism is in effect internationalism'.[54] He then adds, 'Nationalism within a plural society is itself a disruptive force, tending to shatter and not to consolidate the social order.'[55]

Federalism is the solution favoured by Furnivall. He commends the Dutch, who recognized the problem with the notion of 'dual society'. The closest the British have to this, says Furnivall, is 'the theory of the dual mandate'.[56] Here the metropolitan power is 'doubly charged with a duty to the world in the exploitation of the economic resources of the dependency and a duty to the people to consult their welfare and ... to devote especial care to the conservation of the native social order by a policy of Indirect Rule ... this may be termed the Federal solution ...'[57] At which point my exposition of Furnivall neatly comes full circle: at the end of the book he recalls his Preface – the Europeans have a duty to bring the colonial territories into the broad stream of modern life.

Brookfield, writing about dualism, begins by remarking that: 'It is a matter of simple observation that the economies of a great many developing countries are organized in two parts . . .'[58] and a little later notes that whilst this is a fact attested to by 'other writers and by Western businessmen and planters in every bar in every colony there has ever been . . . to say this is not to accept any particular explanatory theory.'[59] With Boeke and Furnivall we are offered two rather similar explanations which have now come to be regarded as classic texts. The theories they offer do differ in detail, as we have seen: Boeke focuses his analysis upon the cultures and economics of these societies, whereas Furnivall focuses upon the politics and economics. Both theorists, treating the same territory, have recourse to what I have called, in discussing modernization theory, dualistic strategies of explanation and I have argued to some length that such strategies have grave defects. The detail of Furnivall's work I have not critically reviewed. To do so would be rather repetitious: his overall strategy – allocation of the population into sharply distinct groups, interacting minimally and in what we would now call an economic zero sum fashion, and requiring thereby the guiding hand of the colonial power – is not, in broad outline, so very different from Boeke, although their particular intellectual foci are different, as are their policy proposals. Both theorists argue cases from the stance of colonial administrator-scholars – their theories have, so to say, a 'family resemblance'.

The theories of Boeke and Furnivall, as practical exercises in making sense (as they were most certainly intended by their authors), were rendered otiose by the Second World War. The future was inherited by the nationalists whom Boeke and Furnivall viewed with disfavour. Nonetheless their work has considerable interest both as specimens of a style of theorizing and as the base upon which Evers would have us believe a Southeast Asian theory of development could be erected. It is to this argument that I now turn.

3 The basis of a Southeast Asian approach?

I want now to consider briefly the collection of essays presented by Evers. This collection was offered, let us recall, to adumbrate the essentials of 'South-East Asia's indigeneous contribution . . . to . . . social science'.[60] I will review, in a fairly simple fashion, this collection of essays and ask whether or not Evers actually secures his claims.

The collection begins with the issues of the *diversity* of Southeast

Asia: and an authoritative historical review is cited. That Southeast Asia *is* diverse is fairly easy to grant; but what is not discussed is whether or not Southeast Asia is any more diverse than other parts of the world. When a key claim in your overall argument[61] is going to be the appropriateness and usefulness of the concepts fashioned locally to deal with this diversity, then it is necessary to show that the area actually is unusual. Resting content – as this argument (essay collection) does – with *illustrating that which strikes you as obvious* is a weak beginning.[62]

The argument then shifts to look at the work of Boeke, which is presented via a series of extracts from his 1940 text *Indonesian Economics*. The core of the argument is thus displayed: the irruption of capitalism into agrarian Eastern societies has generated the pattern labelled 'dualism' and this requires an economic theory to go with it. Boeke's work is then discussed via a series of commentators and, it must be said, this sequence is well fashioned. The opening commentator, Koentjaraningrat, reviews the debate as to whether: (a) Boeke got the story (facts) straight; and, (b) a more central concern, it seems, for commentators, whether Boeke was right to argue for a new economics. This commentator offers no view, but the next one does. Thus Higgins offers a trenchant critique from the position of an orthodox economist. All rather naive, so far as I could see. Not so the contribution of the third commentator, Yamada, who calls Boeke a Don Quixote of economics and reviews his arguments sensitively, systematically and critically. Yamada remarks at the end of his piece that what is needed in talk about Southeast Asian development is a clarification of 'the structural interrelationships between economic social and cultural factors'.[63] He immediately adds: 'This problem is exactly what Boeke was vainly trying to emphasize and solve'.[64] The subsequent contributions collected by Evers add little to the foregoing.

I think we can reasonably say the following in respect of the argument (collection) thus far: Evers's collection is discussing the pros and cons of dualism. This is an interesting issue interestingly presented. However, I wonder if he has not asked one very interesting question (is 'dualism' a part of the base of a Southeast Asian approach to development?) and then gone to answer a rather different question (that is, is dualism interesting, and so on?).

In the second section of the argument (collection) attention turns to Furnivalll, who first speaks for himself through an extract from the text I cited above. We then have an apparently rather disconnected series of readings which after a while resolve themselves into a discussion of the issues of social coherence and control. This is appropriately Furnivallian.

Rex looks at Myrdal, Malinowski and Furnivall as thinkers who have rightly picked up culture-contact/conflict as an issue for modern society. Wertheim looks at how the Chinese emigrated to Southeast Asia and how they have settled into various socio-economic circumstances. This is a tale of conflict and accomodation with 'host' populations in the context of new nation-state-making: a fragile situation. Evers himself looks at nascent class conflict in the burgeoning urban centres of Southeast Asia. The situation in Malaysia and Indonesia is looked at in terms of ethnic cleavages, and finally the use of the idea of pluralism in the *West* Indies is reviewed.

At this point the question raised above can be repeated: all this material is interesting and Furnivall-relevant but what has it got to do with the pursuit of a novel Southeast Asian approach? I cannot see that it has any direct bearing upon the problem.

In sections 4 and 5 we meet the debates surrounding John Embree's characterization of Thai society as 'loosely structured' and Clifford Geertz's notion of 'involution'. Again the central argument presented by Evers is not advanced. Finally, in section 6, we have pieces on culture, class and dependency and, at this point, the coherence and force of the argument (collection) finally shrinks away to nothing.

4   Boeke and Furnivall's theorizing and the project of a Southeast Asian Sociology

I began this discussion of dualism/pluralism by saying that out of the various 'routes' through the material which was available I would pursue the intriguing claim made by Evers that these ideas formed some sort of a basis for a distinctively Southeast Asian contribution to sociology. *In my terms*, Evers was looking for an independent Southeast Asian theory of development and, as I have by now made clear, it strikes me as bizarrely inappropriate to begin such a laudable search with the work of two colonial administrator-scholars who *both* rejected the nationalists, who could be taken as a rather more plausible start-point for an independent theory (see below) *and* who did not look to any social/political future that would be recognizably plausible today but instead to either a continuation of colonialism or a reversion to some romantic vision of an undamaged past.

In this concluding note I will offer explanations of why the case argued by Boeke and Furnivall cannot form the basis of an independent Southeast Asian approach to theorizing development; of how Evers comes to offer such a hopelessly flawed argument; and who must construct a Southeast Asian approach and what I think will be at its core.

I remarked above that I thought that both Boeke and Furnivall were prospective and general social theorists looking to interpret the world in a practical (political-policy) fashion. When interpreted in this way their work is of considerable intrinsic interest. However, I cannot see that it is sensible to read them as uncommitted contributors to a 'general science of the social' – the orthodox image of social science. Their approach involved the two crucial elements of: (a) a presentation of the 'gross facts' based upon familiarity with the area; and, (b) the realization that a new economic-political theory was needed. What they did, to repeat, was argue *circumstance-sensitive and problem-specific cases*. The question to be asked – bearing in mind Evers's suggestions – is '*whose case?*'. And the proximate answer to this question has already been given: they were administrator-scholars and they argued the case of responsible, concerned (etc.), *colonial administrators*. This 'case' cannot provide the base for an independent approach to Southeast Asian development. In social theorizing conceptions and intent are inextricably intertwined and their views of how the future ought to be shaped by their subsequent theorizing. This is *not* to say they were 'biased', it is to say that *all* theorizing is necessarily value-suffused and that such 'values' both help fashion and direct analysis. Fact and value cannot be separated in any simple fashion such that we could say yes, they had many *facts* correct, even if their colonial values are no longer satisfactory; rather we are confronted with, so to say, 'package deals' and in the *first* place we either accept or reject the 'package' and only *thereafter* can we search for any valuable elements.[65] If we are looking for an 'independent Southeast Asian package' then it is of little use looking to Boeke and Furnivall.

I can offer as an example of what I take to be an 'independent approach to development' an intellectual-political product similar in overall form to what I take Evers to have in mind – the Latin American dependency school of development theory. In this case the experience and circumstances of Latin America are apprehended using both 'established' and 'novel' social scientific ideas in a way that places these factors at the *centre* of enquiry.

Evers fails to find his Southeast Asian analogue to dependency theory for two broad reasons. The first is that he uses a starting point which is shaped – and shaped quite obviously – by colonial interests; this is the point I have made several times above. The second reason, it seems to me, is the way in which he casts his own work and his prospective Southeast Asian theory in essentially orthodox empiricist terms. In the argument that Evers presents there is no hint of any appreciation of social theorizing as being *necessarily* lodged within a context: a set of disciplinary traditions and social circumstances which together constitute the ground upon which the theorist builds. Theorists construct arguments designed to make sense; theorizing is thus circumstance- and problem-specific. If Evers had followed this view of theorizing then he would not, I feel, have produced a text comprised of debates by outsiders about theories produced by outsiders.

To conclude: I think the question raised by Evers is a thoroughly interesting one, but it seems to me that he has looked for an answer in the wrong place and in the wrong way. Against Evers's view I would suggest that any indigeneous Southeast Asian approach to development will only be discovered (if it's there) in the work of *local* scholars, commentators and social activists.

4   Arguing on behalf of scholarship: Barrington Moore

I want to consider in this chapter the mode of engagement of the critical humanist scholar, and I have taken the obvious figure of Barrington Moore as my example. In the post-Second World War career of development studies Moore's text *The Social Origins of Dictatorship and Democracy* is justly celebrated. This work represents an example of what I think of as 'revisionist modernization theory': the attempt made by a comparative handful of figures to accommodate to the evident flaws in the early simplistic formulations of modernization theory. The substantive interest of Moore's work lies here. But for the present I am interested in Moore's work insofar as it instances a particular mode of social theoretic engagement. I will review Moore's work with this interest of mine in view: thus little of what I say about Moore *per se* will be novel in itself. I will consider the following: firstly, his milieu and intellectual style; secondly, the substantive arguments of *Social Origins*; and, thirdly, the nature of the contribution made by Moore. Against the familiar social scientific habit of measuring contributions against the imaginary standard of a 'general theory of development' (or, here, modernization) I will endeavour to characterize and evaluate Moore's work as a particular mode of social theoretic engagement.

In a discussion of Walt Rostow,[1] I offered two reasons why his 'message' had been listened to – timing/origin and content: in brief, he said what people wanted to hear and did so from a position of authority. If we look at Moore in a similar way we find a much more intriguing situation: his 'message' was listened to but generally with considerable irritation. How did he manage this?

Moore's book was published at a time when surety in respect of the world role of the USA as guardians of the 'free world' was beginning to crumble; and as confidence in the justice, vigour and harmony of US society itself was also failing. Social theorists in the US at this time had to revise their rather complacent schemes[2] and tackle the issues of conflict and change. The response of the mainstream theorists was to invoke ideas of neo-evolutionary change and conflict theory.[3] It is an unsatisfactory strategy of 'ad hoccery'[4] and it's this approach that leads to the familiar US textbook absurdity of labelling Marx a conflict theorist. In contrast Moore did *not* adopt a strategy of *ad hoc* revision, rather he effected a partial return to the classical tradition of social theorizing and began the whole analysis to some extent afresh. What he presented was, in *Social Origins*, a comparative historical approach which was sensitive to the value-ladenness of social theorizing.

Moore's response to the problems of conflict and change was much more fruitful than that of the mainstream modernizers and this ensured the text a hearing: so much for the timing and general strategy of analysis. What of the content of Moore's 'message'? It is here that irritation was most easily expressed: if effecting a partial return to classical social science was problematical for the mainstream then what Moore had to say about conflict and change was even less welcome. In contrast to the orthodox story of the rise of the modern world which had largely 'read out' conflict, Moore made conflict between classes, civil war, and revolution all crucial to any plausible analysis. Moore was also sharply critical of contemporary US society. On the business of the 'receipt of message' we can note that there are those who can be labelled and dismissed (and this is a familiar strategy – call someone a 'left-winger' and dismiss their arguments or, contrariwise, call someone a 'right-winger' and dismiss them) and there are those who cannot be dismissed in this a cavalier fashion. Thus Smith notes that whilst Herbert Marcuse's *One Dimensional Man* (1964) was dismissed as 'left wing', Barrington Moore could not so be treated:

> Here was a man who actually *believed* in the proclaimed values of liberal democracy and did not think that the existence of capitalism was a fundamental obstacle to their achievement. The very Americanness of Barrington Moore made it difficult for radicals or conservatives to ignore him.[5]

Moore's partial return to the classical tradition of social theory is, so far as I can see, the crucial reason for his continuing interest. Smith, in his commentary on Moore, makes this point and suggests that Moore was a member of a 'scattered . . . intellectual resistance movement'[6] to orthodox US social science. Another member was C. Wright Mills who, to recall, had argued that 'what may be called classic social analysis is a definable and usable set of traditions . . . its essential feature is the concern with historical social structures . . . its problems are of direct relevance to urgent public issues and insistent human troubles.[7] Moore follows this view.

Moore's work as a social theorist spans some thirty years from the 1950s through to the 1980s and, in addition to *Social Origins* (1966),

he has produced a series of other texts.[8] Endeavouring to characterize
in a brief way his underlying concerns is not easy, for not only does he
follow Mill's injunction but he does so in a perfectly obvious way.
That is Moore *addresses problems*, he does not ply the trade of this or
that disciplinary specialism within social science. Both in the body of
his work and in *Social Origins*, in particular, he takes the roles of
methodologist, political theorist, moral analyst, historian, sociologist
and so on as and when the problem at hand dictates. However, a brief
summary of his underlying concerns can be advanced – but let us
note that this is a considerable simplification of what is complex
analysis. Moore is interested in how his style of history-making can
'. . . be used by men and women in order to comprehend and master
their destiny within the limits of their moral and rational development
and the stage of evolution reached by the societies and the global
order to which they belong.'[9] This summary, from Smith, seems both
correct and somewhat restricted – Moore's concern for, as I put it,
'making sense' was substantive and not, as the quotation implies,
rather formal or technical. Moore looked to understand, using his
'historical and comparative' approach, the general nature of liberal
democracy: the role of the intellectual was the dispassionate display of
the truth and the moral touchstone of enquiry was the elimination of
unnecessary misery. It is interesting to compare this characterization
of the cognitive and moral position of the intellectual with that of
Habermas.[10] Moore's 'critical theory' is based in his comparative
historical studies of the rise of the modern world, as he puts it, and
not, as is the case with Habermas, in a philosophically sophisticated
Hegelian Marxism. This difference in starting point and style has
considerable implications for the coherence of the analyses presented: Moore's 'empiricism' and commitment to liberal democracy lead
him into trouble, as we'll see.

Moore's characteristic approach follows the classical tradition of
social science in that it derives – in its own fashion – from the
Enlightenment. The role of the scholar, as we've seen, is characterized by the morally engaged pursuit of the truth (about liberal
democracy in Moore's case) and this entails a series of tasks for the
social scientist: how the world changes; what the scope is for effective
human action and upon what moral base such action can be
established. Evidently this procedure is going to issue in a 'dense'
analysis – an example might now be helpful. In his *Social Origins*
Moore begins with the English case, discussed under the heading
'England and the Contributions of Violence to Gradualism' which at
the outset is evidently rich in irony. Moore's analysis opens thus:

As one begins the story of the transition (i) from the preindustrial to the modern world (ii) by examining the history of the first country to make the leap (iii) one question comes to mind automatically. Why did the process of industrialization in England culminate in the establishment of a relatively free society? (iv) That contemporary England has been such for a long time, (v) perhaps even considerably more liberal than the United States in the crucial areas of freedom of speech and the tolerances of organised political opposition (vi) seems plain enough.[11]

This passage is typical of the way Moore's enquiries into history are conducted so as to illuminate the present: it is 'critical'. It is also, evidently, the work of a literate man – there is no recourse here (or elsewhere in Moore's work) to any self-consciously 'scientific' procedure: Moore pursues his problems directly and does so upon the base of a complex set of intellectual, ethical and political commitments. Thus (i) he speaks of *the transition* to the modern world: on Gellner's scheme[12] an unsatisfactory episodic model of change. He (ii) distinguishes pre-industrial and modern: the sort of dualistic scheme familiar in modernization schemes. If history is a 'before' followed by an 'after' then (iii) someone had to leap first: again a modernization/orthodox position. Moore then poses a question (iv) which is typical Moorean strategy – inviting the reader to join the process of discovery: the particular claim is both studiously vague (relative to what other societies?) and uncritically accepting of UK polity. This orthodox view (v) of the UK is repeated and used as base for a sharp criticism of the USA: Moore routinely offers explicit moral judgments. The perceived tolerance of UK polity to dissent (vi) again lets Moore *read-in* ethics and politics. In sum, what we have is a comparative historical, ethically engaged, pursuit of an understanding of the present situation of liberal democracy – and, by implication, the chances for the future.

Moore's analysis in *Social Origins* runs to some 500 pages, all written in the above-illustrated 'dense' style. Happily for my expository purposes the author summarizes his own argument in a brief preface, which I shall refer to.

Moore declares that his book

endeavours to explain the varied political roles played by the landed classes and the peasantry in the transformation from agrarian societies . . . to modern industrial ones. Somewhat more specifically, it is an attempt to discover the range of historical conditions under which either or both of these rural groups have become important forces behind the emergence of western parliamentary versions of democracy, and dictatorships of the right and the left, that is, fascist and communist regimes.[13]

Moore is thus interested in the *variety of routes to the modern world* and he identifies four.

'The first of these leads through what I think deserve to be called bourgeois revolution . . . a necessary designation for certain violent changes that took place in English, French and American societies on the way to becoming modern industrial democracies.'[14] The three sets of violent changes are respectively: the English Civil War of the seventeenth century; the French Revolution of the eigtheenth century; and the American Civil War of the nineteenth century. We can usefully expand on this a little. What Moore is doing is looking at the industrial and commercial bourgeoisie gained political power in each of the three states. This attaining of political power was: (a) necessary to securing a liberal democratic version of industrialism, and (b) shaped by the particular concatenation of class forces holding in each of the three sets of circumstances. Moore takes for granted the historically progressive role of the bourgeoisie (in fact he collapses their role into an evolutionary logic of a modernization theory type, that is, the whole process is retrospectively viewed as inevitable – so don't bother too much with the bourgeoisie – and what is interesting is how circumstances (rural classes) helped or hindered) and looks at how their route to power shaped their societies route to the modern world. The particular character of existing societies (USA, UK, France) is to be approached by spelling out how their respective pasts shaped them.

The second route identified by Moore

> has also been capitalist, but culminated during the twentieth century in fascism. Germany and Japan are the obvious cases . . . I shall call this the capitalist and reactionary form. It amounts to a form of revolution from above. In these countries the bourgeois impulse was much weaker. If it took a revolutionary form at all, the revolution was defeated. Afterwards sections of a relatively weak commercial and industrial class relied on dissident elements in the older and still dominant ruling classes, mainly recruited from the land, to put through the political and economic changes required for a modern industrial society, under the auspices of a semi-parliamentary regime. Industrial development may proceed rapidly under such auspices. But the outcome, after a brief and unstable period of democracy, has been fascism.[15]

Moore does not discuss the case of German fascism on the grounds that others have said all he would wish to. Elsewhere[16] I have briefly reviewed the historical experience of Germany: unified under Bismarck's authoritarian dictatorship, the bourgeoisie failed to attain power after his departure from the scene. Max Weber devoted much of his efforts to identifying to the German bourgeoisie their 'historic responsibilities' – he failed and liberal democracy was eventually *implanted* in (West) Germany by the victors of the Second World War. And in the case of Japan – the first of three Asian examples considered by Moore – we have a similar tale of authoritarian reform establishing a capitalist industrial system but no democracy: Moore speaks of 'Asian fascism' and here I will fill in some of the detail.

Moore begins his analysis by comparing Japan, China and Russia. In the seventeenth century relatively stable governments came to power in all three countries but, whereas in China and Russia revolutions eventually occurred, in Japan a version of reform from above occurred. Moore asks 'why this difference?' – and answers in terms of the class dynamics of Japanese feudalism and that system's response to the irruption of Western influence in the nineteenth century.

The Tokugawa Shogunate (1600–1868) established peace, and politically it was concerned with 'the maintainance of peace and order'.[17] It was on Moore's account a feudal system of rural lords (daimyo), aristocrat-warriers (samurai), and a rural peasantry that supported the whole system. The system worked, but contained within it the seeds of its own demise:

> By the time Commodore Perry's ships appeared in 1854, the Tokugawa system has suffered substantial decay. The decline of the old order, together with attempts to preserve the privileges of the agrarian elite, had already given rise to some of the social forces that eventually culminated in the [1941] regime . . .[18]

The key factors were two – 'peace and luxury'.[19] Thus peace 'permitted a commercial way of life to emerge not only in the towns but also in the countryside'.[20] And luxury weakened the power of the nobles whilst simultaneously giving assistance to the towns and depressing the peasantry: the warrior-aristocrats were marginalized through this period and became (some of them) reactionary.

It was the irruption of the West that fatally disturbed the processes of this precariously balanced system. The Meiji Restoration of 1868 was essentially a backward-looking attempt to create a unified state in face of outside pressures. This it did – but the restored monarchy then pursued a 'modernizing' strategy. Moore asks: 'what prompted this largely feudal revolution to carry out a program with many undoubted progressive features'?[21] His answer is that the Meiji Restoration enabled a section of the landed aristocracy to seize power and force through a revolution from above that involved the key aspects of unified nation-statehood and industrialization. Moore comments: 'The Tokugawa in their victory of 1600 had laid the foundations of a modern centralized state. The Meiji completed the process.'[22]

The warrior-aristocrats had not bargained for this as they pressed for the return of the emperor, and so rebelled – the Satsuma Rebellion of 1877 – and this was 'the last bloody convulsion of the old order'.[23] It took, says Moore, only nine years (1868–77) for the Meiji government 'to dismantle the feudal apparatus and replace it with much of the basic framework of modern society. This was indeed a revolution from above...'[24] This reform in the face of outside challenge and internal conflict, and cast within a deferential and hierarchical status-conscious culture, did not produce the upheavals in ideas that the changes in the Western 'routes' had: there was no peasant revolution and there was no bourgeois revolution either – the upshot was the fascism of the 1930s.

The third of Moore's 'routes to the modern world' he calls communism. The two examples presented are Russia and China. As with the German case in 'route two' so here in 'route three', Russia is not discussed directly. But both Russia and China are taken to exemplify peasant revolutions – culminating in authoritarian communist regimes.

Moore's analysis of China begins with a discussion of the rural-bureaucratic system of Imperial China: a system that could not, importantly, contrive a creative response to the depredations of the West in the nineteenth century. In the absence of a Chinese equivalent of the Meiji restoration, the system disintegrated slowly and in 1911 collapsed. The Kuomintang vaguely resembled the fascist alliance of Europe but rested content with a defence of the status quo. This absence of reform, and continued exploitation of the peasantry, made the latter fertile soil for communist cadres. Eventually it was the communist party, led by Mao, that attained power in 1949 after a long-drawn-out war against both the Kuomintang and the invading Japanese.

To complete this brief exposition of *Social Origins*, we can take note of Moore's discussion of India. Moore himself is uneasy about this material – it provides a 'fourth general pattern',[25] but not another 'route', as Moore's point is precisely that India has not yet 'arrived' in the modern world. More unfortunate still is the fact that it does not seem to be advancing. Moore observes: 'In the country so far there has been neither a capitalist revolution from above or below, nor a peasant one leading to communism. Likewise the impulse toward modernization has been very weak.'[26] Moore's analysis of India is of considerable interest for my purposes – the most striking thing is that India is the only specimen tackled of a general category of cases to which the theorists of modernization paid attention – the *new nations*

of the Third World created by the business of colonial withdrawal.
However, what Moore says about India is pessimistic: the surplus of
the peasantry has to be used to create an industrial economy, but
there is no sign of the political force that will achieve this. Muddle,
drift, slow improvement and a lack of effective political will are the
essentials, so far as Moore sees, of the present situation of India.

Now, after the historical analyses Moore goes on to look at the
'theoretical implications' of his work. In this section he considers the
following: firstly, the circumstances which give rise to democratic
route; then the nature of the route of revolution from above; and,
thirdly, the general conditions and characteristics of peasant revolution. The implications/lessons of the three main 'routes' are
considered and finally, in an epilogue, the nature of ideas about
change (cultures and ideologies) are discussed. This whole section
does indeed pursue the general implications/lessons that can, in the
light of this remarkable comparative historical study, be made about
the process of modernization. In this section we find, amongst much
interesting detail, the following major concerns:

(1)   an affirmation of Western liberal-democracy as the model of a
      'modern polity' – others are ranged against this;
(2)   an affirmation of the role of Western feudalism in both
      contributing to the rise of liberal democratic states and its
      absence elsewhere being a significant reason for 'failure'
      elsewhere;
(3)   a consideration of the 'class' dynamics of the shift to the
      modern world – crown/landed aristocracy/towndwellers –
      where responses to impulses to commercialization were
      crucial;
(4)   a consideration of the above in terms of 'actors' choices' where
      these are spelt out in terms of ranges of possibilities – what
      groups could have done and what they actually did – and
      patterns of conflict:
(5)   in respect of (4) these matters are considered with reference to
      issues of structure and agency comparatively from country to
      country and where (1) provides the model to keep enquiry
      coherent, and core social arrangements are distinguished from
      superficial factors;
(6)   a summary of (1) through (5) in guise of a specification of the
      condition for the development of democracy;
(7)   a consideration of the authoritarian/fascist route of Japan and
      Germany in terms, again, of the concatenation of class forces
      present;

(8)   a discussion of the logic of the system of fascism – how it came about, worked, understood itself;

(9)   a promotion of the peasantry from the status of 'objects of history' to 'actors in history' again in terms of the logic of their situation;

(10) a discussion – in the Epilogue – of the 'role of ideas in history' which concludes by suggesting that both liberal democracy and communism are now historically obsolescent.

I have said that Moore's work is in the 'classic tradition' of social science: in its characteristic style his work reaches back into the late eighteenth century 'Enlightenment': the nature of his argument is historical, comparative and morally engaged – I called it a 'dense' style. Judging the value of this sort of work is *not* a narrowly technical matter – it requires that we grasp in a single move the 'work as a whole' before we offer comments. I have offered my characterization above – a 'revisionist' or 'intelligent' modernizer – and now I will offer a few comments upon the argument of *Social Origins*. I will offer six points by way of 'strength' and the sixth point will be the hinge upon which my discussion turns – it will lead to my list of 'weaknesses'.

Firstly, Moore adopts an historical approach to the issues of modernization, and identifies the different groups involved and seeks to interpret their behaviour. The typical modernization theorists' 'logic of industrialism'[27] is thus significantly improved upon: instead of a mysterious evolutionary process sweeping all before it we get some idea of how various groups contributed to it. However, Moore does remain an modernization theorist, that is, evolutionist, and nor does he tell us what criteria of imputation he is using to interpret his actors behaviour.[20] Secondly, Moore picks out patterns of conflict within the historical social systems he is analysing. Further than this he discusses the 'logic of conflict and revolution' – that Moore saw that good could come of violent change was one of the reasons for the irritation of the orthodox! Thirdly, Moore uses comparisons between different countries and periods to vary great effect: they generate questions to put to his historical data and they provide a means for revising his general formulations of historical data. Fourthly, Moore's wide-ranging analyses – in time and geography – let us grasp the *scale* of the changes he is discussing. It is difficult to embrace a Rostovian analysis centering upon a twenty-year 'take-off', after reading Moore. Fifthly, Moore judges: the work is morally engaged; indeed the pursuit of a compelling set of arguments' evidence for the broad tenets of liberal democracy does seem to have been one of the wellsprings of Moore's work as a whole.

Sixthly, (i) Moore makes his analysis coherent; there is a concern to run together sociological generalization with historical detail in a self-conscious manner. This coherence is achieved by: (a) affirming the model of liberal-democratic society as *the* model; (b) identifying the 'route' from the pre-modern world to liberal-democratic societies *and* specifying its conditions; (c) considering other 'routes' similarly and in relation to the liberal-democratic touch-stone.

(ii) Moore ends up with a set of models (implied, never quite spelt out) of patterns of group logics and dynamics arranged around the model of liberal democracy.

(iii) Moore presents all this via explicit questioning and argument: he invites us to join in an enquiry-in-progress and not merely passively consume his finalized conclusions. Relatedly, we can say that Moore is a sophisticated and critical scholar and not an aspiring social technician. The business of social theorizing, for Moore, is the pursuit of the truth, and reason is emancipatory.

Turning now to the 'weaknesses' of his enquiry, we can focus on this point (6) – coherence.

Firstly, the ideal-type of liberal-democracy, around which Moore's scheme revolves, is based upon the model of the experience of the UK and Moore's version of this experience simply is not plausible. Moore follows the orthodox received version of the UK's history: this is a history that stresses gradualism and plays down conflict.[29] Secondly, the pursuit of a 'set of models' is, to my way of thinking, methodologically unsophisticated (even though his work is most intriguing). As a way of arguing a case, which is clearly what Moore is doing – on behalf of liberal democracy – this strategy is limited: crucially it restricts the attention the theorist pays to reflexively investigating his own premises. In Moore's case liberal democracy is largely taken for granted.[30] Thirdly, Moore (a) looks at the *internal* dynamics of those societies he discusses and thus neglects the external forces impinging upon these societies; and (b) except for brief notes on India, neglects the Third World of new nations created by the dismantling of colonial empires: this is a massive neglect.

Moore is first and foremost a comparative historian and I think the value of his intellectual contributions to the study of development flow from this *and* from his moral concern and scepticism. In *Social Origins* his comparative history is conjoined to an approach to development which, perhaps inevitably, draws heavily upon modernization theory. Nonetheless, Moore's work does represent one specimen of that grouping I have called the 'revisionist' or 'intelligent' modernizers, so he is not only in good company (eg. Gellner, Bendix, Rex and others of the 'middle period' of development studies[31], but indeed has contributed massively to the only worthwhile legacy of modernization theory.

It is in this area that the substantive continuing interest in Moore's world lies. But for my present purposes it is the mode of engagement of critical humanist scholarship that is interesting: here again is a *particular* engagement with the world. It has to be judged – as I have briefly done – firstly in its own terms and thereafter located relative to the classic traditions of social science. Measured against the then contemporary work of orthodox modernizers, Moore's work is evidently superior – he *argues a case* rather than offering technical elaboration upon a taken-for-granted frame. However, the return to the classical tradition effected remains partial simply because his escape from the confines of modernization theory was incomplete. His neglect of the new nation-states of the Third World and his surprisingly uncritical acceptance of the tenets of liberal democracy (and the model of the UK!) meant that he never reached the intellectual area inhabited by today's reflexive-minded development theorists. Issues of cultural, cognitive and ethical relativity, matters of the nature of the exchanges between rich and poor nations, and so on and so on, were simply not identified.

5   Arguing on behalf of 'the planners': Chen, Fisk and Higgins

Orthodox social science typically argues in a policy scientific manner. Its particular commitments to 'scientificity' entail what is essentially a manipulative orientation to the social world and, relatedly, a preoccupation with securing the 'possessive mastery'[1] of the world, the knowledge, necessary to buttress this stance. The orthodox stance routinely involves the social theorist (academic, research institute fellow or planning agency employee – etc.) operating with the often unacknowledged assumption that social theory translates into practice via the work of planning agencies.

That they should argue thus ought not now to surprise anyone. Any social theory must necessarily have an 'agent of theory execution' – an assumption about how theory is to be translated into practice – otherwise it fails to engage with the social world.[2] The natural agents of execution of a manipulative policy science are prescisely 'the planners', be they state officials, international agency workers or the employees of private corporations.

The way in which these social theorists actually shape or express their central commitments to 'the planner' varies somewhat. There are those who eschew any close identification and instead stress the scientific aspects of their work. In this case the commitment to 'arguing on behalf of the planners' acts as an epistemological and methodological precept. Other theorists suppose that academics and those close to scholarship can make a distinctive contribution to the work of 'the planners' and the familiar political role of the expert emerges: both 'of' and 'above' the mundane world of the bureaucratic preparation and execution of plan documents. These experts understand themselves from within the ideological framework of policy science: thus they invite their audiences to see them as the social science analogues of the natural scientists; that is, detached, disinterested, and possessed of the expert knowledge necessary to the technical manipulation of complex systems.

I have said elsewhere[3] that I regard real world planning systems as both historically inevitable and politico-socially ambiguous and it is this ambiguity that I wish to pursue in this present chapter. I will not be offering any further theoretical reflections here but, instead, a series of examples of the way in which the theme of 'planning' presents itself in the work of the orthodox.

Thus in my first example, that of Chen,[4] we find a commitment to planning that is restricted to an epistemological/methodological precept. So the author offers an apparently dispassionate social scientific review of certain matters but at the same time evidently centres his work on a commitment to planned social change. Chen's study deals with the development of Singapore in the post-colonial period, yet, paradoxically – given Chen's stance and the corporate nature of contemporary Singapore – the author does not explicitly grant the role of planning in Singapore. The upshot of all this is a curiously 'flattened' discussion which at times begins to read like an apologia for the PAP. Chen's work I briefly contrast with that of two other local scholars who adopt explicitly critical criteria in their discussions of Singapore. In my present terms neither 'argues on behalf of the planners'.

In the second and third examples we find a couple of experts, and both treat the situation in contemporary Malaysia. The first expert, E.K. Fisk,[5] offers a characteristically styled prescriptive analysis of Malaysia that is, to my mind, both (unintentionally) amusing and utterly implausible. My second expert, Benjamin Higgins,[6] offers an apologia for certain recent planning débâcles in Malaysia: this text is similarly revealing in that after telling a tale of incoherent thinking and apparently incompetent action the author proceeds to call for *more* power to the planners!

It seems to me that if we are to properly understand the real possibilities of planning – itself a key issue in a distinctly authoritarian corporatist Southeast Asia – then we need to disentangle both the various expectations that have been held of planning; and, relatedly, the way in which this complex set of positions has intermingled and cross-cut with orthodox conceptions of social science. The three illustrations presented in this essay are notes towards such disentanglings.

The essay entitled 'Singapore Development Strategies: a model for rapid growth' by Peter Chen[7] is, so far as I can see, essentially an orthodox one both in its substantive characterizations of Singapore and in the conception of the role of social scientists exemplified. Chen's mode of engagement has the effect of tending to fuse scholarly social science with policy science. Thus we can see in the present example of the work of Chen an unstated commitment to arguing on behalf of the planners – it is in the nature of an epistemological precept. What is especially intriguing in the case of Chen's essay is his apparent reluctance to grant the substantive point

that Singapore is a planned society. To underscore the nature of
Chen's analysis I will add a brief note on contrasting views by citing
the work of Chan Heng Chee and Noleen Heyzer.[8]

Chen's essay begins with the note on the resource scarcity of
Singapore. The city depends on its geographical position and its
people. Statistics of economic growth in the post-colonial period are
presented. Singapore is presented as 'one of the most outstanding
models of development'.[9] Thus far the material is rather familiar, but
now we have an unexpected qualification to the claim that Singapore
offers a model for rapid growth which, implicitly, others could copy.
Chen remarks:

> But it is also felt that the economy of Singapore is dominated by
> regional and international factors . . . that its social discipline is
> formulated by the government and is not the spontaneous creation
> of individual citizens . . . [and that] the stability and prosperity of
> Singapore depend heavily on the political leadership, and not on
> the political system per se.[10]

This complex qualification to the claim that Singapore is a model for
growth is, it seems to me, thoroughly ambiguous. The problem stems
from the phrase 'but it is also felt'. One could ask, felt by whom – the
community of Singaporean social scientists, social scientists generally
or the PAP administration? It is not at all clear at this point quite
where the author stands and thus how he would have observers judge
development in Singapore. This unclarity persists throughout the
essay and it seems to me that the reasons for this can best be
elucidated by noting the tendency of the orthodox to argue for or on
behalf of the 'planners'. Chen follows this style and argues for the
'planners' who in this case happen to be the PAP administration.

This model of growth is further characterized by references to the
policies of the administration: sometimes 'foreign experts' (unspecified) see them as overly rigid and sometimes overly flexible. This
confusion is resolved via the invocation of the phrase 'contradictions
and conflict'. Thus Chen argues that Singapore's development track
has been laid out as a result of a series of specific policies each having
their own goal and that 'Contradiction and conflict are methods used
in the process of achieving these specified objectives.'[11] Thus what
looks from the outside to be incoherence, vacillation or opportunistic
pragmatism is in fact the creative use, in pursuit of particular policies,
of 'contradiction and conflict'. I must confess that I cannot
understand Chen at this point. However, matters become clearer as
the administration's approach is further explained by reference to the
'national ideology'.[12] So, whilst there are no long-term plans as such,
there are a set of principles governing the actions of the adminis-

tration. These principles are 'multi-racialism, multi-culturalism, multi-lingualism, meritocracy, and a self-reliant (rugged) society.'[13] At this point it seems that we are touching on how the administration actually makes sense of its circumstances – or would have its citizens believe it makes sense (see the critics below). But this self-understanding (or self-presentation) is not directly pursued by the author and instead we have a report on how the PAP administration has run together capitalism (the pursuit of economic growth with a free market) with socialism (provision of welfare, especially housing, health and schooling). Chen remarks: 'Superficially, these integrated policies are contradictory to each other[14] – surely an understatement. However, Chen regards this as evidence of that creative use of 'contradiction and conflict' noted above.

This model of development has been constructed by the efforts of the administration. Additionally Chen notes the contribution of the colonial legacy (unspecified), the use of English and the fostering of native enterprise – particularly Chinese business skills and links. The state is the key and this is made evident in the subsequent three areas of more detailed discussion: economy, society, and political sphere. I think Chen is entirely correct to stress the role of the state, but paradoxically this role of the state/PAP is never directly addressed.

In respect of the economic sphere Chen rightly uses the word 'interventionist' to characterize the administration's approach. Singapore is indeed a planned society. Thereafter we are introduced to the major elements of the economic system.

(1) Government involvement in industrialization projects is extensive – setting up development boards or companies. The overlap PAP (political party), bureaucracy (state servants), and industry (private enterprises) is typical not only of Singapore but of many Third World nations.[15] So Chen is right to stress the pre-eminence of the state/PAP in the economic sphere. However, what he fails to do – and this might flow from his casting his discussion in terms of three sub-systems – is pursue this evident truth about Singapore, that is, that the whole society is utterly dominated by the state/PAP.

(2) The government, it is reported, also offers 'fiscal incentives' – tax reliefs and so on – to new firms to encourage them to set up/start up. All of this is fairly unremarkable Keynesian-style material and the report on it is cast in simple descriptive terms.

(3) More novel is the final element of the economic approach – the curbing of the trade unions. This episode is reported largely without comment: the legislation of 1960 and 1968 effectively broke the Singaporean trade unions. Chen comments: 'This is because the government believed that the success of the industrialization programmes rested on low wages and a disciplined work-force.

Employers in Singapore and foreign investors responded positively to these new labour laws.'[16] This is a very narrow reading of a problematical episode in Singapore's history: once again the tone is detached and dispassionate. In contrast, in the work of Heyzer this curbing of union power will be seen as a necessary condition of PAP's buying a particular package deal of development, that is, inviting in the multi-national companies. Heyzer's reading evidently opens up many additional issues which Chen's treatment misses.

After reviewing the economic sphere, Chen turns to the social which is considered as an adjunct to economic growth.

> Many studies have demonstrated the point that socio-political factors and economic factors are not separate but are closely related in the process of economic development. Social and political stability will contribute to sustain economic growth which, in turn, will strengthen the social and political stability in the country.[17]

He then reviews the administration's 'track record' in the fields of housing, community development and communication/education.

The building record of the HBD (Housing Development Board) is in simple quantative terms hugely impressive. It is also cited by Chan Heng Chee,[18] as we will see, as the major basis of PAP's claims to be socialist – it is then an important area. Chen reports on the activities of the HDB in a completely uncritical fashion and the place of housing in the PAP's political credentials is not treated. Nor does Chen have anything to say about the social engineering aspects of the HDB's operations.

In the matter of the community centres and community development there are two points to bring out additionally to the author's descriptive report. Firstly, the community centres existed prior to the PAP; when the PAP attained power it quickly seized control of them, thereby destroying a vehicle for the formulation of local, that is, non-party, opinion. Again Chen's treatment misses out apparently relevant material. Secondly, we can note that the idea of 'community centres' is familiar in the experience of First World planning – and they didn't work too well there either. Another instance of 'social engineering' is thus not tackled.

Thirdly, the author turns to the business of education and the mass media. Having briefly touched upon the very sensitive issue of language policy, he goes on to remark of the mass media that 'all . . . are either placed under the control of the government or closely guided by national policies'.[19] Again, much more could be said but is not.

This section is summed up thus:

> With the combined efforts of the government, the public and the mass media, Singapore has developed into a highly disciplined and well planned society with a strong sense of national identity in the short span of only fifteen years since Singapore became an independent state in 1965.[20]

Once again one is left wondering how one is to separate out policy scientific description for approval. Chen's particular style has the effect of 'flattening out' his discussion and one is sometimes at a loss as to whether apparent approval – generated by his 'arguing on behalf of the planners' – actually is real political approval.

We can pursue this point a little by looking at his treatment of the third sub-system, the political. Here Chen speaks of an elite and interventionist approach. I remarked above that there was an unclarity which ran throughout the essay and in this section we find both an unacknowledged diagnosis of an authoritarian regime and apparent approval of it. The issue is difficult to pursue, as I've noted, because of Chen's epistemological commitments.

Chen picks up the issue at the outset – planning and the policy-oriented, rather than five-year plan, approach – and he remarks: 'All major national policies and development priorities are decided by the cabinet . . . meetings are . . . held in secret . . . deliberations are not generally reported in the press.'[21] It is a 'top-to-bottom' decision-making process. He continues: 'Norms and ends are selected by the political leadership and the bureaucracy, and they are usually supported by the elite and accepted by the masses.'[22] The author then notes, 'there are controversies over the style and extent of democracy'[23] but we are told nothing of these. Chen then discusses the issue of democracy with reference to a couple of planners![24] Planners have nowhere, so far as I am aware, been recognized as obviously fitted to talk about democracy.

Chen's general position seems to be contained in the following paragraph which is the effective conclusion of his analysis. Thus he says:

> Apart from the fact that Singapore is, economically and politically, highly vulnerable and susceptible to changes in external conditions, Singapore is also an elite oriented society in which efficiency, productivity, pragmatism and meritocracy are highly valued by the elite and the masses as well. Moreover, there has been one party in power in Parliament for the past fifteen years. Therefore, the arguments for the top-to-bottom approach are pervasive in the decision making process both at the national and community levels, and the results of this approach judged by

Singapore's social and economic achievements over the last fifteen years are unique and remarkable.[25]

This paragraph represents, on the face of it, something close to an explicit defence of the PAP administration. It begins with an element of the 'official ideology' in the appeal to high vulnerability. It claims that Singapore society is elite-oriented and thus both completely misses the issue of how this came about and is maintained, and avoids the issue of the consent versus the acquiescence of 'ordinary Singaporeans' – other commentators might prefer the phrase elite-ordered. The pursuit of goals of 'efficiency and productivity' and appreciation of 'pragmatism and meritocracy' all evidently revolve around a narrow economic notion of progress. That arguments for top-to-bottom decision-making are pervasive does not say anything about whether they are persuasive. Finally, we have a familiar 'appeal to track record' – but, clearly, the success (or otherwise) of the administration could only be established by critically inspecting its 'track record', which requires in turn that we distinguish: (a) what the administration did do; (b) what it could have done but didn't; and, (c) what others might have done in the same situation. This appeal to an extant 'track record' in the absence of a critical review establishes little.

In sum, Chen's essay represents a broad, orthodox-type review of Singapore's development experience. The 'gross facts' of that record are reported and the principal characteristics of the 'Singaporean model' are clearly presented. It is the way these matters are subsequently handled that seems to be unsatisfactory. Chen's presentation of his material in terms suffused with a commitment to social science as policy science has the effect of 'flattening out' his discussion. The broader traditions of scholarly criticism are not invoked and the essay resolutely sticks to the realm of narrowly technical criticism – and even this is muted. It is around the issues of interventionism and elite control that we can begin to offer both a different interpretation of the experience of Singapore and point up the limited nature of Chen's approach. I will begin with the political scientist Chan Heng Chee and go on to look at the work of a development specialist, Noleen Heyzer.

Chan looks at the political system and political change in Singapore and begins by rejecting familiar schemes of 'political modernization' which issue in the view that Singapore is highly developed: Chan reports that she finds this judgment unhelpful and instead proposes to look at Singapore's history directly. Enquiry is to be structured by reference to the notions of 'authority and accountability', 'participation', and 'distribution'. At the outset then we can see that Chan's work – in sharp contrast to Chen's – does have built into it the potential for critical commentary.

On the issue of 'authority and accountability' Chan adopts a very broad historical perspective – the analysis begins with a reference to Raffles! However, the early colonial years are not investigated in detail. Instead we find a discussion of the PAP administration. Chan notes: 'It is really from the PAP's assumption of power that one begins to look for real and qualitative changes in the exercise of authority and the meaning of accountability.'[26] In 1959 the PAP came to power and it quickly began both previously announced reforms and attacks on the political left which was eventually disposed of. Chan notes the fact of PAP's subsequent election victories and goes on to say that:

> If the extent of authority and legitimacy has remained essentially the same from 1959 till today, the exercise of the authority has altered considerably. . . .Political power and authority is considered to be a monopoly of the ruling leadership and is exercised with increasing authoritarianism.[27]

Chan goes on to unpack this claim and details the way in which PAP has systematically silenced all its critics and simultaneously deprived the masses of alternative sources of ideas, with the result that they can do little but acquiesce. Chan ends her brief analysis by remarking:

> The relationship between government and society in the last fifty years in the exercise of authority has not basically changed. Authority was enjoyed exclusively by the colonial authorities in consultation with local community leaders and business interests. . . .Authority is now enjoyed in the same way by the PAP government.[28]

The comparison with Chen's sanguine treatment of 'top-to-bottom' decision-making is stark.

In respect of participation Chan, interestingly, distinguishes two varieties: (i) permitted participation where the masses are invited to comment on or respond to decisions that are already either taken or at the point of being taken; and (ii) mobilized participation where there is mass political support and action for change. In the period 1955–9 the PAP adopted the second strategy and when it came to power quickly moved to the former position. The upshot of the rule of the PAP government is, argues Chan, that a new political culture has emerged: 'It is a culture which discourages conflict, confrontation and bargaining, emphasizes stability, low risk and petition. Responses to political pressures and demands are at the largesse of the ruling leadership.'[29]

On the matter of distribution, the last of Chan's trio to themes, she remarks that the PAP came to power as a 'left wing democratic socialist government'[30] and amongst its social reform proposals was a housing programme. The governments record in housing is its 'major claim ... of adherence to its socialist principles.'[31] The reality is rather different, thinks Chan, and the present picture is of a 'definite class system with a great or growing gap between the classes.'[32]

If we consider these three areas of criticism then, quite evidently, the characterization they offer of Singapore is very different to that we met above with Peter Chen. Chan speaks of a 'depoliticization'[33] having taken place. Political power is not the sole prerogative of a small elite which rules, in an authoritarian manner, over an inegalitarian society. Peter Chen's essay was optimistic for the future, thus he says that Singapore's 'leaders and people can look ahead to the 1980s with satisfaction at the past and confidence in the future.'[34] In contrast Chan is more pessimistic: the abolition of politics is likely to foster longer-term instability because short-term stability based on depoliticization 'also means a loss of effective representation'[35] and pressures for political change cannot forever be contained by an elite. She adds that if there are no channels for political life to express itself the only other alternatives are 'disruptive violent means.'[36]

Turning now to my second critic: Heyzer is interested in the cultural, political and social consequences of Singapore's development strategy and moreover this is to be considered by reference to an explicit stance. Thus Heyzer states that the idea of 'development' must encompass 'social development for the working poor'[37] and not just economic growth.

The history of Singapore she compresses into a note on the conflict between the Chinese-educated union-based 'populists' and the Western-educated PAP elite who together formed the independence movement. After independence it was the Western-educated elite that gained power and they adopted the strategy of 'inviting in the multi-nationals'. This strategy was possible as the MNCs had begun to engage in multi-national production. Singapore thus became integrated into the world economy as a subsiduary manufacturing centre for the MNCs. Evidently a very different story to that presented by Chen.

Heyzer then pursues the social, cultural and political consequences of this strategy of development. She remarks: 'Central to the penetration of foreign big business in Singapore is the creation of a government-industrial bureaucratic network,'[38] which encourages overseas capital and allocates local capital to a subordinate role. Local capital tends to drift away from manufacturing and into services, property or small-scale industry. This strategy of development has created a definite pattern of employment and reward:

> The nature of foreign industries in Singapore and the bureaucratic network that has grown up side by side with industrialization have . . . [seen] . . the creation of a technocratic elite . . . the formation of a group of middle-level bureaucrats and technicians . . . the growth of a group of skilled workers and a mass of workers employed as cheap labour.[39]

She continues: 'In other words . . . the emergence of class polarizations.'[40]

Singapore is thus characterized as an unequal society and consequently faces the problems of 'potential instability derived from the social experience of inequality'.[41] Heyzer identifies, quite correctly, as a response of ruling groups the promulgation of a legitimating and defensive ideology. The ideology of the Singaporean 'New Society' contains, it is argued, four elements. Firstly, a claim that there is no alternative – and this presumably involves notions of Singapore's economic vulnerability and lack of resources. This was the point from which, as we saw, Chen began. Secondly there is a manipulation of 'images':

> The first set is bound up with technology. . . .The images of the 'New Society' are 'modern', 'technocratic', 'disciplined', 'realistic', 'rational', and 'pragmatic'. The second set of images . . . [identify dangers] . . . 'The Communists', 'The Enemy Within', 'The Real Threat', 'National Danger', 'Subversion', 'The Continuing Threat'.[42]

Thirdly the equation of dissent with disloyalty. Fourthly, the construction of a new 'identity', a general recipe of what it is to be a Singaporean. Finally, we may note that the other strategy for maintaining stability is to suppress other channels of communication: Heyzer speaks of the 'cooption'[43] of the trade unions. Likewise the independent press and individual critics have been curbed.

Heyzer concludes that the administrations strategy is the result of three considerations: the Singaporean economy was always orientated to the world market and 'independent development' would be difficult; the MNCs offered a readily available 'package'; the local political scene demanded results be produced quickly. The PAP administration's actions are thus perfectly intelligible, but the package does have a price tag. Thus Heyzer notes:

> the state and its bureaucracy has developed a highly authoritarian character, disallowing actions and programmes that do not fit in with a

state or elite-defined social reality . . . [there had been] . . . the
creation of a highly stratified system. . . . To conclude, if we take
development, in the broadest sense of the term to be the
banishment of human suffering and the promotion of human
creativity, the development of Singapore leaves much to be
desired.[44]

Again Heyzer, like Chan Heng Chee, offers an analysis that is
based on reasoned and explicit premises. Where Chen's recourse to
the strategy of arguing on behalf of the planners has the effects of
'flattening out' his discourse to the point, indeed, of creating what
sounds from time to time like an apologia for the PAP, Heyzer and
Chan can offer explicit critical judgments.

Turning now to the work of Fisk and Higgins, we find a rather
different exchange between notions of social science and planning.
Where Chen tended to fuse social science and 'arguing on behalf
of the planners' at an epistemological level, Fisk and Higgins are
more explicit in their commitments to a definite social scientific
praxis. Orthodox social science is routinely taken to translate into
practice via the authoritative manipulation of social systems and
Fisk and Higgins embrace this position: thus they adopt the
specific role of 'the expert'.

Fisk's discussion of Malaysia rests on the view that: 'economic
activity . . . is an integral part of the very much wider social system of
that community. Moreover, it is our belief that the economic part can
only be examined properly in the context of that total system.'[45]
Evidently this is a 'social economics' position like that of, say, Myrdal.
And like Myrdal, Fisk's treatment of politics is weak. Generally the
tone he adopts is that of the expert offering congratulatory reports on
Malaysian progress so far. Prescriptions are also offered for further
progress. Analysis of the system begins with matters economic.

Fisk asserts that: 'economic factors are of special significance for
this totality'[46] and Malaysia's track record according to the –
admittedly rather general statistics – is good. The expert offers a
preliminary conclusion: 'From the economic view this sounds quite
satisfactory. . . . However, there are many aspects of Malaysia's
adjustment that urgently need improvement. . . . However, from a
purely economic point of view, Malaysia can be deemed to be doing
pretty well.'[47] This tone of the 'approving expert' continues right into
the introduction to a problem area, Fisk notes: 'the Malaysian
planners have done pretty well. There is nothing in the mode sets of
difficulties . . . that a tightly united little nation could not take
comfortably in its stride. But here we come up against difficulties.'[48]
Fisk's paper then turns to these matters and, after a brief note on

general economics problems – skill upgrading to lift the economy's level – the issue of distribution is introduced.

Fisk observes that a major problem is the 'polarization of economic and political power on racial lines'.[49] The recognition of the issue of ethnicity is expressed in the New Economic Policy (NEP) inaugurated in 1969. The business of what Fisk calls 'polarizations' is then pursued and I think that this is a proper concern. However, we can take note of the way in which he presents the whole issue: he adopts the typical social economics style. I have noted elsewhere how Myrdal reduced politics to planning.[50] Fisk observes:

> Polarization is the development of differences along an axis of change, which become a source of conflict and tension to which people are forced to adjust. The source of conflict leads to action, and especially to political action, and is an engine of change. The energies developed by these tensions build up when polarizations have been ignored or inadequately taken into account in planning, and are liable, sooner or later, to reach an explosive point, as they did with the socio-economic polarization by race in 1969.[51]

Fisk's appeal to planning to tackle a political issue is, as with Myrdal, amusing. The NEP addressed the economic/cultural/ethnic divides in Malaysia. Fisk then goes on to look at the consequences of the policy in terms of further polarizations. Fisk views Malaysia as a very dynamic system and seeks to grasp these patterns of polarization/change so as to make government policy. Four polarizations are identified and Fisk reviews them in turn.

We should note at the outset, however, that Fisk's notion of 'polarization' is not as clear as it might be. It seems to be a mix of structural-functionalist analysis of 'system disturbance' and consequent need for the 're-establishment of balance', plus a distant hint at social conflict as progressive when he speaks about change.

With the first noted polarization of rich/poor we discover that this division has tended to be the same as Chinese/Malay. It is noted that this may be changing as a new Malay component of the urban proletariat emerges; and, moreover, in the rural areas there are now Malay middle classes. Fisk has little more to say on this issue: 'class' is a matter that his approach lets him acknowledge but which at the same time is marginalized in analysis.

Fisk's approach reveals a further ambiguity when he discusses the rural/urban polarization. Thus he begins by observing: 'Associated with the changing composition of the rich/poor polarization has been a series of important changes affecting the rural/urban dichotomy.'[52] Here we can point out that the dynamic notion of polarization is not at all the same thing as an urban/rural dichotomy. Talk of dichotomies is notoriously static: I remarked above in respect of the notion of polarization that it was unclear precisely how we were to understand it and now this doubt must be reinforced. Fisk then goes on to review briefly the changes that have taken place: put simply a drift to the town and a drift from ethnicity towards class is the obvious line of social cleavage.

Fisk then speaks of the East/West Malaysian polarization – peninsular and island Malaysia – and again takes note of potential sources of conflict due to differences. However, quite clearly, what we have here is a slide from the very specific use of polarization given at the outset (ethnic-economic), to a broad descriptive one. Again one wonders about Fisk's precise analytical stance. It seems as though he might just be listing potential sources of problems for planners in an *ad hoc* fashion and that all the talk of social systems and polarizations is summary description rather than theoretical language.

Fisk then turns to religious polarization and is back with a more recognizably social scientific usage. He begins, in expert mode: 'The idea that religion is not an important and proper element in the formation of public policy is one of the absurdities of the last half century. It is an idea that is now collapsing around the world.'[53] Fisk evidently sees religion as one more matter to plan: his optimism in pursuit of an ordered life is impressive, but his substitution of planning for politics is not plausible: religion has often been a mode of political expression and there are many obvious and contemporary examples in Asia.[54] Fisk then reviews the religious scene and notes:

> There are three factors in the situation at the beginning of the 1980's that seem to make the development of some degree of religious polarization a possibility in Malaysia. First, there is the external influence . . of. . . fundamental Islamic revival . . .
> Second, . . . the very effective programme of rural education which has replaced the village religious schools . . . Thirdly, a remarkably large number of the younger generation of rural Malays . . . have left the kampungs during the 1970's to become town dwellers . . . more influenced by fashionable foreign-based teachings.[55]

This is a vague and rather contradictory note but, once again, we can observe that the matters are presented as potential sources of trouble for policy-makers.

Having considered his four 'polarizations', Fisk then returns to economics and the NEP. This is characterized, in its present stage, as reformist/redistributive, that is, 'imbalances' are to be tackled from growth, not the redistribution of present resources. Fisk comments: 'By the beginning of the 1980's there could be little doubt that this joint policy has had some success,'[56] but there are underlying problems and soon 'Malaysia will have to solve its problems of poverty and imbalance or be left to tackle them when financial and trade conditions may be considered less favourable.'[57] Recent favourable circumstances were oil-related prosperity. Fisk concludes: 'Malaysia has gained a most valuable respite through its good fortune, but it is essential that it be recognised as such and the opportunity taken to prepare for the time when the respite is over.'[58] As regards the bumiputera programme – the thoroughly contentious heart of the NEP – Fisk notes it neutrally and adds that this is a part of 'the environment to which people adjust'[59] and that it 'can be changed by legislation and administration'.[60] Again politics is turned into planning and the key state programme of social and political action becomes not a central aspect of the contemporary dynamic of Malaysian society but merely a technical matter which may, or may not, require some adjustment.

In conclusion, Fisk notes that the subsequent chapters (in the text of which his essay is a preliminary) will deal with the factors

> underlying the policy decisions to be made in the 1980's and 1990's. . . .The actual decisions required at any one time will be dependent on a manifold of circumstances . . . and cannot be forecast in any scientific way . . . however the issues raised . . . must form the framework within which most policy decisions will eventually need to be made.[61]

Thus, finally, the policy orientation of the expert is reaffirmed.

Having looked at the 'experts' prescriptions' it is to a 'planner's apology' that I now turn. As with Fisk, we find the role of the expert embraced, but, whereas Fisk is looking optimistically to the future, Higgins is obliged to consider the recent past, a past that has on his own account seen grave failures of planning. Benjamin Higgins's essay has five major parts which I consider in turn.

Higgins begins with a discussion of the background to development planning – his concern in this paper – and offers the view that the Malaysian colonial experience s was both comparatively benign and laid out the pattern of a basically 'appropriate' development pattern. Much of this was plantation and thus: 'it was natural for Malaysian development planners to think in terms of land use. . . .From the beginning of formal development planning in Malaysia urban and regional planning has played a (special) role.'[62] Higgins thinks that within the context of this relatively satisfactory colonial legacy planning has been quite successful, and he cites GNP figures to support this. From this general level he then shifts to the particular.

In step number two of his argument he introduces 'One dark corner . . . in the picture of Malaysian economic and social development,'[63] and that is ethnicity. By this he means the complex religious, geographic, cultural and economic circumstances that issued in the 1969 Kuala Lumpur riots and thereafter the NEP. Higgins says: 'In a sense all development plans and policies undertaken in Malaysia since 1970 may be regarded as part of the NEP . . . the political response to the situation described above.'[64] The NEP was a redistributive and reformist strategy and economic growth was to be the key to drawing the 'Malays more completely into the industrialization process.'[65] Now we move to step three.

Here we find a discussion of the rationale of planning. Higgins notes that pre-NEP work, the First Malaysia Plan 1966–70, was 'competently done and reflected the thinking about development that characterized the 1960's. It was essentially a macro-economic plan.'[66] With the NEP work there is a significant shift to specific goals:

> The Second Malaysia Plan for 1971–5 had a more clear cut ideological foundation and a broader view of the development process in terms of underlying theory . . . .It provides policies, projects and programmes to modernize rural life, encourage a rapid and balanced growth of urban activities, provide improved education and training programmes at all levels, and above all to ensure the creation of a Malay commercial and industrial community at all levels . . . with the aim of bringing Malays . . . into the economic life of the nation as full partners.[67]

This is certainly a broad and ambitious programme. What the SMP introduced in terms of theory was the growth pole concept: this concept was picked up and used in the Third Malaysia Plan, according to Higgins.

In the TMP, 1976–1980, there was an attempt to adopt an integrated approach to planning to link national, regional and urban aspects. The new approach also adopted a disaggregated strategy of analysis in place of the aggregative modelling favoured in the FMP. Indeed, within discussion of development there was throughout the late 1960s and into the 1970s a switch towards models which used more variables – hence, disaggregated. And in the case of Malaysia it seems that the growth pole concept was picked up and used.

The idea of growth pole theory, reports Higgins, was that the state planning agencies could intervene in the national urban pattern and introduce entirely new urban/industrial areas that would invigorate their surrounding areas via 'spread effects'. On the basis of this theory the major effort in Malaysia was to be made in the rural, predominantly Malay, east coast region: thus urban, regional and national objectives were served.

But – and here is step four of Higgins's essay – it did not work.

Higgins offers three strategies of apology for this: the government could not cope administratively; the planning teams could not cope organisationally; and, finally, the theory was no good anyway. This is quite a remarkable series of admissions.

(1) The growth pole based integrated approach required – as in principle all planning interventions must – a large measure of 'clarity of vision' in respect of what was to be attempted, plus 'widespread understanding' amongst those called on to contribute to the programme. These conditions simply did not hold: which is to say that the planners had not appreciated the complexities of the social patterns they were attempting to manipulate. The planners' approach to putting their programmes in place within the Malaysian economy and society was simplistic.

(2) The project required a degree of plan integration as the elements of the overall plan were produced by separate units, often overseas agencies. Higgins reports that the various regional master plans simply did not add up. He notes:

> The consulting teams came from a wide range of countries, had different backgrounds and compositions, used different approaches and techniques and operated at different times . . . Fashions in regional planning methodology have changed rapidly during the past two decades and the changes are all too apparent in the series of Master Plans . . . provisions for assuring a common methodology and techniques for integrating regional plans into national plans . . . were totally inadequate. . . .The inevitable result was that . . .[assembling]. . . the Third Malaysia Plan by adding up existing regional plans . . . proved virtually impossible.[68]

This is, of itself, a quite remarkable admission: to this is to be added the information that not all the regions were studied with the same intensity and this did not help matters. Additionally, reports Higgins, integration of regional and national planning within the government was poor.

(3) There is a further point yet to be made; Higgins reports: 'The final reason for the incomplete translation of the theory regarding an integrated urban-regional-national development strategy into an implementable Third Plan was that the development pole/growth centre upon which it was based turned out to be rather vague.'[69] This is an even more remarkable statement: to the general unreadiness of government and non-competence of experts Higgins now adds in lousy theory![70] Looking in more depth at the failure of the theory, Higgins speaks of the use of an 'adulteration'[71] of the approach, and then admits that the original theory was 'highly non-operational'.[72] Thus what began as an abstract critique of neo-classical economics in

relation to land-use patterns ended up being used as an urban-regional planning approach.[73]

Thus far, to recap, the story is as follows: theory, plan preparation and implementation were all defective. Higgins now asks after the lessons of the episode – this is step number five.

Higgins begins with general matters and remarks: 'One reason why attraction of new industries to 'development poles' may be less effective in diffusing growth throughout the entire urban hierarchy in Malaysia than elsewhere is that the urban structure is itself defective.'[74] This strikes me as a quite fantastic claim: Malaysia, we are being told, needs to get itself organized before it can properly be planned. He continues: 'Malaysia is short of cities in the 100,000–250,000 category.'[75] But how does he know this? We have just been told that the growth pole theory was wrongly understood and wrongly applied and if this observation about defective urban hierarchies is based on some other theory then we are not told what that theory is. Higgins, it seems, is first blaming the victim and then raising the stake: 'There can be little doubt that in order to carry out the sort of development strategy underlying the Third Plan, the entire urban structure, and not just a few "growth poles" must be strengthened.'[76] This is absurd.

Moving on to more specific matters, Higgins then reviews what happened (went wrong) in the growth pole adjacent to Kuantan, a scheme that attracted attention as a large-scale, novel, experiment in 'spatial engineering'. It did not work and the decay of optimism amongst planners is detailed. Higgins speaks of 'simplistic. .[and]. . naive'[77] efforts, but, again, he responds by calling for more of the same: 'The entire hierarchy of cities and regions must be both planned and managed together as a single system.'[78]

In conclusion, Higgins says (rather surprisingly one might think): 'Malaysia provides a praiseworthy example of effective development planning within a parliamentary democracy, a federal constitution, and a mixed economy.'[79] It is granted that errors have been made, but Higgins reiterates that 'the whole system must be planned and managed as a unit.'[80] Given that this step five of his discussion is concerned with learning the lessons of experience, there is precious little evidence of learning to be found. The only sign is a vague remark to the effect that maybe a move towards 'bottom-up planning that would involve the target population'[81] might be a good idea. I'm not sure that Higgins is not contradicting himself here (and with an arguably internally contradictory notion at that!) but if by this call Higgins actually does mean a shift away from expert intervention towards democratic politics, then I would approve and suggest that this would let him begin a broader and richer analysis of Malaysia than the foregoing 'arguments of behalf of the planners'. However, I am far from convinced that Higgins is all that far along the road to a cure to his planners' hubris.

It seems to me, by way of a concluding note, that this trio of examples of how the general notion of planning can find expression within social science can usefully serve as a preliminary to a more detailed review of these matters. It is surely evident that 'argument on behalf of the planners', as I have characterized it, is familiar within social science (and indeed wholly prevalent within development theory). It seems to me that these patterns of argument are in themselves profoundly confused and must be identified and dispelled as prerequisites both to the pursuit of social scientific scholarship and to the identification of specific, restricted sets of expectations in respect of the real world possibilities and costs of 'planning'.

6 A.G. Frank: the mode of engagement of the 'political writer'

1 Introduction

In this chapter I want to offer a 'formal defence' of the work of A.G. Frank. I will argue, firstly, that the character of Frank's work has been routinely misunderstood by academic social scientists, and, secondly, that when his work is properly understood then it can be seen to be both coherent, legitimate and powerful. This essay draws on arguments I have presented elsewhere[1] in respect of social theorizing and scattered comments of Frank's work in particular: it is consequently an exercise in re-presentation rather than anything very novel.

2 Theorists, interpreters, commentators and spokesmen

Social theorizing I take to be generic to human social life: its instances are many and divers. As social scientists we need to be able to 'map' this diversity so as to be able to keep track of the varieties which the 'real social world' offers to us and to locate our scholarship within this swirl of action and thought. This last is vital if we are to be anything more than 'just another' style of theorizing. This 'map' I have given preliminary expression to in terms, first, of specified historical exemplars of particular modes of social theoretic engagement and, second, in terms of a schematic framework of 'roles'.[2]

The exemplars I have specified are Marx for his critique of political economy based construction of a delimited-formal ideology, and the Frankfurt School (with Habermas in particular) for their extention of the marxian critical project into the sphere of the cultural. In this case the attempt to dissolve pervasive-informal ideologies entails that ideas of democracy, critique and ideology ranking come together in that the latter pair suppose an 'ideal speech situation' which in turn supposes an open democratic society. This offers a characterization of what I understand to be the major thread of the 'classical tradition' of Western European social science. Other modes of social theoretic engagement – efforts to make sense of particular problematic situations – we can rank against this core tradition: these might include further contributions to the elaboration of the initial marxian project, successive reformulations of it, positions dissenting from it and work of a similar sort produced in other traditions (and here a major line of theorizing would be orthodox economics). Nor need we restrict our attention to self-conscious formal social theorists – journalism, party politics, arts and letters, reformist programmes, and mass movements of public view and opinion might all be treated (and in the wide literature of social science often *are* treated). In this fashion we can *both* acknowledge what is trivially obvious (once we shrug off the incubus of the 'received model' of the natural sciences and the injunctions in respect of its extension into the sphere of the social) about the human sphere of social theorizing – that it is centrally concerned with *making sense of the social world*, for particular groups, at particular times, in particular places, and with reference to particular resources – *and* yet retain the coherence and systemacity of enquiry which are, *inter alia*, the mark scholarship.

Related to this strategy of mapping via 'exemplars' is the business of roles – the variety of roles which might be taken, *a priori*, to be available to (more or less self-conscious) social theorists. This systematic framework is convenient in that it lets us grasp in a preliminary fashion the work of otherwise unfamiliar scholars or groups, or movements. Construing social theorizing broadly (as including action as well as the production of texts) we can offer the triune scheme of theorists, practitioners, and interpreters. Each can be taken to embody a particular mode of social theoretic engagement.

Thus the 'theorist' operates before the fact of social change; which change he endeavours to characterize and effect via the production of delimited-formal ideologies; the orientation is thus prospective and Marx, Ricardo, J.S. Mill, Spencer, Popper and the lately fashionable Hayek, can stand as examples.

The 'practitioner' engages directly with the social world so as to actively secure change, and this engagement can be more or less self-conscious and the results secured more or less as anticipated: here we can instance Lenin, Mao, Castro, Khomeini; or, indeed, following a remark of Kilminster,[3] Adolf Hitler. A more mundane figure here, and one whose social theorizing we must construe narrowly, essentially the production of texts, might be George Orwell, whose political writing, always direct and engaged, both effected social change and left a legacy of interpretive work for latter social theorists.[4]

The business of interpretation is the last of my trio of roles: the interpreter's orientation is retrospective and concerned with the task of elucidating the arguments/examples offered by the foregoing pair.

And this is the role I have further sub-divided into 'commentator' and 'spokesman' – allocation of a given social theorist to one or other category being dependent upon the social theorist's overt relationship to those whose work is interpreted.

This dual strategy of mapping the field of modes of social theoretic engagement – even in its presently underdeveloped state[5] – lets us offer a characterization of the work of A.G. Frank which both locates him *vis-à-vis* the 'classical tradition' and reveals his work to be a quite particular mode of social theoretic engagement. The last-mentioned point is the basis of my above-noted assertion that Frank's work has been *routinely misunderstood*. Frank's work is, it seems to me, best regarded as that of a political writer. In my terms he is a 'spokeman/ theorist' and that, I think, is how he sees himself.

3   The model of engagement of the 'political writer'

The foregoing schema of 'exemplars' and 'roles' is drawn from a mixture of reflection upon the work of the humanist marxian tradition, the sociology of knowledge (closely linked of course), and my own work in the sphere of post-Second World War theories of development. Any discrete effort of social theorizing, of making sense, we can analyse, it seems to me, in terms of *conception* and *intern*. The former designates the subject's understanding of how enquiry ought properly to be pursued and the latter indicates the subject's expectations in respect of the manner in which enquiry will engage practically with the social world. The two are of course interlinked – most simply as an 'agent of theory execution' is a necessary element of any social theorizing. Any particular mode of social theoretic engagement – which can be located in respect of exemplars and characterized in primary fashion by citing roles adopted – can thereafter be analysed in detail via this schema of conception/intent. This lets us explicitly treat social theoretic efforts as active engagements with the social world rather than, as is more usual in the orthodox style, essentially passive accommodations to the social world as given. (Indeed this orthodox self-conception strikes me as fairly transparently false given that most, for various reasons, seem to be disposed to argue on behalf of the planners.)

In A.G. Frank's case – as I will try to show in a little detail below – we have in the main the role of spokesman/theorist to consider. If we begin with Frank's intentions, then what is strikingly obvious is his *overt political commitment*. This is not incidental to, or extra to, his work. It is not an adventitious deformation of enquiry. It is *utterly central*. Frank's work is to be translated into practice as polemic; and here he adopts the appropriate role: the author is his own agent of theory execution. Given this intention, Frank proceeds to argue his case directly, illustratively, and persuasively. He adopts a neo-marxian analytic frame as the vehicle. Thus in conception his work is interpretive and in intention (initial) critical.

It is interpretive because he aims to make clear to his readers the situation of the dispossessed groups in Latin America, where his work generally is focused; it is initial critical because whilst the intention is critical – to effect an emancipatory change of view amongst his audience – the theoretical machineries adopted are relatively simple. However, things are not quite so straightforward. Frank would have us read his work as marxist analysis of development and under-development: thus one would want to say that his work is marxist in conception (deployment of historical materialist analytic strategies) and marxist in intention (that is, offering emancipatory knowledge to objectively effective groups).

Yet the exchange in any social theorist's work between conception and intent is going to be complex; the distinction itself oversimplifies the exchange of these elements in theorizing. The elements mutually interact – it is not a case of clearly visible analysis linked in mechanically obvious fashion to clearly visible intentions in respect of action. Further, in Frank's case, to compound confusion, there is a lot less 'marxism' than the author supposes. Lastly, of course, Frank's precise 'role' shifts – just like anyone else – as his attention moves through his material: polemic and social science intermingle. This is a point I follow up in a related fashion with Peter Worsley below.

The position advanced by Frank *draws on* the work of other social scientists – historians, economists, political philosophers, sociologists, and so on – and *contributes to* their work (hence the critique entitled 'Sociology of Development and Underdevelopment of Sociology'), but nonetheless it stands as a separate and distinct mode of social theoretic engagement. I'll return to Frank in detail in a moment, but now it would be helpful to sketch out formally this role of spokesman/theorist. Elsewhere I have sketched out this trio of 'roles', but I have not gone on to elaborate this scheme to any great extent.[6] What follows is a further note towards that fuller statement in respect of my schema of 'modes of social theoretic engagement', rather than any finished view.

A.G. Frank's work, considered in these terms, makes use of the roles of theorist and interpreter. It is the latter element that is to the fore. The role of the interpreter generally is concerned with learning the lessons offered by events and/or theorists: the orientation in contrast to the other pair is thus retrospective. Typically the question put to events will be 'how did it come about that?' whilst the question typically put to a theorist would be 'what is the present relevance of

X?'. The circumstances which Frank wishes to interpret to a wider audience are, in particular, the systematically disadvantaged position of Central and Latin America in contrast to the USA. This point was made clearly by David Booth[7] in his review of Frank's work. It is this interpretive intention that generates one key strategic stylistic element of Frank's work – that is, its repeated appeal to the 'lessons of history'. The orthodox view of Latin America – and the wider public view also – as DCs struggling rather ineffectually to modernize, to shift from a hardly changed 'original condition', is engaged with directly and pragmatically. Thus the simple claims of the orthodoxy (professional and public) are taken on one by one, as it were, and rejected by offering Frank's counterview. The strategy is thus direct and, by virtue of operating within the ambit of common sense, pragmatic. Frank offers a detailed answer via historical examples to the question 'how did it come about that Latin America got where it is now?'.

Additionally, of course, to the deployment of historical material, there is an analytical framework – Frank's work is much more than a denial of the standard view. The interpretation is also critical: that is, it offers a coherent counterposition to the orthodox stance. This is where Frank's use of the theoretical machineries of Baran comes into play. What is taken from Baran's political economy is a simple set of notions whereby the historical material can be ordered. Frank is concerned not merely to interpret but further to act as a *spokesman* to particular groups within the systematically disadvantaged Latin American scene: he argues for the *dispossessed*.

At this point the role of the *theorist* becomes marginally more important. The sets of concepts used to order the historical material now take on the guise of a set of concepts whereby *present* social circumstances can be understood. The understanding generated is, again, simple and direct: the message of Frank to those of his audience who are Latin American is that the established order needs must be overthrown before any significant democratic development can progress. Again Booth pointed out that Frank was very much influenced by the experience of the Cuban Revolution.

I noted above that conception and intent are intermingled. In Frank we find the mix of interpretive criticism ordered around neo-marxian concepts deployed characteristically as political writing or polemic. This introduces a further way of considering the interpreter generally: what is being interpreted, for whom, and why at this particular time rather than some other. Frank's work as a spokesman for the lessons of the Cuban Revolution in particular had both an intra-Third World audience, as noted, and a First World audience. If we ask just who this 'audience' was, then it seems clear that we can say that it was not obviously the Western academic scene. Rather it was, we can hazard, the US public scene, or informed opinion in the US. Frank moved in his particular sphere to counteract the demands of what Caute called (in a not altogether dissimilar context) the 'patriotic imperative'[8] – this, I think, lets us begin to understand the reason for Frank's *emphatic* style of writing. Many commentators have observed that public politics in the US has, amongst other things, an element of religious fervour in respect especially of 'communism'. Thus we have recently had President Reagan's 'empire of evil speach' where he characterized the USSR as responsible for the evil in the world. Media commentators dubbed this the 'Darth Vader speech' (the other noted effort being the 'Star Wars speech' that started what is now called the SDI programme). This posture has been called 'manichean' – seeing the world as split into good and evil. Denting this sort of reading of the world necessitates *emphatic repetition* of a simple counterview. I'll pursue this point in a little while by citing other critical commentators.

But for the moment I give a summary of the points made in respect of the *role of the interpreter*, which is concerned with the retrospective elucidation of the nature of events or theory. It will have an audience in mind – and thus the style of the message will vary. It will have some reason for having been presented now rather than some other time: thus Frank was inspired by the Cuban Revolution – Latin America's position *vis-à-vis* the USA long pre-dated this event. This general role of interpreter can be divided: commentator (and whilst I've said little about this version here we find detached interpretation and probably social scientific scholarship, in its detached 'moment', is to be lodged here) and spokesman – arguing a case for a particular group or theorist. As regards the role of the 'theorist' – present intermittently in Frank – we have the presentation of (or contribution to the formulation of) delimited-formal ideologies, or 'theories' commonsensically understood. I'll not pursue this role formally any further here but what I will do is to look at some other noted political writers so as to elucidate this role of 'political writer' and secure my claims that this is how we should regard A.G. Frank.[9]

4   Chomsky, Orwell and Peter Worsley

I have picked these figures more or less at random. The first pair are, for slightly different reasons, obvious choices. Peter Worsley is an interesting comparison because it is clear from his recently published scholarly text, *The Three Worlds:Culture and World Development* (1985), that there are significant underlying resemblances between scholarly interpretive commentary and the explicitly politically engaged work of my 'political writers'; there are also, let's note, very significant differences.

I'll begin with the work of Chomsky, as it has the most obvious stylistic resemblances to Frank's material: I am assuming that this is occasioned by their shared background in the US intellectual/ political scene, although I have not presented here – or anywhere else – the sociology-of-knowledge-based discussions that would establish the point.

Chomsky is certainly more often noted as a theorist of linguistics and philosopher of language rather than as a socialist polemicist, but in recent years that latter role has been quite evident in both journalistic and essayistic guises. I'll look briefly at specimens of both – again culled fairly unsystematically from the material available.

In his essay 'Intellectuals and the State' (1982) Chomsky looks at the role of the liberal intelligentsia in the USA and diagnoses an extensive and severe case of apologetics both for the capitalist system of the USA and its war role in Vietnam. The intellectuals' role is analysed in terms of often crude ideology-mongering – they are seen as technicians restoring the hegemonic forms (belief in the USA's generosity, honour, leadership of the free world, etc.) that were damaged in the Vietnam War period when significant groups genuinely and visibly dissented from the standard view. The media generally is slated as substaining a *spurious debate* : a subtle control of the agenda of debate offers an apologia for US force.

Chomsky talks about the role of propaganda, the *engineering of consent*, which is a process to be sharply distinguished from persuasion via open debate, and argues for a convergence of US (and Western) manipulation of citizenry with the totalitarian strategies of the Eastern Bloc. In substance, he adds, the western strategy is more difficult to combat simply because the method is more subtle. Indeed at this point Chomsky seems to be alluding to a notion of 'repressive tolerance'. One point he makes explicitly is that the orthodoxy routinely distinguishes between responsible technocratic policy analyst intellectuals and value intellectuals and dismisses the latter as unreliable; Chomsky comments: 'It is also striking that subservience to the state and its doctrine is not regarded as a "value", but merely the natural commitment of the intelligentsia or at least its more honourable representatives.'[10] As I have remarked in another chapter in this book, the orthodox habitually 'argue on behalf of the planners'.

In style Chomsky's writing is argumentative and often *brutally direct*: opponents are identified and unequivocally dealt with. Thus, for example, Senator Eugene McCarthy is *dismissed* as an opportunist riding the back of the anti-Vietnam War protest, who neither contributed to the movement before his bid for the Presidency nor after his failure to win the nomination. And McCarthy, he notes, was widely seen as the liberal of the US political scene. To the reader schooled in the modest tones of European academic and political commentary all this looks very combative. This style is repeated in all the essays in the collection: in the title essay, 'Towards a New Cold War' Chomsky argues – again with brutal directness – that orthodox intellectuals are servants of politicians who are cold war warriors serving local and international capitalism via the permanent arms economy. The US – and its hegemonic technicians – supports counterrevolution around the globe so that the world can be kept safe for US business. A summary of US power imperialism is offered in a *New Statesman* article entitled 'The Shadow of the Great Satan'. It is vigorous material and, as I noted, it is out of the same general background as Frank's early work.

Turning to the work of George Orwell, we find an English polemicist of comparable power to Chomsky and, more pertinently, of a controversial status more akin to Frank. The work of Orwell has been extensively debated, during his lifetime and afterwards, especially by social scientists and political theorists and comment-ators. I will first call attention to the character of Orwell's writing and to his own understanding of it and then I'll look at how it has been subsequently received.

Wain[11] begins by speaking of the old-fashioned style of literary criticism that focused on *kinds* of writing: this style identified particular 'kinds' and measured given work against them – correct elements or not. He then goes on to say: 'It is impossible to criticize an author's work adequately until you have understood what kinds of books he was writing.'[12] Just so. Wain goes on to observe that: 'The kind to which Orwell's work belongs is the polemic. . . . A writer of polemic is always a man who, having himself chosen what side to take, uses his work as an instrument for strengthening the support of that side.'[13] This is precisely the point I would make to the majority of Frank's critics.

In the case of Orwell that observation is, however, merely the starting point of much subsequent debate as to (i) the nature of Orwell's message; and (ii) the explanation of how he came to present such a message. Some commentators also add: (iii) how the message has subsequently been taken up into public political consciousness.

Orwell – to address (i) – saw himself as a *political writer*, (I have borrowed this term from him), and as a 'democratic socialist'. Bernard Crick cites Orwell as writing 'What I have most wanted to do . . . is to make political writing into an art.'[14] And Crick goes on to construe 'political writer' both as a specific mode of engagement, writing on various matters and all of it suffused with politics, and as a general term embracing 'philosophers, statesmen, publicists and pamphleteers'.[15] Of Orwell's work Crick notes that eventually it came to have a very particular style because he stressed what he termed 'plain speaking':

> And plain speaking always meant to him clear writing, communality, common sense, courage and a common style. He saw his literary and his political values as perfectly complementary to each other . . . even if plain style . . . limited . . . the development of his own more theoretical ideas.[16]

Crick goes on to add, I think revealingly, 'Obscure, pretentious, or trendy language was to Orwell always a sign of indecision or deceit'[17] – and in this, given the complexity of the social world and the difficulty of grasping it, Orwell was in my view just plain wrong. Worse, he was, as is made clear in his own writing and in Crick's biography, anti-intellectual and this is a dangerous flaw in Orwell. Again Crick revealingly notes, 'His politics were left wing, but many of his prejudices were conservative.'[18] Orwell's work, *per contra* Frank, was untutored and the result, substantively, was that Orwell provided several key ideas to the post-Second World War *cold war orthodoxy of the West*: quite an achievement for a professed socialist.

On the matter of this 'plain style' Raymond Williams speaks of the invention of *Orwell the character* – in contrast to the man. Orwell the character was offered as 'the plain man who bumps into experience in an unmediated way and is simply telling the truth about it'.[19] The stance is a fraud: 'For the key point about the convention of the plain observer with no axes to grind, who simply tells the truth, is that it conceals the social situation of the writer and conceals his stance towards the social situation he is observing.'[20] Orwell's self-conscious stance of unself-consciousness masks an obverse of reflexively generated theoretical understanding – he has in place merely a set of common-sense notions, or, more harshly, upper-middle-class prejudices curiously displaced to a working-class context. Williams goes on to say that the interesting questions about Blair's invention of Orwell is why a style came to be so widely imitated. 'The next generation received the form as wisdom, achievement and maturity, although it was false to the core.'[21]

In my terms the mode of engagement of Orwell's invented Orwell is, in inspiration and style, not really engaged at all: Deutscher, as I note below, regards it as quietist and he speaks of the overall pessimism of Orwell's work as the 'mysticism of cruelty'.[22] However, I will treat the writing of Orwell more simply, granting, as Crick does, that there is a distinctive political writer at work here. The deeper questions about Orwell *per se* has best be left to an essay on Orwell.

E.P. Thompson – moving on to (ii) – speaks of Orwell as a man 'raw all down one side and numb on the other'[23]: he is hypercritical of the left and neglects the right. Thompson goes on to argue that this obsessive denigration of the left is both quietist (Orwell withdrew from genuine political engagement after Spain into mere venting of his spleen), and, as noted, a major contribution to cold war NATO ideology. Thompson sees Orwell as a *poor* social commentator and as a political renegade rather than ally. In answer to the question of how Orwell's particular message came to be formulated, a sketch of an answer would involve his anti-intellectualism and upper-class background – after early moral rebellion Orwell reverts to type. The type is *familiar* in the UK. Wain, an admirer, remarks that Orwell 'was in no sense an abstruse thinker. His political ideas were of the simplest ... he believed in the necessity of being frank and honest, and he believed in freedom for everyone.'[24] Crucially, he thought these values were *directly accessible*. Julie Burchill, commenting on the recent 'daughtergate scandal', notes that the episode involved a conflict of class cultures between 'the lower middle, where honour is nothing and respectability is all, and the upper middle, where the values are reversed.'[25] Parkinson came from the former and Sara Keays the latter. Orwell seems to have understood 'honour', and that it came to have the target and expression it did is a biographical accident of his rebellion and return to origins. Certainly, as Crick noted above, there is no theory, and Deutscher, seeking to understand how he came to argue as he did, notes that 'He found himself incapable of explaining what was happening in terms which were familiar to him, the terms of empirical common sense.'[26]

As regards (iii) the story is of the avowed socialist becoming the darling of the political right – Thompson sees him contributing to NATO ideology: certainly the presentation of Orwell's two books (written during the war when, as a matter of simple record, the USSR bore the brunt of the war against European fascism) *Animal Farm* and *1984* as the definite anti-socialist tracts has been familiar in the Western world. More than this I'll leave to another time, except for an illustration of his work and a footnote.

George Orwell's work has been valued by political sophisticates – both those who agree with his message and those who do not – for its trenchant argument. I'll offer a specimen here as a reminder of its flavour. Then, as a footnote, I'll present a specimen of the work of Germaine Greer who offers a brilliant attack on Thatcherism as a symptom of the decline of political culture in the UK – one of Orwell's targets in a way.

In the second part of *The Road to Wigan Pier* Orwell discusses socialism and declares himself one: problems of socialist failure to prosper are discussed in terms of style – to this he counterposes his own view. Problems of 'presentation' are noted, famously: 'One sometimes gets the impression that the mere words "Socialism" and "Communism" draw towards them with magnetic force every fruit juice drinker, nudist, sandal wearer, sex maniac, Quaker, Nature Cure quack, pacifist and feminist in England.'[27] Orwell scorns not only the 'fringe groups' but the intelligentsia – 'the theoretical book trained Socialists'.[28] Again, 'On the one hand you have the warm hearted unthinking Socialist ... on the other .. the intellectual .. who understands that it is necessary to throw our present civilization down the sink and is quite willing to do so.'[29] Socialism must be presented simply, as simple decency. Orwell's view of socialism in practice is distinctly rural[30] – a simpler life, and healthier life; often he calls progress a 'swindle'. In modern terms all this is romantic. Says Orwell:

> We have reached a stage when the very word 'Socialism' calls up on the one hand a picture of aeroplanes, tractors, and huge glittering factories of glass and concrete; on the other, a picture of vegetarians with wilting beards, of Bolshevik commissars (half gangster half gramophone) of earnest ladies in sandals, of shock-headed Marxists chewing polysyllables, escaped Quakers, birth control fanatics, and Labour Party backstairs crawlers.[31]

Again and again Orwell calls for simplicity – in life and argument. It is very powerful and has been hugely influential, as Thompson noted.

A contemporary polemicist is Germaine Greer: she analyses present UK politics via the persona of the Prime Minister, Margaret Thatcher, whom Greer urges is the 'Nanny of the Nation'.[32] Greer traces the fashioning of the nanny (elocution and restorative dentistry plus appropriate clothes and bosom control) and characterizes the role as reserving unto nanny all decisions and knowledge, all values, and the rest are children who must be told what to think and do. Greer comments:

> Nobody really resents the subliminal message that underlies every statement that Mrs Thatcher makes that Nanny is the only adult in the nursery. Those people who have fussed over Mrs Thatcher's bullying and insensitivity have failed to see that Mrs Thatcher thinks of them as not yet grown up, or to use her nursery lingo, as wets.[33]

Thatcher's ability to carry off this role is evidence, for Greer, of a degraded, often infantilized, polity – that of the contemporary UK. But now let us move on.

These texts generally demonstrate: (i) the power of political writing; (ii) the apparent necessity of simple direct language (in A.G.F. characteristic neologisms and repetitions achieve this end); (iii) the necessity of theoretical sophistication (which Orwell did not have but the others and Frank do have). An elaborated discussion of, especially, Orwell and Frank would, I think, be most interesting but that lies outside my present sphere of interest. Rather, I turn now to the work of Peter Worsley so as to consider the resemblances between Frankian political writing and scholarship.

I remarked elsewhere[34] when looking at Frank that he shifted his position in his writings when in *Dependent Accumulation and Under-development* (1978) he endeavoured, in response to criticism of earlier work, to fix the theoretical base of his material firmly in place. In my terms Frank shifted from spokesman/theorist to commentator/theorist: Foster-Carter, regarding this sceptically, dubbed the claim the 'Two Franks Thesis'.[35] My point was, and is, that there are various roles available to any theorist. And the present relevance of that argument to Worsley seems to me to lie in the way academic social science can be tugged in two rather different directions: to the disinterestedness of scholarly exegesis and the engagement with the world entailed by notions of critique. Worsley offers a text that is *clearly scholarly but is also in an understated way critically engaged*. I'll look at Worsley as a contrasting style of writing politically to that of Frank.

Worsley's *The Three Worlds: Culture and World Development* (1984) seems, on review, to be compounded of three elements: perspectives form the marxian tradition (thus he speaks of capitalism and exploitation); orientations to extant patterns of life which seem fairly directly anthropological (thus he enjoins attention to, and anthropological equality for, given patterns of life rather than any simple measuring against First World standards); and, lastly, English social reformism, which is to my mind evidenced in the text's discursive style. The declared objective of the study is a synthetic review of the post-Second World War experience of the Third World and its theorists such that present problems and appropriate theoretical formulations can be identified: the work is thus critical in two senses – political and social scientific, or scholarly. Overall the text, as I've said, leans strongly to the scholarly.

Worsley's revisions to established theoretical views and procedures begin with Marx, or, more particularly, the distinction between base and superstructure: this, it is suggested, has actively misled theorists into seeing the economic as the key issue and, relatedly, to the neglect of culture. Worsley proposes a 'dialectical sociology' (which he seems to take to be a genuinely scientific study of society). All this I take to be largely acceptable and rather overstated.[36] Moving on, the substantive core of the book looks, in turn, at the peasantry, the working class and ethnicity/nationalism.

The peasantry are rescued via the anthropological insights of the author from, so to say, second-class social scientific citizenship and re-presented as actors having a coherent cultural form and an active role. However this cultural form is in the process of disappearance as the urban-industrial world (of capitalism and socialism) advances. In this advancing sphere the proletariat are tackled: Worsley here disaggregated the poor into discrete sub-groups each having a particular relationship to the capitalist world system. Patterns of resistance are, consequently, taken to be complex and the old 'immanentist myth' of the unfolding of revolutionary class conflict is dismissed. Again Worsley is presenting his views on social scientific theorizing and its results as he offers a political critique of present circumstances: there are, to oversimplify, continuities as well as discontinuities between the work of Worsley and Frank.

A final section deals with ethnicity and nation and begins, rightly, by noting that Marxists have generally struggled with both ideas: additionally to anthropological insights centering on the social construction of images of ethnicity and nation, Worsley ventures (unhappily) into political science with a discussion of nations and states. Nonetheless once again we have a mix of arguments in favour of reformulating social scientific approaches to issues with substantive comment upon the issues themselves. Thus reflections on theorizing are suffused with reflection on political action in the world.

The text concludes with a pessimistic review of present circumstances, and this material we can usefully consider rather more carefully. Thus in Worsley's view decolonization has been followed by various occasions for pessimism: neo-colonialism; opportunistic and incompetent new elites; fatuous claims to socialism; outside intervention (especially First World); and generally a slide into authoritarian polities. This is Worsley's agenda for present and future discussion. *Evidently this is both an agenda for scholarly analysis and represents a series of substantive political judgments.*

One can speculate, after the fashion of those commentators on Orwell cited above, about the occasion for this deepseated pessimism, and I think, to pursue this material just a little further, that there are perhaps two sets of reasons that can be adduced. The first relates to the nature of the passing of the milieu within which Worsley, and many other First World theorists, have moved during the post-Second World War period. The second relates to the particular mix of elements within Worsley's own work.

Of the first mentioned one can call attention to the attempts of the orthodoxy to constitute 'development' as an independent discipline having its own 'object' and 'method' appropriate thereto: marxists offered an analogous discourse centered on political action – Worsley's 'immanentist myth'. The common error, as I have pointed out,[37] was to suppose that the whole complex business of 'development' could be simplified and grasped as a single coherent process, the stuff certainly of academic disciplines but not of this reality. Worsley's material is a product of this particular, and now past, historical juncture: there is no one object or process to understand with manipulative intent (be that plan or revolution making); rather there is a complex of historical processes of varying interest to a multiplicity of groups. Scholarly commentary has to begin by acknowledging this or else we are just one more group. Worsley's text punctuates the transition of two periods: it both marks the end of the discourse that shaped it and gestures to the process of supersession of that discourse.

Secondly, and relatedly, we can ask if the more specific trio of marxism, social anthropology and social reformism actually fit together. On the evidence of Worsley's text there must be some doubt, given the rather different intentions of each style of enquiry. It seems to me as if there might well be a confusion of understanding and intention in Worsley's text. Indeed this confusion, arguably, continues explicitly in his commitment to a 'dialectical sociology' – where Worsley can grant the multiplicity of forms of life he seems unable to grant, as I would urge, that social theoretic engagement is similarly diverse. Social theorizing is not all of a piece – and nor is his own work.

However, to recap, with Worsley we find a thoroughly scholarly text which nonetheless contains a very clear set of political judgments. There are, it seems to me, significant resemblances between Worsley and Frank (and the other political writers): I'll try to elucidate this when I turn to A.G. Frank, whose work instances a discrete mode of engagement but which nonetheless draws on, and contributes to, scholarship. More generally, it seems clear that it is both sensible and helpful to speak of 'political writers' as a group, or available role, within the overall sphere of social theorizing, which is rather closer than might otherwise be expected to scholarly social science.

5   A.G. Frank's 'political writing'

Frank is probably the best-known theorist working within the general marxian line and his writings have been both influential and contentious. Frank is often taken, it seems to me, as a 'universal baddy': attacks on the broad 'radical' tradition often cite Frank in order to attack a whole spread of ideas. Critics of the broad radical tradition often fail to draw elementary distinctions between Latin American dependency (with its several rather less obvious sub-divisions) and the neo-marxism of Baran, Frank and Wallerstein (a trio whose work is, again, not all of a piece). Additionally there is now post-neo-marxian work to consider.[38] As a consequence the attacks of these critics often fail. There are also critics of the left – those who would sympathize with Frank's overall orientation but who dispute much of the analytical detail and political proposals of his work. Many of these theorists also fail, but for the rather more interesting reason of confusions in respect of 'roles'.

It is not really very surprising that Frank should have drawn these attacks upon himself, for both his style and message are unpalatable to the orthodox thinkers of the First World – who prefer to offer modest arguments on behalf of the planners – and to those over enthusiastically rigorous marxists who tend to the view that there must be *one* correct mode of engagement and related analysis. Some of the hostility to A.G. Frank's work flows, as I have been saying, from a fundamental failure to note the *kind* of writer he is; but, equally, more than a few of the attacks are positively invited by infelicities of formulation within Frank's work itself. In the following section I will try to illustrate Frank's characteristic style of political writing, with its links to and differences from scholarship, and note some of the criticisms made and invited.

Frank's background is of an economist turned political activist.[39] The decisive events in Frank's career centre upon his experience of Latin America in the early 1960s. Booth, as I've noted, sees a sharp change in both work and commitment as a result of these experiences[40] – the earlier orthodox training is simply dropped and a new approach embraced (itself a remarkable manoeuvre). Out of the general milieu of long-term foreign, especially US, dominance of the area and the experience of the Cuban Revolution and within the context of a rejection of orthodox approaches mediated via exposure to structuralist economics, Frank conceives the task of contributing to a revolutionary critique of orthodox theorizing and expectations of action. In a text written in 1963 Frank presents his intellectual-political manifesto in these terms:

All serious study of the problems of development of under-developed areas and all serious intent to formulate policy for the elimination of underdevelopment and for the promotion of development must take into account, nay must begin with, this fundamental historical and structural cause of underdevelopment in capitalism. Indeed all serious study of development must take into account the fundamental relation the development of development has had, and continues to have, with the development of underdevelopment. All serious study of capitalism, or its manifestations in the development of the metropole and of that in the underdevelopment of the periphery, and especially the study of the contemporary single world capitalist system and its development in the past and future, must begin with capitalism's unity and its fundamental internal contradiction, which has always and everywhere expressed itself in diffusion and exploitation, development and underdevelopment.[41]

The fundamental contradiction I take to be the private appropriation of socially produced wealth and this is pursued in the fashion specified in the context of Latin American historical experience. The familiar Frankian schema emerges in his 1967 text *Capitalism and Underdevelopment in Latin America*, where the fundamental contradiction is further elucidated via the three contradictions which characterize the dynamic of capitalist development of underdevelopment. These are:

the expropriation of economic surplus from the many and its appropriation by the few, the polarization of the capitalist system into metropolitan center and peripheral satellites, and the continuity of the fundamental structure of the capitalist system throughout the history of its expansion and transformation, due to the persistence or re-creation of these contradictions every where and at all times.[42]

With this basic position sketched, Frank goes on to review the history of Chilean and Brazilian incorporation. A series of stages are identified beginning in the sixteenth century and culminating in the twentieth century, which is characterized in terms of the incapacity of national bourgeois groupings to fulfil their classical historical role of nationalist capitalist development. A condition of dependent and deformed '*under* development' has been generated and only a regime wedded to socialist ideals can now advance matters.[43]

It is at this point that we can begin to take note of Frank's characteristic style. Above with Orwell *et al.* we saw that 'political writing' apparently required a simple analytic frame, directness of debate/enquiry (together giving simplicity of argument), plus many repetitions and illustrations of the message. Offering a counter-position to an established 'conventional wisdom' demands this sort of approach – neat tidy chains of logical argument not only will not work but they don't even get purchase. Wittgenstein remarks in the *Philosophical Investigations* (1974) that to overthrow myths you need multiple examples of the error before those in error can see. With

Frank we have two characteristic elements: the analytic framework taken in the main from Baran and the detailed attention to history.[44] These we can usefully pursue: they are evident in his 1969 text *Latin America: Underdevelopment or Revolution*.

Of these essays Frank declares: '[they] were written to contribute to the revolution in Latin America and the world.'[45] The central argument or political position is that,

> Underdevelopment in Latin America . . . developed as the result of the colonial structure of world capitalist development [which has] penetrated all of Latin America thereby forming and transforming the colonial and class structure of underdevelopment . . . the development of underdevelopment will continue . . . until its peoples free themselves . . . by violent revolutionary victory over their own bourgeoisie and over imperialism.[46]

And subsequently history and theory are pursued. If we take the first essay, we can look in detail at Frank's style.

In 'The Development of Underdevelopment' Frank advocates an approach that is sensitive to history and that grants that societies and theories change through time. He argues that an 'adequate development theory and policy [requires] first learning how their past economic and social history gave rise to their present underdevelopment.'[47] This injunction is used to consider orthodox material: there has been a gross neglect, argues Frank, of the episode of colonial empire. He says, 'for this reason most of our theoretical categories and guides to development policy have been distilled exclusively from the historical experiences of the European and North American advanced capitalist nations.'[48] A lack of knowledge of history, argues Frank, results in an inadequate theory; one which neither fits the facts nor displays the options for the future, instead we have theorems of recapitulation: the Third World will travel the same set of stages as the First World did. Frank thinks this last claim, generated by an ignorance of history, is ridiculous and the conclusion he draws is that 'consequently, most of our theory fails to explain the structure and development of the capitalist system as a whole and to account for its simultaneous generation of underdevelopment in some of its parts and of economic development in others.'[49] Now this simply presents Frank's counterview to the orthodoxy: instead of an argument from specified premises, we have the deployment of comments about the historical inadequacies of the orthodox which are shaped – as we find out – by the Baran-inspired framework. To be strict Frank introduces his own positions in a distinctly misleading fashion because history, of course, does not tell its own story. From this point Frank unpacks his position in a question-and-answer style.

Firstly, he remarks that 'It is generally held that economic development occurs in a succession of capitalist stages,'[50] where the presently developed are the model and all other countries are, being underdeveloped, fated to repeat this sequence. Frank observes: 'Yet even a modest acquaintance with history shows that underdevelopment is not original or traditional . . . the now developed countries were never undeveloped though they may have been underveloped.'[51]

Secondly, Frank notes the widespread view, amongst orthodox theorists, that 'contemporary underdevelopment of a country can be understood as a product . . . of its own economic, political, social and cultural characteristics.'[52] Once again Frank invokes history and remarks that 'historical research demonstrates'[53] that underdevelopment is generated by the world capitalist system. The repeated appeal to history is typical, as is the above tactic of offering simple distinctions – under/un-developed – which surely Orwell would have approved of!

Thirdly, Frank continues by noting the orthodox thesis of the diffusion of growth impulses via contact with the developed nations and he denies it: '[An] historical perspective . . . suggests that on the contrary, economic development in the underdeveloped countries can now occur only independently of these relations of diffusion.'[54]

Fourthly, Frank considers and rejects the dual society thesis. This leads, fifthly, to a general declaration of his positions: 'A mounting body of evidence suggests, and I am confident that future historical research will confirm . . . [the development of underdevelopment].'[55] Again and again Frank makes this appeal to history. The history being read in the light of the theoretical machineries taken from Baran: the presentation, via the appeal to history, is designed to persuade. The only problem created by this technique is that it permits others to misread his work as straightforwardly academic – which makes it crude scholarship – rather than, as is the case, sophisticated political writing.

As Orwell appealed to the common sense of the unreflective working classes so Frank appeals to history. In narrowly scholarly terms it is an unsatisfactory procedure, but as a device to *undermine* the established view and win over people to his own viewpoint it has been most effective – it is the demystificatory strategy of simplicity and repetition in action. The appeal to history is structured by using Baran-derived marxian schemes and the developed marxian counter-position is, simultaneously, sketched in its outline.

Now I want to take note of how history and explanatory frame come together *persuasively*. In 1972 Frank published his short book *Lumpenbourgeoisie – Lumpendevelopment*. This text represents a first reply to his critics and the first reconsideration of his thesis in respect of the historical development of underdevelopment.

The text begins with a preface entitled 'Mea Culpa' in which he lists a series of criticisms made of his earlier work. He notes that he has been accused of being overly schematic, historically shallow, neglectful of class, and too emphatic in respect of external aspects of dependency. Frank denies these lapses and offers his present text as a clarification of his position. He declares that he will defend three major claims: first, that 'the conquest placed all of Latin America in a position of subjection and colonial and neo-colonial economic dependence in relation to the single world systems of expanding commercial capitalism',[56] second, that 'this colonial or neo-colonial relationship to the capitalist metropolis formed and transformed the economic and class structure, as well as the culture of Latin American society, with the transformation in national structure occurring as a consequence of changes in the forms of colonial dependence';[57] and third, that 'this colonial and class structure established the very direct interests of the dominant sector of the bourgeoisie. Using governmental cabinets and instruments of the state, this sector spawns policies of economic, social, cultural, and political underdevelopment for the nation and for the people of Latin America.'[58]

The dominant class of Latin America, with its self-interested alliance with the centre, Frank dubs the 'Lumpenbourgeoisie' and the politico-economic consequences of their role 'Lumpendevelopment'. And in respect of the criticisms of his earlier works Frank notes that 'instead of discarding the methodology or rejecting the thesis I should attempt to strengthen the methodology and clarify the dialectical relationship between the actors and their changing setting.'[59] This is the task of the 1972 text. At which point one might note, again characteristic of Frank, that his material is presented as contribution to debate in progress – not in the style of academic work which presents its results in a more measured style. For A.G. Frank, his writings are direct contributions to immediate and demanding problems. Further than this, it is clear to me that in pattern of argument little has changed in this text, although Frank does follow up these discussions and 'reformulations' to produce a *political pamphlet*, of no little elegance and power, which interprets the historical experience of Latin America in line with his central notion of the active development of underdevelopment. In the text Frank again declares himself politically; thus lumpendevelopment and its characteristic set of problems can be resolved 'with the only true development strategy: armed revolution and the construction of socialism'.[60] In this text Frank stands revealed as a political writer and activist. This is evidently a quite distinctive way of making sense of the social world, and it certainly has little obvious direct connection with orthodox-type arguments on behalf of the planners which are backed by appeals to the natural sciences, notwithstanding Frank's confusing habit of appealing, orthodox style, to history. I hope that it can now also be granted that this mode of social theoretic engagement demands initial attention in its own terms, lest we dismiss by misrepresentation.

The characteristic elements of this mode – in the case of A.G. Frank – are, to recap: the central strategy of the appeal to history; the Baran-inspired claims in respect of the requirements of 'serious study' (the framework deployed); and the combative argument style.

Frank makes much of the alleged 'neglect of history' and he uses this to make a whole series of points – some critical of the orthodoxy directly and some constitutive of his counterposition. Thus the neglect of history has the effect, he claims, of denying the real history of the Third World. This neglect allows foolish theorems of 'recapitulation' and allows analytical machineries to be taken from the experience of the First World, thus inevitably skewing analysis. In these claims A.G. Frank is both surely right and in wide company – members of the tradition of dissenting economics could and would grant all these points. What Frank did that was, arguably, rather special was to enunciate the point with his own particular verve: the idea that the orthodox position effectively abolishes the real history – and indeed any history – of the Third World nation-states is a telling formulation. Galbraith has pointed out[61] that, notwithstanding the vested interest we have in hard-gained knowledge, eventually intellect rebels when asked repeatedly to swallow nonsense. On the matter of the reading of the history of the Third World Frank's criticism undoubtedly struck a chord for many theorists.

The 'neglect of history' also allows schemes of diffusionism to gain credence, for simple attention to historical data, claims Frank, will suffice to reject any optimism in respect of the spread of growth impulses from the developed to the underdeveloped. Similarly misconceived in principle and unhelpful in practice are schemes of dualistic analysis: here again A.G. Frank's views would (in their analytical moment, if not political) command wide support. The orthodox have operated with – in various forms – a simple traditional/modern dichotomy and, as many have noted, it simply won't do. Others[62] have argued that the dualist strategy is intellectually broken-backed. The trouble with these notions – like others – is that they allow the orthodoxy to ignore the sorts of global capitalist circumstances, as Frank would have it, which circumscribe and shape the economic and social patterns of dependent elements of the world system, in favour of a self-serving focus on internal circumstances.

Frank takes this to be a variant of the old strategy of blaming the victim. Overall, the neglect of history allows the orthodox to conjure up a totally misleading scheme of underdevelopment – taken as an original and comparatively degraded form of life which with First World expertise and aid can now be remedied. A.G. Frank, with another of his brilliantly simple rhetorical moves, argues that the Third World never was initially underdeveloped, but instead may be regarded as having been undeveloped. Further, it is precisely the history that the Third World does have – of colonial incorporation into the global capitalist system – which is the cause of present underdevelopment. Thus Frank overthrows the myths of the orthodox and substitutes his own notion of the development of underdevelopment.

The strategy of writing in the history that the orthodox routinely write out entails the presentation of historical material and this is given form by the peculiar mix of Latin American theories and the work of Baran. Frank declares early on that 'serious study' demands that a trio of issues be confronted: the centrality of 'capitalism' as an explanatory category; the importance of exchanges between centres and peripheries for an understanding of the latter (and, rather like Furtado, by implication for the former also); the continuity through history albeit in various guises of the logic of capitalism. The requirements of theory are further unpacked in his schemes of contradictions. We might note, in passing, that Frank's intellectual background is quite clear. Rejecting the orthodox neo-classicism (learned in Chicago of all places), Frank runs together aspects of Latin American dependency (structuralist economics) with the material of Baran, in particular the notion of surplus. The political reformism of ECLA is rejected in favour of a left activism inspired by the experience of Cuba (indigenous and established CPs do not seem ever to have impressed Frank). The result of this melange is a wholly distinct formulation: a part of the 'neo-marxian' position, certainly, but to be judged *both* independently *and* in the particular context of political writing in which it is working.

The arguments Frank derives from the 'neglect of history', and those advanced under the broad schemes of surplus expropriation and so on, are translated into practice – engage with the world – as persuasive, politically committed writing. Frankian argument style involves a series of typical elements. Picking out the obvious ones, and recalling Orwell, we have, firstly, the declared commitment to an academic and political critique of the orthodox in the service of revolutionary socialism in Latin America. Secondly, and crucially, we have simplicity of argument and in turn this is compounded of the following elements: one, a simple analytic framework taken, as noted, from, in the main, Baran, which is readily graspable so as to structure the illustrative historical material and point to a developed counter-view; two, the use of arresting neologisms and formulations – development of underdevelopment, lumpenbourgeoisie, lumpen-development; three, a resolute directness of argument in that Frank goes to the point and eschews elaborate formulations; four, as noted, the use of extensive illustrations from history such that repetition can fix his view in place and offer detailed piecemeal corrections for the orthodox story; five, the appeal to history so as to persuade. In sum Frank's work is combative and engaged. Frank is on the side of the poor and he takes himself to be working for them. This is why politics are central to his work: the tone is a relation to the US 'patriotic imperative' and to the manner of public political argument of that country.

In an earlier text[63] I argued that social theorizing was practical – in the sense of being designed to solve particular problems at particular times and places. The theorist, the particular individual contriving particular formulations, is bound by these circumstances. Of social theoretic efforts we can say that circumstances and problems call forth distinct efforts of theorizing – an appreciation of milieu leads us into matters of conception and intent. Recalling Wain above, we have to understand what *kind* of writer we are dealing with *before* we offer any comments. A.G. Frank, it seems to me, has to be read as a 'political writer'.

6   Critical views of A.G. Frank

I remarked above that Frank's work has often been of the form of contributions to debates in progress, rather than 'finished' academic statements. Consequently throughout his work there are scattered 'replies to my critics'. The 'mea culpa' section of *Lumpenbourgeoisie – Lumpendevelopment* (1972) I have noted. Also to be noted are the remarks in his *Dependent Accumulation and Underdevelopment*(1978) which I will come to. A further reply to critics is available in his *Critique and Anti-Critique*(1984).

In this last text he presents an essay entitled 'An Answer to Critics', which seems to be a recently revised version of an early 1970s paper, in which he usefully categorizes his critics: we can begin here.

Frank notes: 'many critics have singled out A G F for his work as supposedly representative of the remainder, sometimes going so far as to claim explicitly or implicitly that a (successful) critique of this one example will do and hold for all.'[64] This strategy Frank evidently, and rightly, regards as ludicrous. Further, he notes, accurately: 'One thing is sure, and has been frankly clarified by the author and universally appreciated by friend and foe alike: the work has been intentionally and consciously political and substantially inspired by the Cuban Revolution.'[65] Frank is a political writer, in other words. From this point he categorizes his critics: '[they] seem to fall into three major tendencies: (1) the backward looking right wing, (2) the traditional marxist left and (3) the forward looking new left'.[66]

Of (1) Frank is scathingly dismissive – as one might expect – seeing them as either blind or biased or both: 'These critics from the right lack either the perspective, the competence, or the interest, or all three, to examine the argument on its own ground,'[67] preferring instead either to nit-pick or to dismiss the entire effort on the positive scientific ground that it's all ideology. Rightly, Frank points out that this is not plausible and he then, most interestingly, adds into this group Bill Warren.

Of (2) Frank is equally dismissive and for not wholly dissimilar reasons: orthodox CPs have not approved of his celebration of the Cuban Revolution and have preferred to stress what Frank sees as reformist strategies. Frank asks just what have the various CPs contributed to the recent renaissance of Marxist scholarship and answers, emphatically, nothing. These critics are seen to be backward-looking both politically and analytically.

It is the members of category (3) that Frank takes seriously, although in this essay he has little of substance to say. He approves of and supports their forward-looking stance and indeed seems to grant that the 'dependency' position he has argued for now stands ready for supersession as circumstances and analytical sophistication both change. Again Frank is joining in debate.

Pursuing these last-mentioned critics, I'll take note of the efforts of Laclau, Brenner, Leys and Palma – all of whom take Frank to be a straightforward marxist *theoretician*. Consequently they miss precisely what is novel in Frank's work. However, we can note their work not only for this point – which illustrated the claims I have been making in this essay – but also because they show that Frank does indeed contribute to theory (and he takes these critics seriously as a consequence).

Laclau argues that the notion of capitalism that Frank uses is not that of Marx and that, consequently, his arguments are not marxian and, further, they are confused. Having characterized the Frankian thesis of the development of underdevelopment, Laclau comments:

> It can be seen that Frank's theoretical schema involves three types of assertion: 1. Latin America has had a market economy from the beginning; 2. Latin America has been capitalist from the beginning; 3. the dependent nature of its insertion into the capitalist world market is the cause of its underdevelopment. The

three assertions claim to refer to a single process identical in its essential aspects from the 16th to the 20th century.[68]

These are considered in turn. Thus the criticism of dualism in the first point is granted, but Laclau adds that it does not follow from the fact that Latin American economies have been market economies that they were capitalist economies. So far as Laclau is concerned, Frank is in error in equating capitalism with production for the market in pursuit of profit, rather capitalism should be seen as a complex social form – the idea of mode of production is preferred. The upshot of the criticism, focusing now on point three, is that Frank's thesis is overgeneral. At which point, following all the above arguments of mine, we can say both *yes* this is probably true *but it is not directly relevant to the Frankian project*. Laclau is offering a technical academic critique of a *particular aspect* of Frank's project.

These technical theoretical matters are pursued by Brenner in his excellent paper[69] where he characterizes the initial dynamic of capitalism in terms of a complex exchange between technical possibility and social pressure/opportunity – thereafter the logic of accumulation proceeds to drive the system. Brenner considers Frank's answers to these questions and finds that: '[Frank] was unambiguous in locating the dynamic of capitalist expansion in the rise of a world commercial network, while specifying the roots of both growth and backwardness in the "surplus appropriation chain" which emerged in the expansionary process.'[70] Brenner objects that this effectively redefines capitalism as an exchange relationship and displaces the dynamism of the system into centre/periphery relations. The result of these errors, so far as Brenner is concerned, is that Frank collapses into Third World*ist* ideology: a view of the present world system that sees the only chance for progressive change arising within the peripheral areas. And again one can say yes this is all probably true but does it really bear directly upon the real Frankian project? If Brenner has read Frank as a 'political writer' then accusing him of collapsing into a Third World ideology would have seemed rather absurd – it is the political commitment that is central to his work. Brenner reads Frank as a careless academic and he shows no sign of recognizing that Frank is offering a quite distinct mode of engagement.

Leys[71] addressed the character of Frank's work generally and, whilst he offers a series of technical criticisms, his discussion is suffused with an appropriate regard for the contribution made by what he terms 'radical underdevelopment theory'. Leys lists the difficulties he has with the theory – its imprecision, vagueness, and 'primitive concepts' – but does add that radical UDT 'stimulated the empirical study of institutional and structural mechanisms of underdeveloped'.[72] More generally he notes that: 'in the context of the early 1960's when UDT emerged as a militant critique . . . its thrust was unquestionably a progressive one.'[73] Leys is right in both these particulars: and a grasp of social theoretic roles would have enabled him to go on a step further and consider directly the issue of the precise contribution of Frank (it might also, apropos of Leys' use of Althusserian concepts, have enabled him to consider his own role).

Finally, Palma[74] in his superb review article assimilates Frank to a general 'neo-marxist' position, which is not unreasonable, and then goes on to lodge these theorists within the broad marxian tradition. Palma, following Brenner, observes that Frank's work in the end is nothing more than an inversion of the views of the orthodox such that peripheral status is necessarily degraded and unprogressive.

Of all four cited here – and others have pursued these matters further[75] – I would reiterate my basic point: what they say may well be true and point the way to building upon Frank's breakthrough, but that A.G. Frank's contribution to the change of perception which they inherited should be acknowledged and this entails granting that Frank was, *inter alia*, first a 'political writer'.

Shifting now to Frank's most extensive reply to his critics in *Dependent Accumulation and Underdevelopment* (1978) we find that the author recalls that he has contributed to the formation of the 'dependency' school and that his early work has been heavily criticized for failing to offer a genuinely dialectical analysis. Of the present work Frank says that it represents 'an attempt to transcend the 'dependence' approach, but without yet abandoning it or the focus on underdevelopment, and to proceed towards the integration of dependence and underdevelopment within the world process of accumulation'.[76] The book tackles a set of questions occasioned by criticisms of earlier formulations. The looked-for revised version of the approach is characterized in three ways: by reference to method, procedure and product.[77]

The method is to be revised so as to encompass the insights of Adam Smith and Marx to produce a holistic and dialectical analysis of the process of the development of underdevelopment.[78] The procedure to secure this reformulation will entail 'scientific examination of the historical evidence'[79] and hopefully will see the emergence of a better formulation of the circumstances of 'subordinate dependence'[80] of Latin America in the global system that generates the development of underdevelopment.

What is clear from Frank's argument here is that this refashioning represents a fairly slight change: the established position is to be strengthened rather than radically altered, and indeed in work published subsequent to this text the 'old' Frank returns. The refashioning offered involves a slight shift in terms of roles as Frank moves towards the stance of commentator rather than spokesman. It was this set of comments that occasioned the sceptical 'Two Franks Thesis' comment upon my views which I noted above. Again I would urge that the 'real' Frank is the political writer and the more academic commentator is secondary.

One final set of comments can be made on the critical debate surrounding Frank and it is to note that the author himself has contributed to the misunderstanding of his own work – at least by academics – in that he routinely adopts a distinctly orthodox tone. Thus he makes repeated appeals to 'history' as a source of facts to validate his position, whereas of course he is offering a particular reading. The mixture of simple appeals to history plus the analytic frame borrowed from Baran do encourage the view that he is operating with a fairly simple notion of 'general theory' – the social science analogue of the presumed results of natural scientific research. Relatedly there are discernable within his work what I have elsewhere labelled 'slides to the general'.[81]

All these accidents of presentation, flowing I would suggest from his efforts to persuade, allow his critics to read him as an academic theorist of rather dubious competence instead of a political writer with a clear, coherent and vigorous message of his own. For if we ask what is the crucial novelty of Frank's work the answer is plain: it is the overt political commitment of his writing. This engagement is utterly central to his entire effort: to review his material as if this were either not the case or reprehensible on methodological grounds is, it seems to me, a gross error. Not only does it prevent any attempt to accurately weigh Frank's contribution, because this must begin acknowledging it on its own terms, but it also confuses the subsequent debate on the value of the technical material he has presented.

More generally I think that we must reject this mishandling of Frank's work as it represents one more attempt at academic closure of debate – against the narrow critics of whatever political stripe. I would suggest that if we treat the *varieties* of modes of social theoretic engagement, then we'll understand not merely A.G. Frank better but also the nature of social theorizing (and scholarship) *per se*.

7 Analysing dependent capitalist development: the Asian NICs

1

In this paper I want to consider some of the recent discussions about states and development that have been occasioned by the apparently successful dependent capitalist development on the part of the NICs. I will argue both that the 'rise of the NICs' does not refute the simpler formulations of dependency theory and that the material necessary to formulate dependency/neo-marxism and produce a more theoretically rigorous marxist analysis of dependent capitalist development already exists.

It is possible to identify a series of *responses* (in contradistinction, for the moment, to issues) to the rise of the NICs by those working within the 'radical' tradition;[1] schematically: radical denial, radical affirmation, and *various* measured theoretical reformulations.

Those disposed to 'impossibilism'[2] might be expected to adopt strategies of denial: A.G. Frank's deployment of the notion of 'ultra-underdevelopment' might, perhaps, be cited as an example. In the context of Frank's concerns for both history and political activism, the present affluence of mineral rich 'LDCs', or MNC fuelled NICs, could indeed look transitory. But it must be said that the Frankian terminology is unappealing even if his basic position – political pamphleteer – still remains coherent.[3] Judged by more narrowly scholarly criteria, the Frankian project itself – let alone 'ultra-underdevelopment' – has received seemingly damaging criticism.[4] One can envision other strategies of denial: all have it in common that they argue that given patterns of change do not *really* count as development.[5] Once the decision has been arrived at to deny that what has happened counts as development then generating rationalizations is fairly straightforward. This decision may well not even be noticed: one strategy of denial is that of simply not noticing what has been happening. Higgot and Robinson suggest that it was the 'impossibilist' tendencies within marxian dependency theory that made simple recognition of dependent capitalist development apparently so tardy.[6]

Warren

Turning to the opposite pole of response to the rise of the NICs, we meet the 'inevitabilists', those who follow Warren in particular, who see not merely the rise of the NICs but industrial development within the Third World more widely as the decisive rebuttal of the dependency line in general and Frank in particular. This rebuttal is taken as the occasion for the re-presentation of fundamental marxist truths about the dynamism and expansionary nature of capitalism. Again, given a positive response to the rise of the NICs being a key element of this position, then a variety of detailed expressions can be expected. These can be labelled strategies of affirmation. The basic message of Warren – that theorists should attend to empirical data and not simply rehash Frankian notions – is, so far as it goes, reasonable. But Warren's own position is little more than a note of Marx's view of capitalism as dynamic plus selective economic data, and I cannot see here any case for the dismissal of the dependency/ neo-marxian line.

More interestingly, so far as I am concerned, we can identify more measured responses: attempts to 'learn the lessons' offered by recent NIC economic success. This interpretive strategy can help to reformulate a marxist view of dependent capitalist development. However, here I will first consider the essays by Bienefeld[7] which both acknowledge change and analyse it in a fashion that is *simultaneously instructive and misleading*. Bienefeld's recent work is interesting in that there is, additionally to a procedure of re-formulation, an evident slide from *commentator*, offering a representation of what he terms dependency theory, to *spokesman* for a social economics policy scientific stance. Re-formulation of dependency/ neo-marxism is not the same thing as arguing for a new policy-relevant position. This apparent confusion of roles may have been occasioned, in part, by the habit of social scientists of 'arguing on behalf of the planners'.[8]

Contrasting with this discussion of Bienefeld's 'revisionist' revisions to dependency/neo-marxism, I will take note of some of the discussions of Southeast Asia which do go beyond the sterile impossibilism/inevitabilism debate whilst remaining within the broad marxian tradition.

Shifting now to the *issues* thrown up by all these debates, I will pick out what seem to me to be the major ones bearing the overall problem of reformulating marxian dependency theory.

The role of the state and the costs of success are the two key points that Bienefeld makes in his ambiguous reworking of what he calls the dependency position: I will begin by looking both at the substance of Bienefeld's 1981 essay and at the role-slide evidenced in his related essays. Here, in brief, I offer a rejection of what one writer has recently termed 'Listianism'.[9]

Much of the present debate about the fate of a 'properly marxian analysis' of development has been occasioned by the economic success of the NICs. I want to look at the Asian NICs so as to underline: (a) the very particular circumstances of their success; (b) the crucial role of the state in these successes; and (c) the ambiguous character of their resultant development.

When we look at this issue of 'states and development' we need firstly to acknowledge that dependency/neo-marxian work must be refashioned to deal with the dependent capitalist development evidenced by the NICs. This is, indeed, an almost banal point: in my view social theorizing is about making sense, in various ways, of given situations. Consequently the history – and future – of social theorizing is the application of sets of concepts to particular circumstances. The NICs represent a particular occasion of marxian analysis – and maybe not all that important either – rather than a chance to stage the high drama of the clash of position taken as definite, or potentially so. Marxists more than most should appreciate the shifting, fluid, discursive character of social scientific enquiry: ours is a reiterative and not a cumulative enterprise.

More particularly, accommodating the NIC experience entails that we understand the *specifics* of the NIC phenomena; their colonial and post-colonial histories; the business of the shaping role of the state; and, finally, the specific costs and likely future sources of change within these societies.

2

I want to begin by taking note of some of the recent arguments amongst students of development as to whether or not there could actually be 'dependent capitalist development'; and, if there could, then where this fact leaves dependency theory/neo-marxism. I'll look at three ways of running the argument.

2.1

One way in which this difficult area has been approached is in very general terms: social theorists have written and spoken of moderniz-ation versus dependency theory. In the literature this is often presented as a simple debate between clearly delineated positions where 'truth' was in principle unambiguous. Thus it was claimed that dependency theory was unrestrictedly *better* than modernization theory. Contrariwise, modernization theorists usually dismissed dependency as vague, sloganistic and impractical. Some argued, more subtly, that when dependency theory was intelligible then it was not really new.[10] Now whilst I would tend to be sympathetic to the substance of the former claims I think that the real story of the relationship of 'modernization theory' to 'dependency theory' is much more complicated and much less clear cut.

Firstly both positions are in fact internally complex and by speaking generally this complexity is missed. Thus Furtado, and Cardoso, for example, tend to be lumped together as 'dependency theorists' just as Rostow, Huntington and Eisenstadt, for example, would be lumped together as 'modernization theorists'. Simplifications of this sort may well assist immediate debate but it cannot help clarity of thought: I think this habit of 'picking out the key ideas' and thereafter speaking generally is unhelpful because social scientific debate often just is ragged, or intellectually untidy. So the exchanges between these two positions – dependency and modernization – were a complex dialogue between internally complex and shifting positions and not merely the attempts by one clear stance to replace another, equally clear, position.

Secondly, and more importantly for my purposes, to the extent that it is sensible to speak of 'modernization theory' and 'dependency theory', then what we are confronted with are different delimited-formal ideologies[11] – both are attempts to make practical and political sense of the world and, evidently, they were constructed at different times, in different contexts and with differing intellectual resources and practical objectives. Any simple comparison is going to be rather besides the point.[12]

If this view is accepted, and I've argued for it elsewhere,[13] then we have to acknowledge that 'dependency' and 'modernization' are better viewed as *separate* areas of intellectual, practical and political endeavour. Consequently each must be judged, *academically*, first in their own terms; that is, how they conceived their work, what their intentions were for it, and how these expectations actually worked out in practice; and thereafter, in terms of the classical traditions of scholarly social science where this will centre on the skill of argument deployed so as to uncover the 'truth' (and this will involve reviewing proffered arguments so as to discover whether or not their target was clearly seen, effectively engaged, and finally whether or not it was actually worth aiming at).

I can perhaps elucidate this point a little further by distinguishing between 'first order' and 'second order' discourse. Thus debates between active proponents of modernization and dependency will be 'first order'. Here the exchange between them will typically be cast in terms of which theory is better than the other at solving the problems which the various proponents insist need to be solved. This debate could be – and often has been – cast in *narrowly technical terms* or, rather more subtly, in terms which stress *reflexivity* as a necessary condition of effective policy science.[14]

Moving on to the idea of 'second order discourse', the realm of scholarly social scientific commentary, typically we could expect to find a range of concerns: the elucidation of patterns of arguments so as to display the conception of proper enquiry adopted and the intentions of enquiry affirmed; the relating of these arguments to their cultural and intellectual milieu; the identification of institutional and other vehicles of expression; and the judging both form and content against those exemplified in the classical tradition of social science.

This distinction seems to me to be fairly straightforward and to flow from my earlier characterization of social science. In our scholarly work, itself context-dependent, we confront a *series* of exercises in making sense and we need to carefully characterize them and relate them to established traditions within classical social science. However, it seems clear that the variety of 'modes of social theoretic engagement' is often overlooked. I do not want to pursue this theoretical point here, but I do want to suggest that there needs to be *clarity in respect of roles adopted*, both by proponents and commentators, in discussions of the impact on dependency/neo-marxism of the fact of dependent capitalist development (what we say depends, in part on whose behalf we argue). At the very least we can then be clear just what is, or is not, at issue.

It must be clear now that I take the view that much of the talk of 'dependency versus modernization' (and the implications for that debate of the record of the NICs) is hopelessly misconceived. My substantive comments are these.

(a) The defeat of dependency theory by the rise of the NICs and the simultaneous resurrection of a version of modernization is not an issue. The claim is simply nonsensical on the *a priori* grounds sketched out above. Again, if the claim is entertained, then it can be shown to be false on detailed grounds – these I'll examine below first with Bienefeld and then in section 3.

(b) The discovery of a 'new improved' dependency theory – a narrowly technical policy scientific version – is not the lesson of the rise of the NICs. A narrowly technical version of dependency always was available within the Latin American dependency line and this scheme always was different from Frankian neo-marxism: they are different modes of engagement.

(c) The discovery of (another) *really* promising approach is not in prospect either. Those who wish to assimilate a reworked dependency theory to the older tradition of 'dissenting economics', which seems to be Bienefeld's position, could attend to that tradition directly.

(d) What is happening in some areas of enquiry is that a marxist discussion of dependent capitalist development is being undertaken. This is the process I call the reformulation of dependency.

2.2

Certain patterns of argument within the marxist camp have been characterized as a debate between 'impossibilitists' and 'inevitabilitists'; and it has been rightly said that this is an unhelpful framework for considering dependent capitalist development. I think it might be useful to speculate as to how debate ever came to be pursued in such terms. I am not interested in politics here, rather I want to suggest that a particular intellectual confusion was present and that this contributed – but was not solely responsible for – the sterile impossibilist/inevitabilist dichotomy. This confusion can be elucidated, in a very preliminary fashion, around the issue of 'general theory'; its character and role within social science, and the possible misunderstandings of that character and role.

Elsewhere[15] I have argued that the common-sense notion of natural science continues to sow confusion within social scientific work and I want to add to those remarks here. The 'received model' of natural scientific explanation has been analysed by Giddens[16] as a particular set of presumptions about natural science and their extension into the realm of the social: it is an essentially positivistic model of natural science. The deployment of this model runs with the grain of post-Second World War social scientific 'naturalism' and with the wider cultural grain of Anglo-Saxon celebrations of natural science as descriptive of the facts of nature. In this tradition – unselfconscious and self-conscious – general theory is taken to be both *complex summary description* and *the obvious goal* of enquiry.

I think that it is fairly clear that pressure to produce 'general theory' is present within the orthodox empiricist camp of social science, but I also think that it operated within the marxian camp – notwithstanding the proponents' affirmation of 'historical materialist dialectics'. Thus 'general theory' is taken to be the product of a developed dialectical science of the social: a sort of exhaustive and finally correct statement about some set of circumstances or other. Theorists sometimes actually pursue this goal, speaking of 'programmatic statements' of enquires needing much further work, and sometimes they rest content with pro forma statements, speaking of 'adumbrations of an analysis', and the like.

However, as I have argued above, in social science there are only successive instances of the deployment of sets of concepts or, as the prime case, the production of delimited-formal ideologies. There is no 'general theory' to be prepared. Marx's *Capital* I thus take to be a time- and place-bound analysis resting on a particular set of concepts. *Capital* made use of the language of political economy to offer an elucidation of the dynamics of capitalism, or putting it another way, it produced a delimited-formal ideology. Marx's *other* writings served *a range of other tasks*: political pamphleteering, academic critique and journalism, and so on.

Any sense we can attach to the idea of 'general theory' seems to be either (a) the illustrative deployment of core concepts, thus (in)famously Marx's 'stage theory' of economic formations presented in *Grundrisse*[17] or (b) the preliminary cashing of the moral stance necessarily embedded in the theorists' work – thus the 'general scheme' (history and judgments) present in the *Manifesto*.

I think this wrong idea of 'general theory' has been present in some subsequent marxian work. It is discernible in the work of Frank and Warren: thus, in part, we can grasp the reason for the vehemence of the exchanges between the proponents of the two positions – what seems to be at stake, but isn't, is the prospect of a definitively correct analysis.

In Frank's case the polemical simplicities of an exercise in political pamphleteering – to the effect that disengagement is a precondition of the replacement of the development of underdevelopment with the development of development – are offered as simple empirically demonstrable truths about the real world. Frank allows others to (mis)read him as offering a 'general theory' (and his empiricist syntax – arguing from the facts of history does make things worse[18]) instead of a highly particular piece of social theorizing.

In Warren's case we find a variant of this situation: he points to the raw data of economic growth in the Third World and to Marx's view of capitalism as dynamic in order to argue that Frank *et al.* were wrong and that development is inevitable. That Warren was right to call attention to dependent capitalist development must now be granted, but his conclusion that Frankian-style dependency is thus overthrown represents merely a confusion as to, first, how social theoretical argument variously works and, second, how dependency/ neo-marxism must be refashioned to work in the particular situations of the NICs. A general theory of the inevitability of dependent capitalism is no more helpful than the (apparent) general theory of its impossibility. Hamilton[19] is surely right that we should avoid this sterile debate and I further think that we should beware the temptation to pursue 'general theories'.

2.3

The final way of considering the 'implications of the NICs' I will treat in the company of Bienefeld. Essentially his approach is regressive: a shift away from the holistic and explicitly value-engaged style of political economy (for example Cardoso) towards a narrower 'expert' role centered on what seems to be a scheme of dissenting economics.[20] However, he does usefully call attention to two issues around which dependency/neo-marxist theory can be reformulated and these are the role of the state and the social-cultural costs of the economic development thus far effected.

In an IDS collection dealing with 'dependency', Bienefeld[21] argues that whilst many of the original claims made are untenable, more especially the 'impossibilist' aspects, nonetheless the questions posed in respect of how 'late arrivals' can integrate into the world economy were crucial. Bienefeld remarks that, whilst advocating state intervention to aid the late arrivals' integration into the world economy, the dependency theorists were led to stress the asymmetrical power relationship of peripheries and centres: and there was a drift into 'impossibilism'. However, Bienefeld wants to off-load all this and re-start debate. Evidently Bienefeld cannnot recognize the role of the political pamphleteers, for he sees them as having merely confused and obscured analytical questions. The unfortunate effect, he thinks, has been that the rise of the NICs has been used to dismiss both pamphleteers *and the good questions*.

Palma is reviewed and Bienefeld speaks of a distinction between 'the possibility of capitalist development, as against the particularity of capitalist development under specific conditions'.[22] Bienefeld wants the latter, 'practical-specific' orientation: so where then is the problem? It seems to me that it lies in the way Bienefeld slides between a practical political understanding and better policy science. Thus we find Bienefeld both advocating the study of specifics and dismissing Palma's support of Cardosa's analysis of specifics via political economic analysis. This use of political economy to analyse concrete instances of dependency is called a 'methodological abdication'. Bienefeld goes on to comment: 'Any advance must begin from the point we have reached to date, and this point includes the capacity to establish some generalizations and some hypotheses, however much these may be in need of refinement and development.'[23] So Frankian enquiry is dismissed, Cardoso-style political economy is a 'methodological abdication' and in place we have a (not obviously spelt out) methodology that looks distinctly 'cumulative'.

This method is to be used in pursuit of the challenge to dependency theory made by the NICs to 'refine its approach'.[24] This refinement is set in the context of the rise of the NICs having strengthened two key propositions: the importance of the international context and national policy (aimed at fostering a more dynamic integration of local into global market). Bienefeld's refinements entail, essentially, his acceptance of a de-politicized dependency theory where dependence centres on the exchange of strong/weak.[25] With these revisions Bienefeld can argue that 'reality' and 'dependency theory' do, after all, 'fit'. He then goes on to add that dependency theory (his version) may fit even more closely with the orthodox stress on the benefits of integration than had been thought. The success of the NICs, he points out, has come from not merely state policy but also from changes in the international division – thus, he notes, integration has indeed fostered economic growth.

However, the character of that economic growth is quietly passed by in this discussion. Bienefeld seems reluctant to judge, and, where a political economic approach would have obliged him to adopt an explicit evaluative position, his depoliticized dependency is cast in partial, 'expert' terms. Dependency theory is narrowed down so as to become merely a technical way of conceptualizing the exchange between established powerful economies and recently emerged weak economies so as to aid policy-making in the latter.

In a subsequent and related essay Bienefeld presents his argument in a clearer fashion – both in respect of his useful reworking of dependency and his unsatisfactory revision of its holistic and engaged approach. Bienefeld begins by offering an argument to the effect that early dependency theorists – and he often seems to mean Frank and at other times Furtado – were wrong to talk about both *disengagement* and *socialism* in their analyses of the position of peripheral economies within the world economic system. Bienefeld argues instead for *specific enquiry* organised thus:

> [we] should ask the question whether or not a greater degree of social control can be imposed on the development process through the mechanism of the state, and whether this control can be (or is being) exercised in the interests (short or long-term) of the great majority of the members of that society.[26]

Then the position of the NICs is reviewed and they are diagnosed as the somewhat fortunate benefactors of competition between capital in the First World. The NICs are taken to *confirm* the dependency theorists' stress on the *nationalist state*: the NICs owe their success not simply to the passive receipt of world market forces but to state-ordered responses to opportunities in the international situation. Bienefeld adds that the inegalitarian, non-democratic forms of the NICs *reinforces* the requirement for a more humane model of development, as the peripheral capitalism on offer in the NICs remains liable to the ethical criticisms lodged against peripheral capitalism by the dependency theorists.

Again, in tone Bienefeld's analysis seems to be not only resolutely non-marxist but is clearly committed to 'better policy science'. I'll come back to this point below. For the moment I'll take note of a thoroughly ambiguous follow-up to Bienefeld offered by Lamb.[27] Lamb seems to grant, like Bienefeld, that world political economic circumstances have ushered in the NICs. Then Lamb goes on to berate both dependency and marxist theorists – unspecified – for not tackling the *politics of dependent accumulation*. This is most peculiar. His remarks on the politics of 'fast-track' developing nations mention: the role of overseas linkages; the breaking of the power of organized labour; and the establishment of authoritarian states with the local bourgeoisies well and truly 'bought off'. But can one not suggest that all this has been said and often, and by, amongst others, Frank?

The apparent slide from political economy to a narrower focus on the policy scientific elucidation of the possibilities for state action appears most clearly in the text edited by Bienefeld and Godfrey. The text is avowedly 'theoretically eclectic'[28] and the editors focus on the contexts for Third World policy planners – how action is constrained by their circumstances as 'late developer'. This is, it seems to me, fairly clearly a type of dissenting economics. The idea of 'dependency' originally conceived as a way of looking at the Third World within the world capitalist system, is now merely an abstract principle – or a good set of questions – around which Bienefeld looks at choices facing actors (states) in the world system. The material is thoroughly interesting, but the focus on policy analysis seems to me to be a regression analytically.

As a final note on this way of debating the 'implications of the rise of the NICs', I will note a recent suggestion – which cites Bienefeld and other IDS workers – to the effect that a new position in respect of development is in process of emergence: the Listian development dialectic. Identified in a recent article by Foster-Carter,[29] List is characterized as having been the first to spot the matter of the problems of national policy-making for late-comers to industrialization. Foster-Carter apparently embraces this pragmatic policy-oriented approach, noting that it does 'synthesize so much';[30] and he goes on to say: 'Thus armed, development studies can come of age ... its prehistory can end and its real history commence.'[31] For the reasons cited above, I do not find this a helpful formulation.

The matter of how NIC phenomena can be accommodated within a reformulated marxism will be one of the subjects of the next section of this essay when I look at the case of the Asian NICs. For the moment, in summary, I will say that none of the three strategies of responses thus far examined are satisfactory: all are both overgeneral and confused in respect of the precise nature of their engagement with the issue.

3

I want to consider here some recent discussions of dependent capitalist development in Southeast and East Asia – the Asian NICs. I want to take note of the very particular circumstances of the economic success of these countries and of the roles played by the various state machines in their respective success stories. I will also note the ambiguous nature of development in the NICs in terms of social, political and cultural changes and costs. These will be the principal substantive concerns here. However, additionally, all this material does offer a sketch of how one can reformulate the dependence/neo-marxian line so as to both (a) interpret the recent histories of the NICs; and (b) clearly lodge analysis within the broad marxian tradition. This sketch follows on from my discussions with Bienefeld above on how *not* to effect such a revision.

Capitalist Southeast and East Asia tends to appear under two headings: the Asian NICs and ASEAN and this has the effect of subtly misdirecting enquiry in that the *labels* invite, respectively, a focus on economic performance and political positions adopted. In both cases we are drawn away from enquiry cast in terms of social, economic, political and cultural change. However this misdirection has been overshadowed recently by the crude 'impossibilist/ inevitabilist' debate. This is evidenced in a very recent review of ASEAN which I will note before turning to consider the important essay by Hamilton.

Limqueco looks at 'the current process of capitalist industrializ- ation [in ASEAN] . . . from the perspective that the development of productive forces and class struggle are the prime movers of society.'[32] This stance is explicitly anti-dependency and anti-neo- marxist (apparently the author, like so many, simply and wrongly assimilates these two). And whilst it is arguably reasonable of Limqueco to simplify his message in order to present the outline of an analysis of dependent capitalist development, the resultant mix of marxist rhetoric and agency data is unappealing.

Nonetheless, Limqueco does usefully point out that ASEAN has played 'host to a great flood of Japanese and American capital'.[33] This has had both a massive impact upon economic development and very particular impact on social and cultural costs. The ambiguity of the post-Second World War patterns of development in ASEAN Limqueco attempts to spell out via the notion of 'structural contradictions'. The first is identified as the problem of labour absorption as the agricultural workforce has shrunk: the pace of change has been rapid and many have been absorbed into 'informal sectors', service and bureaucracies. Limqueco comments: 'The generation of an unemployed and under-employed workforce is a key structural contradiction, which leads to severe social problems.'[34] A second area of hidden problems attaches to the drive to export manufactures: these industries have been import-dependent as ASEAN's contribution has been restricted to the provision of cheap docile labour: there is a drift to indebtedness.[35] The third 'structural contradiction' is that of wages and prices. Limqueco sees the ASEAN regimes as sharply inegalitarian, with the situation of the poor weakening. He comments: 'The consequences in human suffering as a result of the deterioration in income are politically and socially explosive.'[36] Again one can grant that this is generally true of the region, but the claim must be disaggregated to carry real conviction – a point I'll pursue below when looking at the Asian NICs. However, the general approach of Limqueco seems, if crude, appropriate: the very peculiar context of his debate is revealed when he remarks that his data establish the *irrelevance* of dependency and neo-marxian analyses of ASEAN. Better, it seems to me, to speak of re-formulating; and a more thorough attempt at this is made by Hamilton.

Hamilton[37] begins by noting that the NICs have been esteemed by the orthodox as vindicating their optimism and have posed an awkward question to dependency/neo-marxism. The orthodox Hamilton rightly sets aside, remarking that their insistence on focusing on economic indicators and ignoring the social realities of inequality and the political realities of repression is unsatisfactory and he goes on to look at discussions *within* the marxian camp. At the outset he notes that 'The broad consensus of radical economic analysis was that capital in the imperialist centres was alone capable of self-expansion and that any sporadic industrial growth in the periphery occurred solely at the behest of the transnational corporations.'[38] Hamilton cites Warren as attacking this view and rehearses his argument that 'the imperialist powers favoured Third World industrialization, that in any case their ability to restrict the latter has been and is being markedly eroded, and that imperialism will disappear.'[39] This is referred to by Hamilton as the 'impossibilist-inevitabilist problematic'[40] and he declares that he wishes to escape its confines.

The strategy Hamilton adopts, to anticipate, is to deploy what seems to me to be an *economic metaphor* whereby the NICs are taken to

have been 'annexing space in the world economy . . . at the expense
of other capitals . . . [whereas others] have industrialized largely on
the basis of *new* spaces'.[41] This metaphor is then pursued in terms of
linkages to the world economy and internal relationships of class. His
general view of the Asian NICs is that their industrialization was
fortuitous, has exhausted its potential (it cannot annexe any more
space), and is unstable due to the mix of rising expectations and
political repression (where the former is a result of success and the
latter a condition of its continuation).

The analysis begins with a discussion of the world context of the
NICs which, it is reported, have managed to 'occupy a larger and
more diversified space in the world economy by specializing in the
production and export of light industrial goods'.[42] The multi-
nationals have played a role but, with the exception of Singapore,
'*local capital has been responsible*': it has opened up an economic space
which rests on goods having no very great capital or technological
input and whose manufacturing can utilize cheap labour, that is, light
consumer goods. Hamilton then considers the sets of class circumstances that fostered, and now sustain, this particular role.

The appropriate starting point is the colonial period. Korea was
occupied by Japan and played the role of agricultural supplier:
patterns of agricultural life were much disturbed by the colonial
power.

> The traditional Korean landed aristocracy was seriously weakened
> by colonial occupation and annexation of land, but it was not
> destroyed. It continued to exist effectively in alliance with the
> colonizers and was to suffer the opprobrium of this collaboration
> in the future. The twin exactions of pre-colonial feudalism and
> Japanese colonialism caused widespread agricultural
> pauperization.[43]

In Taiwan a similar agricultural role was pursued albeit with less
reworking of patterns of life. In neither territory was there any
appreciable industrialization. 'During the period of intense colonial
rule there was no potential, indigenous leadership stratum to speak
of, except perhaps for scattered cabals of intimidated nationalists. No
strong merchant class could develop, nor was indigenous industry
allowed to flower.'[44]

From this context the shape of the post-war political, social and
economic world emerged. The formation of the new nation-states in
Asia, as elsewhere, was a period of confusion. American concern for
resisting communism was of importance. In Korea the obvious
nationalists were also largely communist: with the defeat of Japan a
series of local political initiatives were taken – factories seized from

the colonialists, local government organizations formed. The Americans arrived a few months later 'and there began the process of crushing all popular political activity'.[45] Syngman Rhee became their stooge figure whose subsequent rule to 1960 was that of a US puppet whose power rested on a police force and bureaucracy both tainted by collaboration. South Korea, like Taiwan, received massive military and economic aid from the Americans. Hamilton comments:

> In both countries, aid constituted the largest proportions of national budgets for several years . . . foreign direct investment was extremely low in both countries until the late 1960s. The effect of US intervention was not only to sustain conservative, anti-communist regimes but also to foster the development of nascent bourgeoisies whose members profited from close ties with [the] US.[46]

Politically in Taiwan the Kuomintang (KMT) came to power with the aid of the USA, who as above, backed them with aid in their fight against communism. Hamilton makes it clear that the KMT were no puppets, but adds that the US had massive influence through aid for reconstruction and development.

In respect of Hong Kong and Singapore the story is simpler: both were founded as trading ports and both European and Asian capital serviced that trading role. Of Hong Kong and Singapore Hamilton has little to say: local nationalism never appeared in Hong Kong and Lee's regime, once established was wholly acceptable to international capital.

The business of industrialization is then considered. It is noted that: 'the role of indigenous capital accumulation varied from relative insignificance in Singapore to the main bearer in Hong Kong, Taiwan and Korea'.[47] Close study reveals, claims Hamilton, that: 'the primitive accumulation of capital is as much a political process as an economic one.'[48] The role of the state is examined and for each of the four it is found to be extensive, especially in enforcing a shift from merchant to industrial capitalism via land reforms, urbanization-industrialization programmes and the use of US aid to build appropriate infrastructure. This drive to industrialize coincided with the post-war economic boom: thus all four were able to carve out new 'economic spaces' for themselves.

The nature of the local capital formed and the industries developed are discussed in some detail by Hamilton. Summarizing his points, we have the claim that local industrial capital was both:(a) firmly backed by local states themselves firmly lodged within, linked to, metropolitan capital – especially the USA; and (b) that local industrial capital was 'inexperienced' and cautious, thus making use of relatively 'low tech' developments having a high labour input; (c) larger scale and 'higher tech' enterprises required more extensive link-ups with overseas capital.

Recent changes in the world economy have, argues Hamilton, posed problems for these four economies. Both the circumstances and nature of their success were very particular. This appraisal forms the basis of Hamilton's view that the path of growth of capitalist industrialization has, at the present, come to a halt. Hamilton notes that their

> entry into the international division of labour has been largely on terms laid down by the dominant capitalist powers, and in consequence the Four have been left with economies which are heavily biased towards a few consumer goods industries, except Singapore where foreign capital has been responsible for a broader, but no more independent industrial base.[49]

Recent attempts to diversify have not broken the mould whereby Asian NIC capital links to world capital via the use of cheap labour. Hamilton judges this – as I noted above – a limited economic space and a vulnerable one. By way of a comment on Hamilton's essay I'll make the following points.

(a) The use of the metaphor of 'annexing economic space' is both pleasing in that it lets us grasp the totality of the various nation-states' recent histories and, arguably, misleading. This is because evidently it is a spatial metaphor. There are two effects here: firstly, success is understood as more/less space, that is, quantitatively; and, secondly, the whole matter is curiously static, thus the ideal implied is of an autonomous space rather than a particular set of relationships, internal and external, which processually – as responding to and initiating movements – implied political and ethical goals on the part of the society. Thus, for example, Chan Heng Chee and Hans Dieter Evers[50] have characterized Singapore as 'modernization theory put into practice': again the Singaporean elite would speak, not wholly implausibly, of 'democratic socialism'. Elsewhere[51] I have argued that 'development' is to be understood as an ethico-political notion. The ideal of development pursued by any ruling group can, in principle, be discovered from looking at both claims and practice. In any case a simple quantity approach to development is not very subtle.

(b) The 'initial conditions' of colonialism are handled in a not wholly satisfactory fashion: Singapore and Hong Kong really are very different from South Korea and Taiwan in terms of their positions within the world economy. Neither began their 'annexing of space' from a situation of, so to say, having none at all. Both territories have always been integral parts of the world capitalist economy. There does seem to be an oversimplification at this point of Hamilton's analysis. Hong Kong and Singapore do not simply contribute cheap labour to the world system; they also contribute as mercantile centres – both are key trading and financial centres.

(c) Whilst it is clearly shown that there has been significant capitalist industrialization in the Asian NICs, what is understated is the social, political and cultural cost of this development pattern. Hamilton does little more than note that three of the four are authoritarian. Related to this apparent neglect is an absence of any real discussion of internal political processes: a 'depoliticization' effected by repression seems to be granted, with a few 'tensions' acknowledged. Surely there is more to be said on this matter.

(d) Hamilton's treatment of 'external linkages' seems to be very schematic, thus the role of the US early on is noted in detail, but the subsequent rise of Japanese economic power is only mentioned in passing. And the historically imminent retrieval of Hong Kong by the People's Republic of China does not seem to be mentioned at all.

However, setting these criticisms aside, what Hamilton does offer is an overview of dependent capitalist development that is thoroughly plausible. And he rightly calls attention to the role of the state. It is to the wider context of state action that I now turn.

In an early essay concerned to look at the metropolitan capitalist response to defeat in Vietnam and oil-price-rise-led recession, Halliday,[52] often borrowing a Frankian syntax, distinguishes between an 'inner arc' and an 'outer arc' of states all centered on Japan: the former being the four NICs and the latter ASEAN. Japan is presented here as the regional representative of global capitalism. This is a useful corrective to Hamilton, for it calls attention to both the real historical fact of conflict in Asia and the central importance for understanding Asian dependent capitalist development of the role of Japan.

Halliday begins a subsequent discussion of the pivotal role of Japan by observing that 'Since 1945 East Asia has been the centre of the world struggle between capitalism and socialism....East Asia has also witnessed some of post-war capitalism's most impressive achievements.'[53] Halliday analyses the present situation focusing on the role of Japan which he sees as crucial. Taking note[54] of the way Asia came in the post-war period to assume its present form – sharply divided between capitalist and socialist countries – the author observes that

> Behind these barriers a remarkable capitalist transformation has occurred, creating a series of new social, political and economic structures. . . .The Taiwan and South Korean regimes achieved what the anti-communist governments in Indochina found

impossible: they established a real social base through land reform, industrialization, greatly increased export earnings, and correspondingly more efficient systems of political repression.[55]

Hong Kong and Singapore are noted as trading and finance centres.

Moving on to consider Japan and this 'inner arc' Halliday notes: 'Just as Japan's restoration and re-insertion into the world economy were precipitated by the fight against socialism, so South Korea and Taiwan were reshaped not only to 'contain' the Korean and Chinese revolutions, but also as Japan's periphery.'[56] Halliday talks of Japan benefiting from the 'hyper-militarization'[57] of this periphery by being relieved of defence-spending burdens and economically through favourable trade balances. The structural relationship of Japanese capital to the inner arc is also tackled. Where Hamilton stressed that capital in Hong Kong, Taiwan and South Korea was indigenous, Halliday presents a rather different view. Whilst *direct* Japanese investment has been low there has been very extensive *credit* involvement, and all in all, thinks Halliday,

> its capitalist periphery has been of inestimable importance to post war Japan, not only because of the size of the markets involved, but also because of the structural integration with the metropolis, the long term trade imbalance, and the dependence of many smaller Japanese firms (aggregated by the shosha) upon the periphery for maintaining profit margins.[58]

Halliday continues and says that in some very real ways both Taiwan and South Korea can be regarded as 'extensions of the Japanese domestic market.'[59] Halliday goes on to draw the conclusion that Japan depends upon the existence of these peripheral capitalisms and would be 'sorely challenged'[60] if other East Asian states followed the DPRK or Vietnam. However, the real threats to Pacific rim stability, in Halliday's view, flow from the fundamental instability of the 'East Asian pattern of capital accumulation through mass repression and super-exploitation'.[61]

Both Hamilton with his 'economic spaces' and Halliday with his 'inner' and 'outer arcs' are using spatial metaphors as an aid to disentangling complex patterns of economic and political change. The problems with the former I've noted; and with Halliday the relevant broader political and historical material tends to be presented in a fashion that falls into an overly simple geo-political scheme. However, we do now have a sketch of the basic elements of a plausible analysis of dependent capitalist development in the case of the Asian NICs. These are, to recap:

1 An historicist and holistic approach – thus the way in which presently extant nation-states, with their characteristic economies and

polities, came into being must be the starting point of analysis.

2 This process of 'genesis' can then be unpacked – patterns of economic growth are detailed and the contributions to this pattern of local capital, foreign aid, foreign capital, and local state reform-for-industrialization are all detailed.

3 To these patterns of economic growth with their precise exchanges of domestic and international capitalism are related matters political – internal reform and repression and the way these strategies were linked to the 'outside', sometimes with reform encouraged (as in the case of Taiwan) and sometimes with reaction defended (as with South Korea), and often with a general indifference to internal politics so long as anti-communism flourished.

4 Appropriately the enabling role of the *states* are identified – there has been economic growth via political action; domestic reform, repression and external accomodation to the USA and opportunism in the global market place.

5 Likely future sources of change are considered – exogenous possibilities such as major realignments of blocs, the recovery of Hong Kong, and the possible recovery of Taiwan, by the People's Republic of China, unification of North and South Korea and so on are all tackled, similarly pressure for endogenous change.

Much more needs to be said to 'fill out' this marxist analysis of the dependent capitalist development of the Asian NICs but, it seems to me, we can safely grant that such an analysis can be achieved: thus may dependency/neo-marxism be successfully and instructively reformulated.

4

The brief examination of the patterns of development of the Asian NICs presented above with reference to the work of Hamilton, Halliday (and Limqueco) is, it seems to me, enough both to refute the pessimistic and analytically regressive conclusions that Bienefeld draws from the episode and to offer a sketch of a plausible marxian analysis of the dependent capitalist development of these NICs. The former point has been more satisfactorily achieved than the latter – a mere sketch only – and I will therefore add a couple of points on this matter.

4.1

The exchanges between Hamilton and Halliday usefully establish (or remind us) that an appreciation of the history and contemporary context – economic, social and political – is a prerequisite to any genuine understanding of their patterns of development. Against the narrowing vision of Bienefeld, with his stress on the 'possibilities of state action', we have a review of the genesis and character of the post-Second World War development pattern of the Asian NICs that is considerably richer in conception.

The disintegration of wartime Japanese power and the parallel replacement of European colonial interest by US commercial and ideological (anti-communist) interest has the effect of fostering a specific pattern of development in these Asian NICs. In the context of subordinate economic and political roles within the capitalist system the NICs carved out their own particular 'economic space', as Hamilton puts it. A measure of partial, fortuitous and socially restricted, but nonetheless genuine, dependent capitalist development has been achieved. The two authors I've cited to establish this point offer differing emphases in their analyses: Hamilton tends to focus on economic patterns of change, whilst Halliday looks to their broader role in Japan's 'inner arc'.

The major role of the Japanese is urged by Halliday: they are *the Asian capitalist power* and their influence is extensive. Hamilton's stress on the indigenous capital nature of South Korean and Taiwanese industrialization is counterbalanced, as Halliday points out by the importance of Japanese economic and political power. Hamilton's argument is also revised in that where he discusses the Asian NICs and the world economy generally, Halliday speaks clearly of the world economy's 'regional representative', Japan. Interestingly, Hamilton's view is also implicitly challenged for the future: these capitalist industrializers may *not* have reached a ceiling because they are to a significant extent locked into the Japanese 'space' in the world economy and that evidently has not reached its ceiling. One commentator, seemingly lending support to Hamilton, has suggested that at the present time the four NICs do seem to be in what for them are unusual difficulties. Bowring[62] argues that the NICs have structural problems and he suggests that 'underlying causes of NIC export success may have waned'.[63] He cites: (i) the situation of maximum penetration by the NICs of the US market – no more space can be carved out, as Hamilton might put it; (ii) recent trading profits derived from oil-exporting countries (either through oil processing or selling manufactures and services) are waning as the oil trade stagnates; (iii) the changing trade patterns between the Third World and Japan in particular may be squeezing out the Asian NICs as Japan and Third World deal direct; (iv) upgrading the technological bases of economies is not straightforward for a variety of technical and trading reasons; (v) loss of capital inputs from the USA is in sharp contrast to previous years. The future looks 'stable' rather than expansionary. Bowring sees the NICs as benefiting in line with overall Asian expansion: their ceiling drifts upward whilst their space remains stable.

4.2

The role of the state in these four countries is an issue that is stressed by both Bienefeld and Hamilton. The former offers what seems to me to be a narrowly technical reading of the circumstances/character of the dependent states of capitalist Asia. 'Dependency' for Bienefeld ceases to be a delimited-formal ideological term denoting the largely external shaping of the local economy and, instead, becomes merely a label for an additional set of problems facing policy planners in the LDCs. A crucial question that is begged is thus the *actual nature of the Third World state and its ruling elite*. It certainly cannot be assumed that the Asian NIC elites have the same interest in development as the 'ideal policy planner' upon whose behalf Bienefeld apparently argues.

It is also true that this business of the *nature of the state* in peripheral capitalisms has been extensively discussed in the marxian literature. I cannot here rehearse these debates, but suffice it to say that: (1) the scope for action genuinely independent of the dictates of the global capitalist system is usually taken to be fairly slight; and (2) the 'nationalist' credentials of many 'replacement elites' in the Third World are also doubted notwithstanding the familiar nationalist developmentalist rhetoric. Against Bienefeld it can be pointed out that the nature of the exchanges between local and global capitalist economic and political (base and superstructural) factors is a matter that has received much attention.[64]

4.3

Related to this business of characterizing the dependent capitalist state is the matter of the possibility of change. Two broad sources of change can in principle be identified: changes arising from shifts within the 'external' global capitalist economy and the world political system, and those flowing from 'internal' developments. I'll set the former aside, having mentioned some of them above, even though it was such broad changes that brought the NICs into being. Looking to endogenous change, it is possible to identify a series of enquiries that have been launched by 'radicals' over recent years.

Thus Feith[65] has argued that there might be elite group splintering around debates concerned with economic and political direction of nations. The consequences of such splintering could be that fractions of the elite will appeal to groups within the newly created middle classes. This would mean that a large grouping, brought into being by post-war economic success, but thus far not extensively involved in decision-making, would be drawn into the fundamental political processes, and in a situation of conflict. Feith is speculating as to possible occasions of movement towards First World models of political action.

Processes of 'liberalization' have been mooted[66]: here following the broad modernization line of thought there are suggestions that as regimes becomes both secure and have established 'track records' of success then there will be progressive removal of machineries of repression and control. The commentators we considered above did indeed point to the dilemmas faced by the ruling groups of the Asian NICs in respect of prosperity-generated demands for political and social relaxation when these economies have depended precisely upon repressive political systems. It must be said that at the present time there is little sign of any meaningful relaxation of established patterns of authoritarian rule in Singapore, Taiwan or South Korea. In this case, as in others, Hong Kong's anarchistic capitalism seems to be something of an exception.

Within the more obviously marxian tradition there has been much stress of late upon class analysis. In part this is a reaction to the simpler formulations of dependency theory which did slide in the direction of stressing exchange relationships to the exclusion of endogenous class forces. So there have been attempts made to reintroduce this aspect of analysis: one problem seems to have been that commentators have seen generally authoritarian societies and have found discussing class in any detail apparently rather difficult.[67]

4.4

The characterization of the polities of the Asian NICs has been a difficult area. The classical marxian focus on patterns of production and associated class and political expressions has rather foundered upon the predominant role of the state. To outside commentators the states of the Asian NICs have looked so brutally dedicated to acting as a committee for the bourgeoisie that analysis has baulked at producing further detail. However this is, as noted above, changing. Here we can note some of the strategies that have been adopted to try to grasp the peculiar characteristics of these states – all are variations on the theme of control.

Thus the term 'authoritarian' has been widely used – calling attention to the concentrations of power in these societies and to the manner in which such power has been exercised. Opposition groups have *routinely* been harassed or suppressed. Trade unions have been broken or so thoroughly coopted as to have lost all identity as separate institutions. Control of the press is widespread. These two aspects together serve to prevent the formation of oppositional groups – they can neither organize nor disseminate their ideas.

A related idea that has been used is that of 'corporatism'.[68] Here is a term with considerable resonances within the European tradition of thought. As a way of characterizing social forms – rather than ideologies or institutional arrangements – it calls attention to factors such as hierarchy, stability, discipline. In their classic Western European guise in the 1920s to 1940s these key ideas cited were also linked to ideas of racial supremity and destiny and expressed in militaristic fashion. One can easily discern the presence of the former trio in all the Asian NICs – sometimes it seems to be dignified with reference to Confucianism and 'Chinese tradition'. The latter traits are also visible, even if less obviously so. The way in which this term can be reworked to designate particular patterns of accommodation between governments, workers and employers is also interesting. These corporatist models of industrial harmony have been fostered and, routinely, the example of Japan is invoked. And in contrast to this usage the term has been moved in the systems characterizing direction in such a fashion as to invoke the European historical example directly; commentators have spoken of neo-fascism.[69]

All of these characterizations are trying to grasp the essentials of these societies in terms of the experiences – social, political, and cultural – of the masses who inhabit these nation-states. A modest attempt at this uses the notion of 'depoliticization'.[70] The power of the state and its various organs is so extensive that debate about the nature of society has largely dried up. Political and social debate is either not conducted in private amongst people known to each other or, in public, it is either not conducted at all or conducted in terms laid down by the governments.

If we consider the work of Hamilton and Halliday, plus all the other writers to whom I have alluded, then we can clearly see the outline of a marxist analysis of dependent capitalist development. The authors collectively treat the historical occasions of the formation of these countries and specify how external and internal socio-economic forces acted to mould the pattern that has existed to date. Patterns of internal conflict are considered and possible future sources of change identified.

In sum, what we need to note, picking up from Bienefeld's 'revision' above, are two points. Firstly, that the rise of the NICs does not render irrelevant or otiose the dependency/neo-marxian line. And, secondly, that the material required to construct a more rigorous marxist analysis of the dependent capitalist development of the Asian NICs *already exists*. I've sketched the outline of that analysis above. For those working within the broad 'radical tradition' there seems to be little warrant for a pessimistic and rather defeated retreat to dissenting economics of the sort advocated by Bienfeld.

8 Constructing nation-states in Southeast Asia

1 Introduction

In chapter 1 I took note of the very general historical conditions which attended, and shaped, the rise of interest in matters of development as they are presently understood. However, a concern for development can be traced back into pre-Second World War days: into the work of colonial administrators (Boeke and Furnivall, for example); into the realms of 'enlightened opinion' in the First World; and, of course, into the sphere of nationalist political movements within the subject nations themselves. To pursue this concern to any further length would have us returning to debates in the nineteenth and, even, eighteenth centuries when earlier 'nationalist developmental' ideologies were presented in the context of the earliest round of nation-state formation. But when we speak today of 'development' it is the Third World we have in mind – as did the theorists of the pre-Second World War period of extensive formal colonial holdings.

Much of the pre-war material is of considerable interest, but in addition to the problem of treating a vast amount of literature which, strictly, is not directly relevant to my concerns here[1] there is the important point that the post-war period is novel[2] in that issues of development were now to be discussed in the context of there being a growing band of new nation-states constructed, variously, from the old colonial empires of Western Europe (and, in one instance, the USA), and constructed over a relatively *short* time span.

So, 'development', in the post-Second World War world has been closely associated with the explicitly voiced hopes of the leaderships of the new nation-states of the world. These sets of ideals and claims I labelled, in chapter 1, the 'ideology of nationalist developmentalism', and I offered a few remarks on the character of the argument thereby presented. In these brief remarks I was interested in sketching how people came to be interested in 'development' and how ideas and circumstances came together so that by the end of the war the demands of 'nationalist developmentalism' could be firmly lodged in political debate. These demands turned out to be irresistible, and in this chapter I want to pursue the upshot: nation-making as a substantive problem. I will proceed in the following way.

I will look first at patterns of withdrawal from empire and sketch out the diverse 'styles' it has taken. In the earliest instances this involves the rebellions of Latin America and parts of North America against the rule of Western Europeans. In Western Europe in the early nineteenth century there is a period of nation-state formation: it's here that we find the familiarly invoked models of nation-states. All this material – the subject of much attention from historians and political scientists – I will present in a brief, and very much simplified form. Then I will go on to look at the post-Second World War period, taking note of the African case, but focusing on Southeast Asia.

This 'tour' of the history of the emergence of nation-states will open up two issues which I want to look at. Firstly, the business of the construction over time of the very idea of nation-statehood. Secondly, the history of the nationalist movements of Southeast Asia.

In this opening section, I want to look at the use of the idea of nationhood/statehood to order and give force to the resistance of indigenous peoples to the political, economic and social position of the colonizers. The idea of the nation was used, as Gellner argues,[3] to legitimate the pursuit of statehood. Once established, the formal power of the *state* was used assiduously to foster the idea of *nation*: it was a notion that could weld together otherwise disparate groupings of people. These remarks might seem fairly banal, but the point is this: the ideology of nationalism includes a basic claim to the naturalness of nation-statehood. As Tivey puts it,[4] one has a nationality just as one has a gender, and it is this taken-for-grantedness of nation-statehood which must be problematized so that we can appreciate the idea of nation-statehood as an 'ideology', to put it crudely, promulgated by particular groups within particular contexts and with particular audiences in view. In the 'developed west' the idea, or complex of ideas, is utterly taken-for-granted: nation-states simply exist. But in the 'developing world' nation-statehood is somewhat more problematic. Ruling elites routinely and carefully foster the idea of nation-statehood as being in process of consolidation (after decolonization) and as self-evidently desirable/inevitable. However, the reponses of minority ethnic and religious groupings to such claims have occasioned problems for more than a few elites. Interestingly, though, the claims of minorities are usually for the establishment of their 'own' state.

The substantive material to have been presented thus far, both theory and history, will lead us to the point of formation of new nation-states. Beyond this we will have to look at the business of nation- and state-making.

Reaching a politico-legal settlement with the departing colonial power was, so to say, the first job. In this phase the attention of all parties would be upon the achievement of independence. Thereafter, forging the new politico-legal entity into an effective nation-state, and for the moment I'll set aside what that might entail, is job number two. Here the character of the elite-promulgated nationalism has changed and the obvious key change is that the 'external enemy', the foreign power, has been expelled. This must therefore occasion a reshuffling of the various elements in the nationalist vision. If we ask how this 'reshuffling' has taken place, and with what result, then we confront a more ragged story. This is so because in the early phase, 'Nationalism I', all endeavours were aimed at a specific target – independence – whereas in the later phase, 'Nationalism II', the target of 'effective nation-statehood' is considerably more complex.

In looking at this second phase the 'theoretical issues' will involve the following: centrally, the pursuit of political, economic, social and cultural coherence, stability and progress. This opens up a series of more particular issues. In respect of 'coherence' we can look at the role of elites and ask: how have 'national elites' been constituted; from where do they draw their ideas; how do they present them to their populations, and how do they secure their acceptance? As regards the masses, we can look at: how they have been mobilized; what they have expected and how they have acted. The military and the bureaucracy are also elements to consider under the heading of 'coherence'. Moving on to the issue of 'stability', we can consider ethnicity and conflict, intra- and inter-state. Finally, with 'progress', the business of national development ideologies can be looked at. The 'historical' material to be considered here will involve looking at the post-Second World War histories of the new nation-states and asking just what has actually happened.

In sum, in this chapter I will look at the historical rise of the idea of nation-statehood and take note of the earliest examples of nation-states. Following this I will look at nationalism in pursuit of independence and then, finally, the concern of successful nationalisms with nation-building.

2   Patterns of achievement of nation-statehood

It will be useful here to offer a general sketch of the business of withdrawal from empire[5] for two reasons. Firstly, to draw attention to the scale of the changes involved. Withdrawal from empire involves, successively, large parts of North America, virtually the whole of South America; the Middle East; South Asia, Southeast Asia; North Africa; and, finally large areas of sub-Saharan Africa. As an episode of political change it was clearly very extensive indeed. Further than this, and in the same 'historical vein' we can also take note that it was also a recent episode in history: the rebellion of the United Kingdom's North American colonies began only in the late seventeenth century[6] and South America fought its wars of independence in the early years of the nineteenth century.

Secondly, I draw attention to the fact that withdrawal from empire was, from the start, cast in terms of nation, nationalism, and statehood. Nation-states are routine taken-for-granteds in present-day thinking but they are recent and novel human inventions. Orridge comments:

> The notion that there is or should be some intimate connection between broad cultural similarities and political organisation . . . would have seemed very strange, and would have been far from political reality, in most times and places before the last two centuries.[7]

The withdrawal was accomplished over roughly two hundred years. By the time the US celebrated its bicentennial in 1976 most of the surface of the planet was allocated to sovereign nation-states – not all, but most. And when Brunei recently 'attained independence' it became the world's 169th sovereign state.[8] The business of achieving the status of nation-state was never straightforward. As I noted above, speaking of the first phase of nation-making, the idea has to be promulgated and accepted: this is a political process and, like all political processes, is suffused with latent and actual conflict. Tivey remarks that 'The achievement of sovereignty involved long and confused struggles and was nowhere a simple process.'[9] Why this should be so is made clear, in principle, if we follow the distinction made by political scientists and historians between nations and states. Seton-Watson remarks, at the very outset of his influential text *Nations and States* (1977), that

> The distinction between states and nations is fundamental. . . .States can exist without a nation, or with several nations among subjects; and a nation can be coterminous with the population of one state, or be included together with other nations within one state, or be divided between several states . . . .. The belief that every state is a nation, or that all sovereign states are national states, has done much to obfuscate human understanding of political realities.[10]

Claims to nationhood are thus not the same as claims to statehood; and when the two claims do not neatly overlap – and more often than not they haven't and don't – then there is scope for much complex tension. However, this will be pursued in Nationalism II: for the moment a brief sketch of the rise of nation-states will suffice to illustrate my two claims – the scale and pervasiveness of the shift to nation-statehood.

The related issues of withdrawal from empire and achievement of the status of nation-statehood can be broken up, in a roughly chronological fashion in such a way as to generate a series of types, or routes to nation-statehood. In the overwhelming majority of cases this 'route' is through withdrawal from a larger encompassing colonial empire. As we'll see even in the case of Western Europe, the familiar pattern of today's states is a result of the slow disintegration of the Holy Roman Empire and, latterly, a series of dynastic empires. Each of the various routes to nation-statehood became, once mapped, available to subsequent aspirant nation-states. Anderson calls the idea of a nation 'modular . . . capable of being transplanted . . . to a great variety of social terrains . . .'[11] What follows is, let us be quite clear, a very much simplified scheme.

The first batch of 'new nation-states' were constituted in the America's – North and South. These areas, unusually in the overall context of our discussion – actually shared a language with the encompassing unit from which they were splitting-off. Language was never an issue. The rebellions in both North and South were occasioned by economic conflicts with their respective metropolitan centres; and problems of geographic[12] and social[13] distance exacerbated these conflicts. These nascent nation-states had the powerful ideas of the Enlightenment to draw on and eventually the claim to nation-statehood was lodged. The lodging and securing of these claims was by no means a straightforward business and in neither continent was independence gained easily. That the metropolitan powers would resist is fairly easy to comprehend and their resistance caused the withdrawal to be long-drawn-out. In the case of the USA, as now is, the war of independence was not a simple matter of Americans fighting British; indeed Seton-Watson says that: it 'was as much a civil war between the people of two territories. In England there was widespread sympathy for the American cause, and in America a large minority of Loyalist supported the British.'[14] The war – which the British had sustained, over what in these days was a vast distance, for five years was won for the Americans when the French lent crucial aid which culminated in the American victory at Yorktown. Even so, the greater part of British North America – in terms of geographical area – remained British: namely Canada. And for years afterwards there was danger that the 'infant' USA might fail as the states pulled in different directions: Seton-Watson speaks of 'a serious danger of disintegration.'[15] The subsequent creation of

'Americans', as an identity, took years, indeed into the twentieth century.

In Spanish America[16] the route to nation-statehood proved to be even more difficult. The Spanish empire had, to simplify, been harsh and inegalitarian. In addition to the tensions between colonial and metropolitan powers (as in the North American case) there were tensions between indigenous Indians and Creoles, between Creoles and peninsulares, between radicals and conservatives, and between secular groupings and the Roman Catholic Church. The wars of independence began in 1809 and Seton-Watson records:

> The emancipation of Spanish America was fought over an immensely wider area than the war of the North American colonies against the British. It was also immensely more painful, with heavy casualties to civilians as well as soldiers, and mass acts of reprisal cruelly performed on both sides. It was spread over nearly twenty years instead of five.[17]

The complex web of conflicts and the extraordinary length of the wars against a debilitated Spain – in 1808 Napoleon had invaded – led Anderson to remark that the nationalist impulse in Spanish America was actually rather weak and uncertain.[18]

The second batch of nation-states require a more complex tale. This batch includes the nation-states of modern Western Europe and the rise of both nations and states (and recall that these are not the same thing or necessarily coterminous) took place over a long-drawn-out period – Seton-Watson, an orthodox historian, speaks of 'from the fifteenth century on'. However, Anderson, who treats the idea of nation as a 'cultural artefact' and as intimately linked not only to language but to formalized print languages, makes the period of fifteenth to nineteenth centuries one of the slow crystallization of national language communities organized, increasingly, into states. The business of the creation of states (as feudalism slowly gave way to capitalism) and nations (as print language slowly created communities of language users) was slow, and their fusion into modern-day European nation-states was in the main a nineteenth-century phenomenon. Prior to that, general patterns of loyalty and self-understandings had not been, as they are today, taken-for-grantedly national.[19] Anderson argues that these nation-states emerged out of various 'dynastic empires', that is, pre-national orders.[20] It was not until the aftermath of the First World War that the last of the dynastic European empires disappeared: Austro-Hungary and Czarist Russia.

In the case of the European nation-states the business of language was very important: the choice of a national language could, and often was, a troublesome business. Over the long post-Renaissance period, as print capitalism acted to 'solidify' vernacular languages, official state languages were, usually, Latin. The change from Latin to a vernacular language as state language was a key – and contentious – step in nation-state building. The choice of languages of state has been problematic for post-Second World War 'new nations'.

At the same time we have the invention of 'official nationalisms'. This, too, is of relevance to the case of the post-war batch of new nations. The old dynastic empires – Russia, Habsburgs, Ottomans, and British, for example – responded to the rise of nationalist sentiment among their various subject groups by inventing 'official nationalisms': these were self-consciously manipulative, in contrast to the earlier nationalisms, and presented ideas of purported member-ship of a community (which was what belonging to a nation was taken to be) which encompassed more than one language-based group. Thus we have 'Russification', the imposition of the Russian language and alphabet over the Czar's empire. Or, again, the deliberate policy of Anglicization by the British in India. This invention – official nationalism – was later used by the post-war new nations. The disintegration of these dynastic empires in the aftermath of the First World War brought to an end the second phase of nation-state formation. And we have the formation of the League of Nations – the forerunner of the UN.

The third batch saw the dismantling of the remaining overseas empire holdings: the Second World War broke the European colonial empires and we have the post-war flood of new nations. These new states borrowed from the examples established by their predecessors. The machiavellianism of official nationalism was used to manipulate often diverse populations in pursuit of effective nation-statehood. When commentators use the phrase nation-*building* it is apposite. The populism[21] of the nineteenth-century model was adopted. Often the republican democratic ethos of the Americans was taken.[22] The route to nation-statehood was rarely smooth and the subsequent business of making the new states stable and coherent was often fraught with difficulties: in this, as in other respects, the new nations resembled the older ones.

In sum, the familiar pattern of nation-states is historically novel: nation-states are inventions of the last two centuries only. The changes from the pre-national dynastic polities to comtemporary national polities has taken place over a brief period of time. It is certainly one key aspect of that complex set of changes which Gellner summarizes as the 'transition to the modern world'. I want now to turn to consider the Southeast Asian experience in a little more detail.

2.1 Southeast Asian withdrawal

I want here to consider the business of withdrawal from empire in Southeast Asia. I will offer a simple overview of the different ways in which this was accomplished. It is useful to take note of the pattern of colonial rule and withdrawal because this has shaped the character of the subsequently established new states. It also, as we'll see below, shaped the character of the nationalist sentiment. Quite how extensive these 'colonial legacies' have been, and just how long lived, are not questions that I will pursue in any very great detail. Read as an invitation to study the detail of the independence and post-independence circumstances of the new nations, the question would take me outside the scope of this text. I will offer here only a few tentative remarks, which I'll pursue in the final section of this chapter when I look at the present situation of these new nations in a general way.

Turning to the history of Southeast Asia, we find a variety of patterns of withdrawal from empire. Pandy[23] identifies four colonial systems: the USA; the British; the French; and the Dutch. These he characterizes in terms of their contribution, via their colonial practices, to modernization. The idea of modernization is not examined and, moreover, tends to lean towards a fairly uncritical acceptance of the model of liberal democracy. Needless to say much of Pandy's history is of falling way. However, he usefully typifies the four powers: the British and American are seen as most politically liberal whilst the French and Dutch are least liberal. Oddly enough in social terms the situation is reversed and ethnic divides are deepest in Philippines and UK territories.[24]

In the case of the Philippines the withdrawal of the Americans had been scheduled before the Pacific War broke out. At the turn of the century the Americans seized the islands and militarily defeated an indigenous independence movement which was fighting – and overcoming – the Spanish. They dominated the Philippines economically and, it seems, had won the acceptance of 'ordinary' Filipinos. The islands were thus firmly tied into the US sphere; and this included the elite. However, when the Japanese arrived the local elite collaborated with the Japanese. This is detailed by Pluvier and Pandy and, amusingly, apologized for by Milton Osborne.[25] Resistance to the Japanese came from amongst the peasantry. However, when the US forces returned, the same elite was kept in power. Formal transfer of power was not as smooth as the US and their elite allies would have wished and the newly independent elite had to call on US assistance to suppress a rebellion from the peasantry, which together they had provoked. Relations between the US and the Philippines have remained close. The descent of the Philippines into the Marcos 'conjugal dictatorship' proved to be no great problem. Pandy saw Marcos as a representative of the very rich elite that has been in place since before the Pacific War.[26] Cory Aquino, who has replaced Marcos, is *another* figure drawn from this elite.

The withdrawal of the British from their quite extensive Asian holdings was generally peaceful – at least in the sense of there being no anti-colonial armies to contend with. The withdrawal from India can be seen to have similarities with that of the US from the Philippines. The British had followed policies of Anglicization which had had some effects. Angus Maddison[27] argues that when the British left they handed over power to an alliance of business, professional, administrative and miltary elements which ensured a significant, and unfortunate (in Maddison's view), measure of continuity in the nature and exercise of authority. However, this smooth transfer was something of an illusion, as the sub-continent collapsed into inter-religious and inter-language community violence. The sub-continent was partitioned into a predominantly Hindu India and a predominantly Muslim Pakistan – a state of two halves separated by over one thousand miles. Pakistan eventually divided and Bangladesh was formed. The last state formed out of this sub-continental holding was Ceylon, Sri Lanka as it now is. Transition to independence was comparatively smooth, but ethnic tensions were never resolved.

Pandy relates the history of the sub-continent as a melancholy falling away from liberal-democratic grace. Scheming, irresponsible politicians are blamed: and Pakistan and Bangladesh quickly acquired military governments. Salman Rushdie takes a similarly dim view.[28]

The circumstances of withdrawal from Burma and the Malay peninsula are, again, complex: additionally, all these territories were occupied by the Japanese. In the case of Burma, nationalist resistance to the British involved a measure of involvement with the Japanese and the establishment of a nominal independence in 1943. However, the Burmese nationalists, lead by Aung San, changed sides late in the war and aided the British. When the British resumed control they soon bowed to the inevitable and Burma became independent early in 1948, and quickly became plagued by separatist movements among certain minority groups. The Burmese rulers have pursued an isolated route towards 'Burmese socialism': the first Prime Minister, U Nu, once declared that he had a marxist base and a Buddist superstructure.[29]

In the Malay peninsula British administration has been arranged in a confused fashion with three distinct strategies being used: the Colony of the Straits Settlements, the Federal Malay States protectorate, and the Unfederated Malay States protectorate. More importantly there were powerful local rulers in place – the Malay Sultanate. More awkward still, there was a large minority Chinese community. This group had expanded at a quite remarkable rate in the early years of the century and by the 1930s there was some alarm amongst the Malays, the earliest signs of the communal organizations which were to be prominent after the war. The Japanese occupation was a further complicating factor. During the occupation the Chinese suffered badly and it was from this ethnic group that a resistance movement sprang: it was a movement that received British aid late in the war. The Malays, in contrast, had rather been encouraged in their national aspirations, so too had the Indians.

At the end of the war the British re-established control and by a series of accidents, it seems, the largely communist resistance movement slid into rebellion. The ostensible point was to block any attempt to revive the pre-war alliance of overseas capitalism and local 'feudalism'. However, after twelve years the 'Malayan Emergency' saw the defeat of the communists and, arguably, the establishment of precisely the type of regime they had feared. With the extinction of the communist rebellion and after several alarums over the new constitution – which eventually enshrined Malay 'special rights' – Malaysia became independent in 1957, and, after an abortive federation, Singapore in 1965. There has been a good measure of stability in these two countries – with the ever-present communalism apart – and Malaysia has had a scheme of elite power-sharing whilst Singapore has had Lee's 'restricted version of democracy . . .'[30]

The foregoing can, with a great deal of oversimplification, be seen as the peaceful route to Asian independence. What conflicts there were were not straightforward colonial wars of independence. And with the exception of Burma – paradoxically as this case was the most peaceful transition – links with the ex-colonial nations have been retained. The circumstances of Dutch and French withdrawal are rather different: here, to simplify again, we find the violent route to Asian independence and the severing of any ties that the colonial episode established.

The Dutch focused their attention, as a colonial power, firmly on profit. Notwithstanding their schemes of indirect rule and their pursuit of the (rather mysterious) 'ethical policy', their regime was thoroughly autocratic – as was the rule of the French in Indo-China. The Japanese interregnum destroyed Dutch power and the vacuum was filled, with a series of twists and turns both during and after the war, with an indigenous anti-Dutch elite. Indonesian independence was proclaimed by Sukarno in August 1945. Subsequently the Dutch attempted to recapture their territory but, significantly, failed to win

US backing, and by 1947 had acknowledged the independence of Indonesia. The country ran a liberal democratic system, then in 1958–65 'guided democracy' and subsequently a military rule of a distinctive 'patrimonial' character.

The French in Indo-China were similarly placed to the Dutch: their rule was autocratic and exploitative. Their credibility and power was broken by the war years, but the French were able to pass off their attempted reconquest as a fight against communism. The USA assisted them and, with the installation of puppet regimes in the South, a quasi-civil war was sustained for some thirty years before the Vietnamese, more nationalist than communist, ejected them. The process of 'normalization' in this area is still to be finally accomplished: certainly the French have no very obvious role to play!

The foregoing treats the processes of withdrawal from empire. To these patterns we must add a note. Thailand never was colonized: it has maintained an independent status throughout the colonial period as a result of its role as a 'buffer state' between French and British holdings. Thailand has been ruled by military dictatorships, in the main, since 1932 when the absolute monarchy was dismantled. In recent years the country has come firmly within the US sphere. However, it can be read as a third Asian route to the present, to add to our violent withdrawal and peaceful withdrawal.

At this point I will set aside further discussion of Southeast Asia. Having taken note of the manner of their achievement of nation-statehood I will now turn to consider the issue of nationalism (in pursuit of independence). After looking at the idea of nationhood, I will return to Southeast Asian material when I look at the varieties of nationalism advanced. In the concluding part of this chapter I will go on to consider the post-Second World War records of the Southeast Asian nations.

3   Nationalism I

The foregoing review opens up two issues for us:

(a) the business of the construction over time of the very idea of nation-statehood; and,

(b) the history of promulgators of that idea – the nationalists of (and here I narrow my focus) Southeast Asia.

3.1 The idea of nation-statehood

It is rather easy to become confused by words in this area of debate. The whole business of nationalism, in particular, has been regarded as peculiarly problematical by social scientists. Terminological difficulties are often compounded by political or ideological commitments: one can see this in Smith below, or in orthodox Marxists for whom nationalism is an indigestible confusion and who respond with various strategies of denial of the phenomena. I will offer a brief note on the key terms used. These notes I take from the work of political scientists.

If we begin with 'society' we find a word which, with its cognates, goes back into the late eighteenth century.[31] This familiar term designates the set of rules and institutions within which social life is embedded. One key institution is the state. Tivey offers a rough definition:

> The state is a specific type of political formation – that is, it is not any sort of polity or political system. For instance, there were in earlier times sets of social arrangements that relied . . . on customary rules . . . [and] no real central authority existed within the community . . . Again, in contemporary times the relations among states make up a political order but there is no supreme state.[32]

Tivey argues that the key to the idea of a state is that there is 'an independent political apparatus distinct from the ruler.'[33] The state, in other words, is a formal politico-legal entity. Tivey goes on:

> The emergence of the modern state brought with it the idea of sovereignty – a single authority for making laws and with the force to sustain them – within a sharply defined and consolidated territory. The first part of the rise of the nation state is therefore the story of the rise of sovereignty.[34]

In Europe this meant a long and complicated struggle to throw off the authority of what we would now call supra-national bodies, the Catholic church in particular. It also involved curbing the power of 'intermediate groups' – nobles, and so on. In most of the rest of the world, as we noted above, the achievement of sovereignty meant the removal of colonial rule.

The other 'part of the story' is nationalism. Where the state is a politico-legal institution, the nation is – in Anderson's felicitous phrase – an 'imagined community'. I will turn to Anderson's analysis below. Relatedly there is the matter of the nationalist ideology of the state; Tivey suggests that there are five key aspects: (a) the claim that it is natural; (b) that it encompasses a community; (c) that it requires its appropriate national polity; (d) that it requires a defined territory; (e) and national 'confidence'.[35]

Thus we have, analytically, three basic elements. Firstly, the state which is a politico-legal institution. Secondly, the nation which is (or claims to be) a community of people and thus, in some important way, shares a common culture. Thirdly, the nation-state which is a community organized into the politico-legal entity of a state. Thus, to recall Seton-Watson's cautionary note, we can have nations without states, or states without a nation.[36] The familiar image that we have – of the long-established, deep historically rooted, culturally homogenous nation-state, is both based narrowly upon the Western European case and is distinctly misleading. The reality of nation-statehood – historical cultural and economic-social – is much more ambiguous: conflict and confusion have attended nation-statehood just as often as community and clarity. For a group to come together, formulate, lodge and secure acceptance of claims to nation-statehood is a long, complex, task.

Thus far, in this chapter, I have looked at the complex notion of nation-statehood in a straightforward fashion. I have discussed the historical occasion of nation-states, generally and, in a little more detail, in Southeast Asia. In this section I am going to look directly at the idea of nation-statehood. At this point some mention of established lines of debate seems appropriate.

In the literature there are a variety of ways of analysing nationalism (the ideology of the nation-state). Orridge[37] notes that the whole business can be treated as a history of ideas of nation lodged within the history of political thought; or it can be treated as a strategy for organizing various politically active groups. Orridge is looking at the way the idea was produced and how it has subsequently been adapted (a theme I have noted). In addition to these various 'readings' there have been attempts to offer 'theories' of nationalism. He identifies two main types: the argument from uneven development, where claims to nation-statehood are lodged in response to perceived economic disadvantage in an unevenly developing world economic system; and, the argument from social cohesion where it is suggested that the complex interdependency of the modern world necessitates the organizational discipline of nation-statehood in place of earlier and 'looser' polities.

A similar scheme is presented by Smith,[38] who identifies two models which he calls the marxist and modernization approaches. The former, marxist, model is reported as characterizing post-Renaissance history in terms of a shift from feudalism to capitalism with consequent changes in the polity (state form) marginalized in a basically economistic scheme. The latter model posits an evolutionary shift from traditional to modern society and once again changes in the polity are marginalized. Smith is of the view that prevailing discussions of nation-statehood neglect crucial cultural and political factors. Be that as it may, what we seem to have are two divergent (rather than opposed) approaches to analysing nation-statehood. One approach centres itself on economic changes and consequent 'superstructural responses' – marxist, to simplify – whilst the other looks at political and social history and sees the nation-state as a contingent, if plausible, response to problems of modernity – liberal, to simplify. I will take as representatives of these two approaches Tom Nairn and Ernest Gellner respectively.[39] Having looked at what they have to say, I will turn to consider Benedict Anderson's approach.

Tom Nairn begins his theoretical discussion by remarking that 'The theory of nationalism represents Marxism's great historical failure'[40]; and in his essay he runs two arguments: one in respect of nationalism and the other in respect of the implications of his analysis for marxism. This second argument I will not consider.

Nairn argues that nationalism is a product of the uneven development of the (industrial) world capitalist system over the last two centuries (though the process does reach back to the fifteenth century). Where the liberal economic orthodoxy anticipated even development via diffusion of modern ideas, techniques and so on, what has, in historical fact, happened is an increasingly acute uneven development. The contradiction of capitalism (and the clue to Nairn's discussion of Marxism) is its simultaneous drawing together of the world into some sort of a single community whilst also occasioning a pervasive discord in nationalist aspirations. These discordant aspirations are occasioned by the attempt on the part of the marginalized undeveloped to try to catch up. Nairn argues that 'nationalism' was all these groups had in their pursuit of development. Thus he reports: 'The peripheric elites . . . had to mobilize *against* progress at the same time as they sought to improve their position in accordance with the new canons. . . .This gave rise to a profound ambiguity, an ambivalence which marks most forms of nationalism.'[41] He continues by arguing that this unhappy 'copying' as he terms it, in the attempt to catch up, has to make use of the *people* of the backward nation. Thus:

> Their rulers . . . had to mobilize their societies for this historical shortcut. This meant the conscious formation of a militant . . . community rendered strongly (if mythically) aware of its own separate identity. There was no other way of doing it. Mobilization had to be in terms of what was there. . . .All that was there *was* the people . . . in the archetypal situation of the really poor or 'underdeveloped' territory, it may be all the nationalists have going for them.[42]

Nairn, to conclude, argues that nationalism is essentially ambiguous: it can present itself in relatively benign fashions or in malign ways – fascism. It is neither, contra Gellner and the 'moralists', inevitably good nor, contra most orthodox marxists, necessarily bad. Nairn remarks:

> nationalism is the pathology of modern developmental history, as inescapable as 'neurosis' in the individual, with much the same essential ambiguity attaching to it, a similar built-in capacity for descent into dementia, rooted in the dilemmas of helplessness thrust upon most of the world . . . and largely incurable.[43]

Turning to Gellner, whom Nairn in fact cites with a modified approval – arguing that he represents those who do see that nationalism is a response to uneven development (even if they don't use this jargon) but who fail to grasp the ambiguity of the ideology and instead collapse into a general moralistic approval[44] – we find an argument about nationalism which is lodged in a thoroughly intelligent discussion of modernization, what Gellner, as we have seen, calls the 'transition'. This particular location is the source of the 'divergence' rather than 'opposition' that I noted above.[45]

Gellner argues that nationalism has escaped the grasp of nineteenth century liberalism and marxism, both of which looked askance at the phenomenon. Reactions to the continued vitality of nationalism have stressed the inevitability and irrationality of the phenomenon. This is rejected: nationalism is a contingent product of the transition; and once constructed it has great plausibility and moral virtue.

The condition of the emergence of nationalism rests upon the rise in importance of vernacular languages: as the transition proceeds it calls forth a vernacular speaking bureaucracy, and this forms the basis of a broad community of language-users. Gellner points out that nationalism thus engendered is at base not sentimental but materially practical.[46] If that is the condition of its emergence then what actually occasions it is the 'uneven diffusion'[47] of industrialization: the transition to the modern world is uneven and nationalism is a response to perceived disadvantage. Gellner continues by suggesting that: 'Nationalism is not the awakening of nations to self consciousness: it invents nations where they do not exist. . . .'[48] The agents of this invention are – as we discovered earlier – the 'intelligentsia'. Finally it is suggested that nationalism is a 'good thing' not only because the goal of progress for the disadvantaged is laudable but also because the resultant pluralism of national units is some sort of defence against tyranny.

Evidently there are many points of similarity in the analyses presented by Nairn and Gellner: and I think that these could probably be elucidated around the opposition of capitalism (Nairn) and industrialism (Gellner). The cursory review I have offered does confirm the reading of Orridge: the two general models centre their analyses upon respectively uneven economic development (Nairn) and the necessity of novel (and aggresive?) forms of social organization in the transition to the industrial world (Gellner). If there are two different centres then much of the areas of enquiry overlap: and disentangling these analyses in a fashion more sophisticated than the not unreasonable characterization of Orridge would entail looking at what's at stake in substituting (as Gellner does) industrial for capitalist. I cannot pursue this argument here. The material of the foregoing sections (on the rise of nation-states) would be, given its simplicity of intellectual level, equally (un)acceptable to both theorists. It represents, probably, a specimen of what Nairn calls the 'anti-imperialist theory'.[49] These general styles of argument I will, however, set aside. My own generic definition of social theorizing specifies the active making of sense. I shall follow this view – at least to some extent – by following the arguments of Anderson who suggests that nationalism is best seen as a 'cultural artefact' and one that, having been made, is easily transferable. This approach does not conflict necessarily with either of the two above schemes: it does focus upon the active business of making nationalist ideologies and this, in addition to being somewhat closer to my dispositions, will enable us to run smoothly into the issue of Southeast Asian nationalisms.

The notions of nation, state, nation-statehood, and the ideology of nationalism can all be regarded as cultural artefacts. A set of resources available for people to use to make sense of their circumstances. This set of ideas has a particular series of episodes of construction and, once made, were available for remodelling for use in new situations. I will pursue this approach to understanding nationalism (etc.) by looking at the arguments presented by Benedict Anderson in his book *Imagined Communities* (1983).

Anderson's approach is this:

> My point of departure is that nationality . . . as well as nationalism, are cultural artefacts of a particular kind. To understand them properly we need to consider carefully how they came into historical being, in what ways their meanings have changed over time, and why, today, they command such profound emotional legitimacy. I will be trying to argue that the creation of these artefacts towards the end of the eighteenth century was the spontaneous distillation of a complex 'crossing' of discrete historical forces; but that once created they became 'modular' capable of being transplanted, with varying degrees of self consciousness, to a great variety of social terrains, to merge and be merged with a correspondingly wide variety of political and ideological constellations.[50]

So, let us begin with the inventing of nations. Anderson, citing Gellner (1964) approvingly – 'Nationalism is not the awakening of nations to self consciousness: it invents nations where they do not exist'[51] – posits three basic elements to the 'imagined community' of nationhood. Thus:

> The nation is imagined as limited because even the largest . . . has finite . . . boundaries, beyond which lie other nations. . . . It is imagined as sovereign because the concept was born in an age in which Enlightenment and Revolution were destroying the legitimacy of the divinely-ordained, hierarchical dynastic realm. . . .Finally, it is imagined as a community, because, regardless of the actual inequality . . . the nation is always conceived as a deep, horizontal comradeship.[52]

Anderson's enquiry is to be historical, the idea of nation is to be studied in its genesis and change. We can contrast this with both the two 'general theories' noted above: Nairn with his economics of uneven development and Gellner with his requirements of social cohesion. Neither 'general theory' is refuted – indeed both are referred to with approval by Anderson – rather we have an approach which is both dynamic and literary-cultural. The historical approach leads Anderson to ask what went before nation-states, and the answer presented, much as the other commentators have, identifies: (a) religious community; and (b) dynastic realms. Around the theme of community (nation) – how they are constituted in practice and with what resultant characters – Anderson looks at the way in which both (a) and (b) were displaced/replaced by the rise of the secular nation-state.

Anderson begins by looking at the 'cultural system' of the religious community. He wants to know how they were constituted in practice; and points to a shared sacred language and common paths of pilgrimage within an hierarchically ordered meta-institution. People with different vernacular languages shared the same sacred language, took the same pilgrimages to express faith, and lodged themselves in the hierarchy according to trans-ethnic rules. Thus was constituted a 'community of believers'.

The world religions declined, in Europe first, from the Renaissance onwards. Over a similar period the dynastic realms were weakened. Simultaneously we see the rise of mercantile capitalism. The character of the dynastic realm does not involve nation – or any analogue. For the moment I will merely note its decline – how it happened we can touch upon later. What is given pride of place in Anderson's treatment of the decline of religious communities and dynastic cultural systems is the role played by print capitalism. It is print capitalism that, on Anderson's account, is the key to the creation of the cultural artefact 'nation'.

Print capitalism, a very early form of capitalist enterprise, had the effect of destroying the primacy of Latin which had been the sacred language of Europe and, generally speaking, the language of administration. It did so by virtue of 'solidifying' vernacular languages. These print-capitalists produced vernacular editions of sacred texts (Luther, in rebellion against Rome, published a flood of material on Protestantism). And they also produced grammars and dictionaries: they fixed vernacular languages in place simply by writing them down, codifying the languages around fixed rules, and by making them available to a reading public. This reading public was also new: it was the educated and not just clerics and bureaucrat servants of the dynasty in power. Prior to this the sacred/bureaucratic languages had been stable, but the vernacular languages had been fluid and changing. Anderson notes: 'These print-languages laid the bases for national consciousness in three distinct ways. First and foremost, they created unified fields of exchange and communication below Latin and above spoken vernaculars.'[53] Thus the 101 Frenches became French. 'Second print-capitalism gave a new fixity to language'[54] – previously vernacular forms were not only various but fluid. 'Third, print-capitalism created languages of power of a different kind to the older administrative vernaculars'[55] – closer to some vernaculars than others; slowly this advantage narrowed down languages to *the* vernacular. Anderson also reports that the existence of recognized European languages today (and presumably this process is still effective generally) depends upon their having successfully been established as a print-language. Vernaculars that never had their grammars and dictionaries withered away to become lower-status language forms. In Europe all this happened 'pragmatically' – in the case of the post-Second World War new nations self-conscious decisions were necessary, with all the attendant problems.

The rise of modern-type language communities, thanks to print capitalism, created the possibility of nation-communities. Now, as religious community was displaced as a central social experience so too were dynastic political orders. This political pattern had to break somewhere – possibility has to become established practice, and it happened first in the Americas. Here Anderson re-introduces the theme of pilgrimage; the religious journey that helps constitute the community of believers. So how was the idea of belonging to a nation initially constituted? Anderson offers an argument by analogy. The particular 'journey' he has in mind is that of bureaucratic journeys. Colonial schools came, over time, to send recruits into colonial administrations. In the North and South American empires of the

West Europeans (British, French, Spanish and Portuguese) the 'journeys' of the colonial born were restricted. As they moved through their careers, to the pilgrimage centres of their bureaucratic spheres – London, Paris, Madrid, Lisbon – they found their progress blocked. Their 'journeys' finished in the colonial territories: they were an 'out group' disadvantaged, discriminated against – and this they came to recognize. Effectively, the behaviour of the metropolitan administrations split them away from the metropoles.

It is this experience, plus, again, a community of readers, this time of colonial newspapers (print capitalism again), that Anderson posits as the germ of American nationalisms. This is how the potential nationalist group was constituted. Add to this the circumstances of vast geographical remoteness from the metropoles, economic disputes, the political and social ideology of the Enlightenment (anticlerical republican rationalism), and a political occasion for rebellion and we have a sketch of how groups came together, formulated, lodged and, after wars of liberation, had accepted, claims to nationstatehood.

To sum up thus far. In regard to this business of the invention of nations it can be seen that at this point a considerable cultural shift has taken place. The experience of the 'ordinary person' had been of: (a) membership of a broad religious community, held together by sacred language and pilgrimage and hierarchical in form; (b) being subject secularly to a loose dynastic authority, a lord and a local noble; and (c) as inhabiting an essentially 'time-less' life-world.[56] But this has changed – for the first to take the step, Americans – and the experience of the 'ordinary person' is now of: (a) membership of a national community held together by shared vernacular language constituted and expressed in the manifold forms created by printcapitalism; (b) being subject to a sovereign republic state authority; and (c) as inhabiting an essentially historical (progressive) life-world.

In brief, the cultural artefact 'nation-state' is finally put together, from a variety of pieces, in the late eighteenth century. It not only represents a radically different way of a person's apprehending the world, but the artefact is now available for others to use.

Anderson's approach to this whole issue is most interesting. It would seem that what we are being offered is an essay in historicalcultural anthropology. How, then, does Anderson's approach sit with orthodox approaches? The two established explanatory frameworks are the 'liberal' – which would see history as concatenations of circumstances, events, process, and be reluctant to see any deterministic patterns. This is a simplification, and simplifying again we can associate Gellner with this position. In contrast the marxists, the other main contender, would identify in history the slow working out of class conflict around the economic core of society. Again this is a simplification, and again simplifying further we can offer Nairn as a representative of this tradition.[57] However, neither theorist is a particularly typical representative and both cited texts are widely regarded as 'novel' and 'distinguished' contributions. Setting this aside, what we find in Anderson is essentially this: that the modern world is (predominantly) a capitalist system is largely taken for granted, but the key to the rise of nation-state is taken to be the particular phenomenon of print-capitalism and the generation of the cultural artefact of the nation-state is largely accidental. Anderson comments: 'My sense is that on this topic both Marxist and liberal theory have become etiolated in a late Ptolemaic effort to "save the phenomena"; and that a reorientation of perspective in, as it were, a Copernican spirit is urgently required.'[58] This, then, is the basis of the arguments advanced.

To continue: above I have detailed Anderson's position *vis-à-vis* the invention of nationalism; now, we can continue and look at the subsequent 'pirating', as Anderson puts it, of the idea. I will not in these cases review the detail rather I will look at the steps made in the various borrowings of the initial notion.

The idea of national communities crystallized first of all in the Americas. This practical example of the establishment of nation-states influenced Western Europe, as did the, roughly contemporary, French Revolution: what was novel about the upheaval was, for present purposes, the extent to which it was *discussed* – in books, pamphlets and newspapers. It was in Western Europe, as I noted above, that the second phase of the division of the world into nation-states took place. It is in this phase that, paradoxically perhaps, we find the paradigm cases of nation-statehood (it is with these cases, for example, that Seton-Watson, perhaps revealingly, begins). In this period the modern nation-states of Europe emerged from the pre-national orders of the dynastic realms.

In contrast to 'phase one' there was, additionally to the discussed models just noted, considerable struggle around the matter of national print languages. Unlike the situation in the Americas in Europe the national language – the language of power – was contentious. We can add two other points to this material. Firstly, that the slow, uneven spread of nation-statehood was inhibited by the continued existence of old-style dynastic empires. The empires of the Romanovs, the Habsburgs, the Ottomans and the Hohenzollerns all lingered on into the twentieth century – they were destroyed by the First World War. Secondly, the period saw the, somewhat contradictory, scramble for empire holdings. Interestingly both the old-style dynastic empires and the new-style colonial empires generated official nationalisms. Anderson identified this as a novel variant of the basic theme and explains it in terms of the attempt by threatened ruling groups to self-consciously generate national feeling centered upon themselves. By the end of the First World War these dynastic empires had broken up and the familiar pattern of European nation-states had emerged.

In 'phase three', the post-Second World War period, we see the dismantling of the formal colonial empires. In this period the status of nation-statehood is worked for by intelligentsias who have shared the colonial pilgrimages of school-bureaucracy, just as the Americans did in the eighteenth century. Secondly, the choice of the language-of-state, of power, is a sensitive issue. The language conflicts of the eighteenth and nineteenth centuries in Europe are now repeated in the Third World new nations. Often an ex-colonial language has been chosen, as this both obviates local conflict and maintains the use of a major international language. Thirdly, the intelligentsias borrow from nineteenth-century official nationalism and manipulative approach to nation-building, and also populist themes.

This, argues Anderson, is how subsequent nationalisms have borrowed from earlier ones. Each new success establishes a model to draw on. Today we find that the fact that there are successful nation-states permits many new states to search for nation-statehood in multi-lingual and multi-cultural circumstances. They conduct this search, as Smith [59] is at pains to point out, often within the irrational territorial boundaries bequeathed by the colonial powers. Generally,

> Nationalist leaders are thus in a position consciously to deploy civil and military education systems modelled on official nationalisms; elections, party organisations, and cultural celebrations modelled on the popular nationalisms of nineteenth century Europe; and the citizen-republic idea brought into the world by the Americas. [60]

So much for Anderson's argument: we are left with a detailed review of the origins and subsequent career of the notion of nation-statehood. We can add that the problems confronted by aspirant nation-builders will be, roughly following Nairn, Gellner and Anderson – firstly, *coherence*, the constitution of a community; secondly, *stability*, the provision of stable governance; and thirdly, *progress*, the pursuit of economic growth (development). That many Third World nations have experienced grave problems with the third aspect is well known. That many Third World nations have proved to be unstable is well known. That many Third World 'nations' have recurring problems of national coherence is also well known. These observations are not a corrective to Anderson: they merely serve to reintroduce, in a more familiarly social scientific guise, the problem of

nation-building. As Anderson remarks, 'many of these nations . .
[are] . . projects the achievement of which is still in progress . . .'[61] I
will turn to all this in 'Nationalism II'. Let us now conclude this
section by looking at the history of nationalist movements in
Southeast Asia.

3.2 Nationalism in Southeast Asia

Southeast Asia is a large area – however you define its boundaries –
and in this section I will concentrate upon the Philippines, Malaysia,
Singapore and Indonesia. I will then add brief notes on Thailand and
Burma. The cluster of issues that I will look at will be: the manner of
incorporation into the colonial network; the character of the colonial
regime; the nature of the nationalist movements; and, the manner of
achievement of independence – and here I will add a simple note
recalling the discussion above.

Now, evidently, this represents a return to more familiarly social
scientific material after the discussion of the idea of nation-statehood
per se. The material here is concerned directly with the substantive
histories of the new nations of Southeast Asia, but what I will offer is
a broad comparative review. The detail of these histories is both
beyond my present scope and readily available in the work of
historians.[62]

The Philippines were colonized by the Spanish in the sixteenth
century and when the colonizers arrived they found an archipelago
which was thoroughly diverse in its cultures and polities. McCoy[63]
speaks, rather misleadingly it is now clear, of dozens of 'micro-states'.
The colonial regime of the Spanish is usually characterized as having
been comparatively economically benign; which is to say that the local
economy was left to its own devices and not systematically exploited
for the benefit of the metropolitan centre. The social and cultural
effects included the growth of a local elite – Spanish-speaking – and,
at the same time, a dispossessed peasantry. The Spanish interest in
the Philippines can be summarized as one of preoccupation with
disseminating catholicism rather than economic gain.

The notion of a Filipino identity, that is, an emergent nationalism,
took shape through the nineteenth century. Coming in the wake of
the period when Spain had been ejected from Latin America by a
series of rebellions and wars, it would seem that they felt disinclined
to give ground to Filipino national aspirations. This is, I suppose,
hardly surprising on one level – the later nineteenth century was the
high-tide of colonial rivalry and no other European powers were
giving up their holdings. Indeed they were still subduing them and, as
we'll note with the USA in a moment, still acquiring them.

McCoy[64] suggests that the background to nationalism was distinctly economic. It is reported that the Filipino elite had emerged from a diverse historical-cultural background and had come to centre its attention upon economic matters (rather than, say, cultural as did, arguably, the Malay Royals). Nonetheless, it became a self-conscious, highly Hispanicized elite, and their economic blocking by an unresponsive colonial power precipitated the formation of nationalist movements invoking European ideas of nation-statehood and looking to the fairly recent example of Latin America. Filipino nationalism is, it seems, associated closely with three leaders: Burgos (in the 1860s); Rizal (in the 1880s); and Bonifacio (in the 1890s). All three were involved in reform movements that were blocked by the Spanish authorities. The last noted, Bonifacio, saw the revolution of 1896. Rizal was also involved but was shot – martyred – by the Spanish. The tale of the rebellion is a confused one: Bonifacio was the early leader but was shot by Aguinaldo, a landowner, who was a later leader. Aguinaldo, after a period of exile established the first national government in 1898. However, the revolution never quite managed to secure itself and in 1898 the USA – in pursuit of the colonial territories which were seen to be appropriate to its status in the world – invaded. After a war of two or three years, the infant republic was extinguished.

The American colonial regime had its own very distinct style. Having acquired this territory in pursuit of the status of 'great nationhood', the US promptly determined to adhere to its espoused democratic ideals and to prepare the territory for independence. This they did – again in their own fashion; this included the tying of the Philippines' economy tightly to that of the US. In time the USA became a popular master, and the local elite had no great wish for independence. In the inter-war period the Philippines pursued a bizarre notion of bi-nationalism: inhabitants of the archipelago were *both* Filipino and American.

The Second World War proved to be – as for most other places – a disaster for the Philippines. As their own independence had been scheduled for the late 1940s, the arrival of the Japanese – fellow Asians and 'liberators' – was not regarded at all favourably. The Philippines' population split: roughly speaking it was the elite who collaborated and the peasantry who resisted.

The experience of colonial days was regarded favourably by the Filipinos – they were absorbed into the US ambit. In the period of withdrawal from colonialism this basic relationship seems to have been both (a) fixed firmly in place and (b) fatally fissured – although this may be a quirk of my presentation: comparing present unrest with earlier harmony when maybe the harmony wasn't there.

Decolonization did not proceed smoothly in the Philippines: here, as in Western Europe, the USA was anxious about the influence of the political left. In the Philippines the 'left' was the Huks.[65] The Huks had, during the war, run a successful guerilla campaign against the Japanese in central and southern Luzon. They had established their nationalist credentials rather more obviously than had the collaborating elite. In the 1946 elections to the new, independent, ruling parliament the Huks won seven seats. This created two problems for the elite/USA: firstly, the Huks were proponents of land reforms which did not endear them to the local elite, and secondly, the seven seats gave the Huks the necessary power to block economic legislation giving the USA's interests a privileged position – this pleased neither the USA nor the local elite. The remedy was simple: the Huks were excluded. The resulting armed rebellion reached a peak in the early 1950s, but a combination of US money and CIA assistance eventually defeated this rebellion. Thus was the Philippines (a) fixed in place and (b) fissured. The Philippines is still a grossly inegalitarian society.[66]

All the historians I have cited in this section are – with varying stresses given their different focuses – agreed upon three things. Very broadly they are: (1) that the Philippines have been economically absorbed into the US sphere and that this was deliberate US policy from the outset; (2) that the Filipino elite has been 'bought-off' by their economic linkages to the US and is now sharply separated from the Filipino masses; and finally (3) that the contemporary Philippines' political scene is 'degenerate'.

The Dutch began trading in the islands that now make up Indonesia back in the sixteenth century: Dutch influence preceded English and French interests in this area of Southeast Asia. The Dutch, most historians record, were, when they came to establish a formal colonial authority, preoccupied with profit, and they ran Indonesia as one vast agricultural holding: indeed it seems they often claimed that they were doing the First World a considerable service by managing this awkward tropical agricultural territory. The impact of the Dutch formal colonial regime – both economically and socially – is usually regarded as having been very damaging: pre-contact patterns of life were severely dislocated. Economically, in the twentieth century the outer islands did experience a 'boom time' in the 1930s but Java – with very heavy pressures of population – declined throughout the period.

The movement towards Indonesian independence is of interest in that, as Reid reports, it is here that we find the first example of a nationalist movement with a mass base. Over the period 1912–1926 Serekat Islam recruited large numbers of members into what seems to have been a self-help organization for Muslims; but, 'At its height ... Serekat Islam had become the voice of national awakening.'[67] The Serekat Islam grouping was also 'open' in character – any one who wished to join could do so. A few Indonesian communists did so, but they eventually broke away to found the Indonesian communist party in 1923. A further element in the rise of Indonesian nationalist sentiment in this pre-Second World War period was the exposure of small numbers of Indonesians to European political thinking (other than Marxism) whilst studying in Dutch Universities.[68]

The Dutch, in the inter-war period, responded to the upsurge in nationalist sentiment with repression. Reid then notes:

> Nevertheless, the national ideal continued to develop rapidly. ...
> Taking from Marxism the opposition to capitalism, from Serekat
> Islam the solidarity of 'us' against 'them', and from European
> scholarship the name of Indonesia and the rediscovery of a
> glorious pre-European past, secular nationalism became the
> dominant political force after 1926.[69]

And, Reid adds, 'alienation from the colonial regime was universal by 1942, and the Japanese were welcomed as liberators'.[70]

It was the Japanese occupation that – as elsewhere – destroyed for good the European colonial empires. In Indonesia Sukarno and Hatta were nationalist leaders who seized the opportunity given to them by the Japanese to preach nationalism. The other signal services provided by the Japanese were, first, a more extensive and responsible experience of administration and, second, a militaristic Youth Movement which provided the core of the (Japanese-fostered) Indonesian army.

As the Japanese collapsed, the nationalists, with Sukarno and Hatta at the helm, declared a republic on 17 August, 1945 and then moved in a hesitant and patchy way to secure their control over Indonesia. The British and Dutch made their reappearance some weeks later and then a confused period of manoeuvering took place. There were manoeuverings within the Dutch camp as to whether to repress or acquiesce to the new republic. Manoeuverings amongst the British who had stumbled into a colonial withdrawal (as it was) which had little to do with them. There were also, rather importantly, manoeuverings within the UN where the Dutch cause was not favoured. Eventually, after two 'small wars', the Dutch withdrew and the Indonesian Republic was formed in 1949.

The Indonesian Army was thus, from the outset, shaped by the experience of anti-colonial warfare: this had a reinforcing tendency for Indonesian nationalism, and the subsequent pattern of development in Indonesia. Reid notes:

> The result was neither socialism nor capitalism but a system in which the state dominated the formation of capital and the crucial relationships with foreign enterprise. . . . The revolutionary experience had weakened or broken most of the political, administrative and economic institutions of pre-War Indonesia.[71]

The new pattern of economics/social patterns/politics has been characterized, as we will see below, as a 'bureaucratic polity'.

The manner of incorporation of what is now Malaysia into the British empire has two major points of presently relevant note. First, the local rulers – the sultanate – were co-opted and the Malays effectively marginalized, and, second, the British encouraged the inflow of immigrants (Chinese and Indian). Bedlington summarizes the (tangled) story thus: 'British policies . . . were designed to mollify and in part co-opt the ruling class, while keeping the Malay peasantry physically and psychologically down on the farm.'[72] He goes on: '[the Sultanate joined] the British Imperial club, with all its pomp and splendor. . . .[As for the rest] the Malay peasantry did not enjoy any substantial socio-economic progress, but remained immured in a separate and unequal, if tranquil, social system.'[73] This general state of affairs persisted largely unchanged (and unchallenged) until 1942. The colonial regime thus pursued the exploitation of the territory in a fashion that minimized the disruption to established patterns of life (of the Malays) whilst simultaneously (by encouraging immigration) storing up very complex problems for the future.

It was in the inter-war period that we can identify the first stirrings of nationalist sentiment. The Malays began to show signs of reaction to the influx of immigrants whilst the immigrant groups themselves looked to their respective mother-countries. They were all, therefore, communalist in character.

For the Malays there seem to have been two sources of these early formulations of nationalist sentiment: first, the inspiration of reform movements within Islam and, second, a rather more political source of ideas from Indonesia. In 1926 the Singapore Union of Malays was formed and this was the precursor of UMNO (formed after the Second World War). However, during this period it seems that comparatively little was accomplished.

For the Chinese and the Indians the models they looked to were in their respective homelands and local politics/ideas reflected home-land politics/ideas. Thus the Chinese began, after the 1912 Sun Yat-sen revolution, setting up KMT branches; after KMT purges in 1927, the local Chinese similarly divided. The MCP emerged in 1929. The Indians looked to India and Congress – but in contrast to the Chinese they did not develop a strong local sense of nationalism:

indeed the Indians rather tended to split 'internally' on status grounds.

The Japanese invasion, as elsewhere, had a devastating impact: the British were swept away and the three communities were left to adjust as best they might. The contribution of the Japanese episode to the formation of nationalist sentiment is complex: Bedlington tersely summarizes the exchanges by saying that the races were forced apart.[74] The Chinese resisted the Japanese, who treated them with particular harshness (they were, simultaneously, fighting in China) and the MCP fought back. The Malays rather tended to acquiesce and there was, it seems, an element of collaboration in pursuit of nationalist goals. Likewise the Indians: the Indian nationalist Subhash Chandra Bose set up his HQ in Singapore during the war.

As the British returned to take over from the Japanese there was inter-ethnic fighting. Lee notes: 'Racial fighting occurred in several parts of the country as Malays exacted revenge upon the Chinese for MPAJA killings.'[75] From this point things became quickly polarized. Thus in 1946 the British proposed the Malayan Union Plan – a modern state with, crucially, equal citizenship. The Malays objected and UMNO was formed, to protect Malay 'special rights'. Eventually this position was enshrined in the 1948 Malayan Federation. The Chinese, thus having been accorded a second-class status, were not disposed to acquiesce easily. The predominantly Chinese MCP – fearing a return to an alliance of feudalism and overseas capitalism – started an open revolt and the 'Malayan Emergency' lasted for 12 years.[76] The other Chinese organization, the MCA, an elite organization was formed in 1949. The Indians had formed a MIC in 1946. Thus communalist politics were 'built into' the Malaysian scene in the early post-war period. Independence, when it came in 1957, saw the establishment of a government based upon an UMNO/MCA/MIC Alliance – which had been assiduously fostered by the British. Such attempts at non-communalist political parties as there have been have all failed.

The subsequent history of Malaysia has been to a very significant extent shaped by this communal split: Chinese/Malay in particular. An early 'arrangement' – political power to the Malays and economic power to the Chinese – broke down in 1969 with the race riots in the wake of the election.[77] A new 'arrangement' was insisted upon by the Malays and the NEP was promulgated. The plan has the objective of alleviating poverty and effecting a shift of economic power by quickly advancing the interests of the Malays. The system has many areas of tension built into it – but the Malaysian economic and political system has, paradoxically, a familiar look to it for First Worlders: it has been said that Malaysia has 'democracy by default'.

Singapore was not incorporated into the colonial orbit in the sense in which we can speak of the above three nation-states (as now are) being incorporated. Singapore was, in contrast, constructed from a small part of the 'traditionally held' sphere of the local sultanate. A Sultan of Singapore was installed to legitimize the British control of the island, but the sultanate was discarded by the British once their hold was secure.[78] Bedlington remarks: 'modern Singapore is an artificial creation born out of imperial economic expansion, and down to the present economic affairs dominate political realities.'[79] Singapore was designed to be, and still is to an extent, the 'middle man' for Southeast Asia.

In regard to the rest of Southeast Asia it was, as we have seen, the experience of the Japanese occupation that – in diverse ways – both destroyed the old order and fostered the new. The situation in Singapore was somewhat different. The territory had, even in 1945, a fairly high proportion of migrants: they serviced the manpower needs and so on, of a great trading port. The step from trading port to independent nation-state was not an obvious one. Such pre-war nationalist sentiment as there was would seem to have been either externally focused (India or China) or couched in terms of membership of the surrounding Malay world. In the post-war period both the eventually dominant PAP and the 'populists' looked, in different ways, to some sort of linkage with the wider Malay world. An independent nation-state of Singapore does not seem to have been in anyone's mind during the decolonization period – late 1950s to early 1960s.

During this period the British, who had held on to Singapore for military and 'geo-strategic' reasons, looked around for a group to whom internal self-rule could be devolved. Initially this was the Marshall government and in 1959 PAP – both of whom had looked for scheduling of independence. The politics of this period are labyrinthine in their complexity.[80] In 1961 the idea of a Malaysian Federation was floated, which attracted hostility from radicals in the two countries (or three if northern coastal states of Borneo are also included) and hostility from Indonesia and the Philippines. Formed in 1963, the Federation disintegrated in 1965 and the PAP adopted, perforce, a 'go it alone' strategy. The subsequent character of Singapore has been shaped by the relentless drive for economic security as a base for political security within a (potentially) hostile Malay world. The upshot has been to create an arguably unique 'city state'. The original nationalist aspirations were cast in terms of an ideology of democratic socialism but the polity has subsequently been shaped by the authoritarian nature of the PAP and its preoccupation with security. The current 'official ideology' speaks of multi-culturalism and multi-racialism but, in reality, Singaporean national-ism is a mixture of an oddly sterile Western-style commercialism/consumerism grafted on to heavily discouraged 'traditional' cultures – predominantly Chinese.[81] So much, for the present, for Singapore and the others. To complete these comparative notes I will briefly look at the cases of Thailand and Burma.

In Thailand we have a case of 'internal de-colonization'. Using Pluvier's[82] detailed analysis, we obtain the following picture. In the second half of the nineteenth century there were attempts at 'modernization' orchestrated by the monarchy. The upshot of these reform programmes was the construction of an equivalent to the colonial economies. Says Pluvier: 'they produced the same social and economic problems as in the Western colonies'.[83] Discontent amongst a Western-trained intelligentsia, the bureaucracy and the army produced, in 1932, a coup d'état which established a constitutional regime. This was essentially a conservative and authoritarian regime, marked by internal faction fighting. With the exception of an interlude of democracy in 1973–76, little has changed. Thailand was never a part of any colonial empire and Thai nationalism has emerged without any external object to provide a particular focus. The elite has, typically, 'bent with the wind' so as to avoid being incorporated into any formal sphere: the extent of Thai 'independence' – in particular from the US, we can consider below.

In Burma there was a well developed nationalist movement from 1917 on, according to Pandy.[84] There were various reform initiatives made by the nationalists (who split and resplit throughout the inter-war period), and in 1935 a Government of Burma Act came into force. This granted internal self-rule and thus drew the sting of nationalist pressure – their point had been acknowledged, the rest was a matter of timing. However, there was dispute amongst the nationalists who tended to split into an older conservative grouping and a younger radical grouping. Pluvier comments: 'At the moment when the older politicians were about to achieve their aims, their superiority in political life was disappearing in face of the growing prestige of the younger generation.'[85] The effective phase of nationalism arrived with Aung San (and, a little later, the Japanese). Aung San led the Burmese nationalists – in opposition to the British, then in alliance with the Japanese and, finally, in alliance with the British as the Anti-Fascist Peoples Freedom League – to independ-ence in 1948 – although Aung San was assassinated in July 1947. The movement was both nationalist in tone and 'advocated revolutionary programmes of economic, social and political change'.[86]

So much, then, for the business of the pursuit of independence.[87] Having reviewed the construction of the idea of nation-statehood and looked at nationalism in Southeast Asia, I now turn to the post-independence business of making new nations.

4 Nationalism II

In my introduction above I said that in considering Nationalism II we were faced not with a broad movement in pursuit of the goal of independence but with the efforts of a narrower group, in particular, to secure the establishment of an 'effective nation-statehood'. That group being the inheritors of power from the colonial authorities. Around the (ideal-typical) goals of 'the elite' we can order both their behaviour and the responses of other groups – both internal and external – to the new nation-state in question.[88]

Above we have seen both: (a) how problematical the cultural artefact of nation-statehood is; and (b) how the routes to independence in Southeast Asia were a mixture of complex active political action and fortuitous historical accident both lodged within an historical movement which now we would regard as inevitable (that is, colonial withdrawal in favour of nation-statehood).

Once we obtain some sort of a detached perspective on how the idea of nation-statehood, as a cultural artefact, was fashioned in the West and thereafter 'exported' worldwide, then we can start to look at the dynamics of new nation-statehood in an historical-scholarly fashion rather than collapsing immediately into adopting the familiar planner-technical stance. We can consider the following: (i) the behaviour of the elites of the new nations in the cultural/ideological sphere; (ii) how to interpret conflicts over choices of national languages; (iii) how to interpret ethnic conflict; (iv) the phenomenon of political instability within new nations; (v) the position of new nations within the world economy, which is predominantly capitalist, and their efforts to improve their positions. Other issues could be added to this list.

We can characterize the goal I have imputed to the new elites – the pursuit of 'effective nation-statehood' – under the triune formula of coherence, stability, and progress. I will begin with this 'theoretical' material and then go on to look at the 'history', that is, at what has happened in Southeast Asia since independence.

4.1 The pursuit of 'effective nation-statehood'

It is appropriate to begin with the issue of 'coherence' as the literature on development is suffused with the assumption that development is specifiable in technical terms and achievable via expert guided action:

it celebrates, to oversimplify, the role of the planner. In respect of the business of nation-building 'coherence' is read, most especially within the orthodox line, as the responsibility of the elite. Nation-building, development and politics are collapsed into a single practice – what Habermas[89] calls a 'technocratic politics'. I will pursue a schematic – or ideal-typical – model of this elite ordered pursuit of coherence by citing the argument of A.D. Smith.[90]

An elite can be variously described, for example as a 'modernizing elite' or, contrastingly, as a 'traditional elite'. Within the marxist perspective many new nations would be considered to have 'neo-colonial' ruling elites: Herbert Feith argues this case in respect of Southeast Asia.[91] Elites, however described, can also be taken to compromise various elements and Smith, presenting essentially a modernization approach, speaks of a 'professional intelligentsia'. We are offered a discussion of the role and internal make-up of a modernizing elite. Smith, so far as I can understand him, offers an argument that follows – roughly – Gellner, whom we have discussed above and who was labelled by Orridge a proponent of the view that nationalism was an aid to organizational coherence. Gellner, to continue, is also an advocate of the rule of the modernizing elite. Says Smith: 'Gellner's account of the intelligentsia appears in the context of his broader theory of nationalism . . . his account of the pivotal role of the intelligentsia and their cultural interests has proved both influential and rewarding.'[92]

Smith begins his argument by observing: 'in Africa and Asia today it has become abundantly clear that the apex of . . . the new political order . . . is occupied by the intelligentsia . . .'[93] The rest of the chapter – which develops the argument – invokes the African example *only*. This certainly helps the plausibility of Smith's argument, but unfortunately it needs more help than this. The core of Smith's rehashed Gellner is a two-stage exercise in definition: botched followed by persuasive.

Element number one proceeds thus:

> Indeed, if we define the intelligentsia as the professional strata . . .
> experts of every kind . . . if we treat the intelligentsia as the
> disseminators and appliers of ideas and paradigms created and
> analysed by the much smaller circle of 'intellectuals' . . .[then]. . .
> the intelligentsia are undoubtedly the leading . . . stratum,
> especially if we include the military among the modern
> professionals.[94]

One only need point out that the words 'intelligentsia', 'intellectual', 'military' and 'professional' all have clear – and separate – meanings, established over very many years, to reveal this exercise in definition for the botch that it is. Doubtless all these social fractions do have roles to play in the politics of nation-building but we will not find out what these roles might be if they are all collapsed into one vague grouping. And element number two proceeds thus; Smith, having produced the above piece of obfuscation, goes on to ask: 'How shall we characterize this new political stratum of professional intelligentsia?'[95] This is the *label* – professional intelligentsia – that he then goes on to use, but it is nowhere properly discussed.

The clue to the interpretation of Smith's argument here is probably to be found in his general position. At the outset of the chapter he makes reference to Karl Mannheim as a theorist of the sociology of knowledge and, later, planning, who originated the phrase, indeed theory, of the 'free floating intellectual' able to rise above the realm of competing ideological perspectives and see the world straight.[96] This position has never been taken all that seriously by most social scientists, but it's easy to see how Smith could be attracted to it. It enables him to discuss what is obviously a crucial issue in a way that lets him avoid the harsher truths embodied in labels such as 'organizational bourgeoisie' – a term he considers and rejects. The truth of the matter, which I will pursue in detail in my later discussion of corporatism, is that most new nation-states are arguably neo-colonial and in any case are lodged in a world *capitalist* economy.

It seems to me that Smith's argument is overgeneral at this point. He neglects the *details* of actual cases that might illuminate matters. What detail he does present takes the form of occasional illustrative references. A more serious weakness is his neglect of the international context of new nation-states, and their ruling groups. It is this neglect that lets him set aside marxist analyses – all of which begin, quite correctly, from the claim that the world is, predominantly, a world *capitalist* economy. I think Smith manages to effect a regression to a 'pre-Gellner' situation: where Gellner confronts and dismisses (wrongly in my view) Marx, Smith evades the issue and reaches back to the wholly unsatisfactory approach of Mannheim. The argument, as I noted above, is made *plausible* by the exclusive focus upon Africa. I rather suspect that Smith is offering an unsatisfactory characterization of African political and social reality (a Gellnerish schema of elite plus mass?) and in any case if we present *Asian* examples – India, Burma, Indonesia, Philippines, say, – then the claim that nation-state building is in the hands of the 'professional intelligentsia' is simply absurd.

However, Smith is right to point to the military, the bureaucracy, some professional groups and the commercial-industrial bourgeoisie (locally oriented and agents of trans-national corporations): the political elite, narrowly understood, will be drawn from and lodged within these groups. If we look at these elements in the Southeast Asian context then we do indeed have a part of the story of nation-statehood, though that story can also be told in terms of the general notion of *neo-colonial states*. Thus, for example, Feith[97] claims that the replacement states and replacement elites simply play the same economic role, in the world capitalist system, as did the colonial rulers. This argument – which I will sketch here – is evidently at *least* as plausible as Smith's claims.

The strategy adopted by Feith is one of asking whether or not the notion of 'neo-colonialism' is useful in analysing Southeast Asia. Feith will argue that the term is useful, and he characterizes a neo-colonial situation as one where 'Key elements of the structure of dependency and unequal exchange characteristic of a colonial relationship are maintained or restored after colonial rule has been ended.'[98] The notion entails therefore the idea of continuity – decolonization is, in some significant sense, not a 'real' change at all. It seems evident that if an argument like this can be secured, then the 'pursuit of effective nation-statehood' will have to be treated very differently to any ideal-typical model: the same applies to the business of 'coherence', indeed the 'coherence' of a neo-colonial regime must look distinctly ambiguous.

Feith reports: 'There are six major trends in the ASEAN states since the mid-1960's which seem to have recreated or strengthened economic, social and political structures characteristic of the colonial period'[99] – and these the author proceeds to review. I will follow him, but stress what he has to say about the elites themselves.

The first point centres upon the role of outside sources of capital, which Feith identifies as 'the principal determinant of the direction and pace of change in the period since the mid-60's ... Cheap labour, has been a principal factor of attraction ...'[100]

The second point made involves the 'entrenchment of established classes'[101] after a period of fluidity around the time of decolonization. During the interregnum there was – and here I'm glossing over the differences in detail between various ASEAN states – a process of elite solidification, so to say, as the active elements of the nationalist movements (Feith even calls them 'intelligentsias')[102] become absorbed into a refashioned ruling group. He comments: 'the earlier flexibility and relatively easy vertical mobility have largely disappeared, with party, regional and factional conflict becoming less important and with the established social strata entrenching themselves into a kind of upper class'.[103] Feith goes on to observe that these elite groups look like new ruling classes: that is, power, wealth and prestige are concentrated in hierarchical social systems having little social mobility. The precise internal patterns of the various elite formations vary, as do their links to overseas capital. Feith sees a cultural/political 'dualism' redolent of colonial days with a cosmopolitan elite controlling, paternalistically, peasant and urban masses.

Feith goes on to take note of the 'accelerated destruction of precapitalist social formations'[104] as 'commercialization' spreads. A curious point this, which sits uneasily with his 'dependency' perspective – Bob Cately, for example, argued that all of Southeast Asia has been extensively modified since the late eighteenth century.[105]

Fourthly, we have the business of politics, where it is argued that, as a result of the role of the ASEAN states in the world economy, there has been increasing repression. Thus Feith claims: 'In each of the ASEAN countries except Thailand, government is more restrictive and repressive today than it was in 1965.'[106] And he adds: 'None of these countries has yet reached Brazilian, Iranian or South Korean levels of oppression and totalitarianism, but the trends in that direction are well established, particularly in Indonesia, and to a lesser extent, in Singapore and the Philippines.'[107]

In element five Feith identifies one possible source of progressive change when he speaks of the 'expansion of middle class groupings'.[108] They are a group that benefits from the economic growth of these nations, but who do not have any interest in the political repression that accompanies elite group closure. Feith thinks that in periods of upheaval 'fragments' of the elite, in competition with other 'fragments', might well come to see the middle-class groupings as a source of allies – a constituency to make appeals to. Not only is this of itself interesting but evidently it is a line of enquiry closed to Smith by his approach.

Finally, Feith looks to the masses in Southeast Asia and speculates that so long a they remain effectively excluded from political processes then there will remain the potential for 'mass protest' – of which, he acknowledges, there is little sign.

It is on the base of these six trends that Feith bases his claim to the usefulness of the term neo-colonial, and whilst there are evident weaknesses in the analysis – for example, much of the argument is based on the case of Indonesia, and theoretically, the idea of corporatism is not discussed, rather he rests content (I think) with a simple neo-marxism – he clearly establishes both that Smith's talk about 'professional intelligentsias' is a nonsense and that the pursuit of 'coherence' is both complex (involving many elite fractions in various combinations) and ambiguous (when we ask whose interests are they pursuing).

The positions of Smith and Feith represent sharply divergent stances: the former is a variety of modernization theory, whereas the latter is a variety of marxist theory. The one focuses on the internal mechanics of nation-state building and the other on the conditioning circumstances shaping the behaviour of new elite groups. And from this point we can go on to consider two things. First, as an example, a detailed argument about a Southeast Asian case – this material again both recalls earlier 'historical' notes and anticipates later substantive remarks. Second, a note on the issue of corporatism: this both summarizes the points at issue between proponents of the lines argued by Smith and Feith and introduces an issue that will come up later and which follows my present concerns fairly directly.

In their essay 'National Identity and Nation Building in Singapore', Chan and Evers[109] begin by observing that in new nation-states, created from dismantled colonial territories, the elites confront the problem of building coherent nation-states. They express the problem thus: 'Replacing primordial sentiments with national ones is seen as a means of fostering stability and order.'[110] And, following this observation, the question arises of: 'which political elites make use of a deliberate policy of national identity formation for the purpose of nation-building; and if they make use of such policy, what sort of national identity will they try to create?'[111] They make Westernized elites the prime case: those who inherited power. The authors speak of a 'decolonized colonialism'.[112]

Chan and Evers propose two strategies of identity creation: the regressive, invoking a distinguished national past (and this of course, following Anderson, will be language centered and involve much myth-making); and the progressive, invoking some future-oriented ideology, often 'socialism' in some variant or other. The authors note, quite rightly, that *both* elements are often invoked. Then they turn to consider the case of Singapore and remark that here is a 'third variant'[113] occasioned by external pressure of regional, and relatedly, 'big power', opposition to both any stressed Chinese identity and any political radicalism.[114] The solution,

> lay in an attempt to create a non-ideological identity, or if this seems to be a contradiction in terms, an identity through an 'ideology of pragmatism'. Discussion of basic questions of political philosophy and ideology, even political discussion in general, was severely curbed until it flowed at a low ebb out of public purview. . . .Some of the main tenets and symbols of this 'non ideology of pragmatism and development' became 'HDB flats' . . . the Jurong industrial estate or the 'keep Singapore clean and pollution free' campaign.[115]

The authors are interested in the long-term viability of such 'pragmatism' and they think Singapore is thus a case which illustrates problems of quite general interest in Southeast Asia. Again, rather obviously, we are pushed in the direction of considering the corporatist aspects of Southeast Asian patterns of development.

With the ejection of Singapore from the federation with Malaysia the PAP had to secure a new 'coherence', that is, in Chan and Evers's terms, 'consolidate a new identity – a Singapore identity'.[116] This was done, they argue, in the light of the three factors of geographical context, ethnic composition, and the examples of Israel, Finland and Switzerland. The upshot was the presentation of the basic socio-cultural strategy of multi-racialism and multi-culturalism.[117] To this was added the central theme of modernization: this has entailed both mobilizing the population for *elite set* goals and monitoring the inevitable inflow of Western ideas so as to remove potentially disequilibrating factors. Chan and Evers note: 'The pragmatic solution was to create a double identity: a somewhat subdued cultural identity based on the respective local language and a national identity based on English.'[118] Opposition has come not from political parties – these were destroyed long ago – but from Malays and Chinese-educated Chinese. This dissent was, and is, suppressed. The authors observe that members of ethnic minorities see the national ideology as merely the expression of English-speaking elite views, whilst those with socialist views see a comprador bourgeoisie. The cases of Indonesia and Malaysia are noted and in both cases 'regressive' ideologies of nationalism are diagnosed. Our authors evidently regard the 'Singapore lesson' as thoroughly ambiguous: and surely they are right to do so. They conclude by noting that Singapore is 'the first to implement many of the features that social scientists have espoused as crucial steps in the process of nation-building. Our case study shows clearly what an authoritarian model in pursuit of nation-building in fact implies.'[119]

Returning now, very briefly, to the theoretical issue of corporatism, we can see how the debate surrounding this term does indeed illuminate our present areas of concern. (*sic*)

Gellner has argued that in today's world their are two kinds of politics: the politics of becoming industrialized and the politics of being industrial. He proposes Myrdal and Galbraith as representatives of each. I will link both Myrdal, Galbraith and Gellner as theorists of modernization of a latently authoritarian kind.[120]

Galbraith, in a trio of books published through the 1960s and 1970s – *The Affluent Society* (1958), *The New Industrial State* (1967), and *Economic and The Public Purpose* (1975) – argues that the modern industrial world has seen power become concentrated in the planned sector of the economy: huge corporations closely linked to government, now inhabit a largely planned system. Galbraith finds this distasteful and instead proposes a rational and humane industrialism ordered by the reasonable men in control of the state machine. As an ethico-political judgment upon modern capitalism, this has much to commend it. However, there is little justification for Galbraith's substitution of 'industrialism' for 'capitalism' and the reform package offered centres upon the role of another elite more to Galbraith's taste. In fact, it is an essentially corporatist solution to a problem diagnosed as corporatism!

Myrdal

Such confusions are found in Myrdal. This theorist is similarly confident about the power of the 'reasonable state' and indeed the key to Myrdalian style development is the state. Myrdal is so confident that he actually equates politics with planning. Again, the route to the future is to be mapped in a technical expert fashion by a small elite.

The general position being advanced flows from the overall theory of industrialism – convergence: an explicitly fashioned alternative to Marx-derived theories which spoke of capitalism and socialism. The theorist Gellner operates within this frame and offers a most sophisticated theorem of the 'transition to the modern world'. This is conceived as amenable to social scientific grasp and technical expert ordering. Gellner indeed posits an emergent dual-ideology: broad legitimating slogans for the masses and technical knowledge (natural and social scientific) for the ruling elite.

The general view presented by Gallbraith, Myrdal and Gellner is both familiar and plausible.[121] It resonates with the common sense of Western societies, where recourse to liberal reformist states is long established; and it represents the common sense of development studies with its taken-for-granted focus on planning. However, and here we begin to return to, and understand, the caution displayed by Chan and Evers, this route recourse to planning has been challenged: both by the libertarian right – whom I'll ignore – and by the libertarian left. Thus Jurgen Habermas[122] who has identified the requirement for the politics adequate to the present – just like Gellner, in fact – has become a stern critic of what he calls 'technocratic politics'. In place of the routine celebration of expertise, Habermas looks to the radical democratic tradition and proposes the establishment of routine public discussion of the decisions which have to be made in industrial-type societies. To conclude: the term corporatism is the established political science notion around which issues of political concentration and control plus related societal forms have been discussed in (usually) a critical fashion. I will return to this business later.

To summarize this section thus far we can note that the pursuit of 'coherence' – of a basic national identity – is the first concern of the ruling elites of the new nation-states. That this should be so will be clear in the light of our earlier discussions of the rise of the world nation-state system and of the idea of nation-statehood. The post-Second World War period has seen the third phase of the establishment of nation-states. It is in this period of the dismantling of the mainly European empires that the new nation-states of Southeast Asia came on to the world scene. I want to continue this discussion by turning to the second element of my trio of new nation-state requisites: 'stability'. In this section I will review the varieties of conflict that are to be found in new nation-states and in Southeast Asia.

The business of conflict is often cited by the thoughtful variety of First World commentators as evidence of the general incompetence of Third World governments. The Third World story of independence is often seen as a story of a 'falling away' from liberal democratic grace. In the case of the conservative First World commentators this general view presents itself in the claim that those who opposed decolonization have been vindicated. It should be clear by now that both judgments – general and particular – are fatuous: the history of the rise of 'world nation-statehood' is suffused with violent conflict. The post-Second World War phase of nation-state making in Southeast Asia has proved to be the same: the critics noted above are not helpful, and nor, in my view, is the response of Third World nationalists which dismisses *in toto* critical comment upon their 'track records'. What I will try to do here is review the varieties and some of the substance of the conflicts that have occurred in Southeast Asia in the period since independence. I will begin by drawing the obvious distinction between intra- and inter-state conflicts.

If we begin with intra-state conflicts, we can identify a series of quite typical areas of conflict. Thus the most familiar type is that of 'ordinary political life'. In all the ASEAN countries, albeit with varying degrees of repression, we find public debate about matters of politics. The business of political pluralism has concerned both local elites and local scholars. To simplify, the former have seen potential disequilibrating social institutions and the latter have looked, generally uneasily, on the decline of political pluralism. The extent to which shrugging-off Western models of liberal democracy actually is appropriate, that is, fits the circumstances/culture of the new state in question, versus the extent to which this represents some sort of failure, is a debate I cannot pursue here. Recalling the brief discussion of ethics in chapter 1, this issue is evidently an intriguing one. However, for the moment let us rest content with simply noting that 'ordinary political life' has, generally, continued. We can pursue this rather obvious, but nonetheless useful, reminder into three particular areas: class conflict; communist-relevant conflict; and, finally, military-civilian conflict.

The matter of class conflicts has been of interest to orthodox as well as inevitably to marxist theorists. In respect of the latter group recent years have seen extensive efforts to re-use the notion of the Asiatic mode of production in such a fashion as to acknowledge the internal dynamism of what has been seen by marxists, as well as modernizers, as rather static societies. The internal relations of classes have been further pursued under the impetus of both Althusserian schemes of modes of production and the somewhat contrary, dependency-type analyses which stress political economic analyses. These approaches have replaced 'classic dualism's' vision of a colonial elite facing a 'traditional' mass with a detailed discussion of the extant class elements: subsistence peasantry, cash-cropping peasant farming, plantation farming, mineral working, national small bourgeoisie and internal-linked bourgeoisie, state bureaucracies, trading and financial groups.[123] Another style of enquiry, essentially orthodox, is that of sociologists like Evers[124] who has looked in detail at changes in Southeast Asian societies and asked if recognizably working classes are emerging. This is a somewhat narrower reading of class than that noted above and, in Evers's case, has been associated with the issue of the decline (or not) of ethnic sentiment.

Related, in a way, to the business of class conflict, is the issue of communist opposition to established political regimes in Southeast Asia. This is a thoroughly tangled story, as there has not only been evident communist activity in Southeast Asia but, additionally, the local example of a communist state in the People's Republic of China. The region has, in fact, seen active communist insurgency in Burma, Malaysia, Thailand, Philippines and Indonesia.[125] Added to this the region saw an extraordinarily drawn-out war in Vietnam, which not only issued in a 'communist' victory but also saw the defeat of the USA. Recently the Vietnamese invasion of Pol Pot's Kampuchea has acted to keep the issue of communist influence alive as has the apparent revival of the NPA in the Philippines.

The business of 'military-civilian' conflict is evident both in the Third World generally and in Southeast Asia. Why this should be so in newly established nation-states is not difficult to comprehend. Often the military are one of the most coherently founded institutions of the new states and can quickly come to compare themselves favourably with the sphere of 'ordinary politics' – a zone of, as they would see it, incompetence, ill-discipline and cupidity. Smith[126] discussed the problems that new elites face in securing, in my terms, 'coherence' and 'stability', observed that 'military-bureaucratic' regimes have definite attractions in that they are convenient (all new states have military machines); identified with the new state (where politicians might be communalist); they provide career structures for elite class members (military 'professionalism' conjoined to ruling the state creates many jobs); and often they are relatively 'modern' in that they have links to ex-colonial powers who are now suppliers of hardware and training.[127] Military-bureaucratic regimes also have their drawbacks, of course, and Southeast Asia's premier specimens – Thailand and Indonesia – have not been conspicuously stable or successful.

However, in this matter of 'stability' – or conflict – the most routinely cited source of tension and difficulty has been communal relations between differing ethnic groups. The matter of ethnicity I will not pursue – I will, instead, rest content with a table drawn (largely) from Tinker.[128]

Varieties of ethnic tension in Asia

Country	Majority community	Minorities	Differences
Sri Lanka	Sinhalese	Tamils, Moors, Indians	Religion/ Language
Pakistan	Punjabis	Pathans, Sindhis, Baluchis	L
Afghanistan	Afghans	Baluchis, Persians	L
Iran	Persian-Shias	Baluchis, Kurds, Bahasi	R/L
Bangladesh	Bengali Muslims	Hindus, Buddhists, Animists	R/L
Burma	Burmese	Karens, Shans, Kachins, Chins	L/R
Thailand	Thais	Malays, hill tribes, Chinese	R/L
Kampuchea	Khmers	Vietnamese, Chinese	L
Vietnam	Vietnamese	Chinese, hill tribes	L/R
Indonesia	Javanese-Sumatrans	Chinese, Outer-islanders	L/R
Malaysia	Malay	Chinese, Indians	L/R

Varieties of ethnic tension in Asia Contd

Country	Majority community	Minorities	Differences
Singapore	Chinese	Malays, Indians	L/R
Philippines	Filipinos	Chinese	R/L
India	Indian Hindu (plus language divisions)	Indian Muslim, Sikhs	R/L

(Source: After Tinker)

Clearly this is a very tangled picture. It is probably fair to say that communalism has been endemic in Southeast Asia for very many years and even today constitutes a major source of instability.

I want to turn now from these intra-state conflicts to the matter of inter-state conflicts. In this case some of the problems, as above, are due fairly directly to the colonial era, whilst others are new problems. There is probably a distinction to be drawn here between intrinsic problems (whether or not they were bequeathed by the colonial episode) and adventitious problems (conjured up out of the flow of events): using this distinction it does seem that many of the problems of inter-state tension are of this second type.

The first type of conflict we should note is related to the colonial past and the manner of the establishment of the new nation-states – that is, out of the larger colonial territories. The boundaries of the new nation-states were drawn by the colonial powers and, generally, they do not follow particularly closely 'natural divisions' such as culture or geography. The upshot has been a rash of boundary disputes. Pandy reviews for us: India and Portugal, over Goa; Indonesia and Portugal over East Timor; Indonesia and Holland over Irian Jaya, as it is now. Indonesia also disputed the formation – and thus boundaries – of Malaysia; and the Philippines has disputed with Malaysian sovereignty over parts of Sabah.[129]

A related sort of boundary dispute has been that between new nation-states central authorities and secessionist groups – often ethnic based. Again Pandy offers a review: 'Tamils in Sri Lanka, the Nagas and Mizos in India, the Baluchis and Pathans in Pakistan, the Shans, Kayahs, Karens, Kachins, Chins, Arakanese and Mons in Burma, and the Muslims in the Philippines.'[130]

Boundary disputes and secessionist movements are, we may suppose, inevitable adjuncts to new nation-statehood; they are – to give these problems a wider geographical and historical context – not unknown in Western Europe. Thus the status of Northern Ireland is a matter of violent dispute, likewise the Basque regions of Northern Spain, and the island of Corsica has violent secessionists also. There is language-based tension in Belgium between French and Flemish speakers which in the past has occasioned violent incidents. There are also 'regional' movements – demanding more powers or even independence: in the UK there is nationalism, in France and Italy regionalism.

Turning from the arguably inevitable to the probably adventitious, we confront the business of inter-state wars. War has been a recourse of nation-states since their earliest formation and whilst the pursuit of national advantage via war (between equals) was probably made impossible in August 1945 – with Hiroshima and Nagasaki – for First World nations, it remains an option, albeit in altered circumstances, for Third World nations. Asia has seen several such wars. India and Pakistan have fought no less than three wars. China has invaded the border areas of India and Vietnam – and has fought a series of skirmishes with the USSR, occasionally severe. Vietnam has launched a complete invasion of a neighbour – Kampuchea. Indonesia also launched an odd sort of war against Malaysia.[131]

Finally, to complete this matter of conflict we have to take note of outside interventions by the 'big powers'. It is in Southeast Asia that the post-Second World War period's most extensive, prolonged and unsuccessful outside intervention was made: the Vietnam war. This episode represents, arguably, the defeat of US containment[132] in Asia. Prior to this the US – with assistance – fought to establish an anti-communist regime in South Korea; armed and backed Taiwan; and formed a network of regional alliance including SEATO. The business of outside intervention is one that bedevils Third World nation-states. Living next door to a 'big power' is evidently potentially rather dangerous – witness, presently, the cases of Afghanistan and Central America – but it must also be noted that 'lower level' adventures are quite familiar. The Russians, the Americans and to a much lesser extent the Europeans dabble world wide. Southeast Asia is presently fortunate, it would seem, in being a zone of low interference.

So much for the pursuit of 'stability'. These first two elements of my triune schema – coherence and stability represented, arguably, the key problems which faced the elites of the new nation-states as they achieved, in their various ways, 'independence'. The stress that I have placed on these two aspects follows on from the extensive discussion of nation-statehood presented above. However, to these concerns for coherence and stability must be added a concern for development – for the material advancement of their populations. We saw in chapter 1 that the idea of development could be interpreted – at an ethico-political level – in several ways but, nonetheless, some broad material advance is implied: the legitimacy of the new nation-states depends, amongst other things, upon successful industrialization. It is enough to note here that insofar as 'development success' is an integral element of the pursuit of 'effective nation-statehood' then, whilst there have been no dramatic breakdowns it is equally true that the record of achievement in Southeast Asia remains deeply ambiguous.

Looking at the three elements together – coherence, stability and development – we can offer some very general comparative comments on the new nation-states of Southeast Asia. I will do this in the following section.

4.2 Southeast Asian nation-statehood – how effective?

The material in this section concludes my look at what I have labelled 'Nationalism II': immediately above I was concerned with an ideal-typical model of the elite-ordered pursuit of 'effective nation-statehood'. Here I want to ask just how successful this pursuit has been. This is evidently a question of great complexity – it should be clearly understood that what follows here is very simplified: here we are concerned with summary judgments. Such judgments are a necessary part of social scientific work: they act to bring into some sort of unified perspective the difficult and extensive material which social scientists deal with. These summary judgments are, if you like, intellectual 'gestalts' – they encompass conception, intent, and 'data' in one simple statement, and thus help keep enquiry coherent.

The first type of summary judgment I want to take note of is the rather pessimistic 'falling away from liberal-democratic norms' position. This is found in the review article by Tinker[133] and in Pandy's history. Tinker's argument is a double one: the familiar 'falling away' position is present in a submerged form. It is submerged with a broader argument which asserts that nation-statehood *per se* is an anachronism. Tinker looks to a United Nations supra-nationalism and regards the nation-state as less than satisfactory in general and of little relevance to Southeast Asia. He comments:

> In Asia, the nationstate continues to be the largest unit that the mind of the ordinary man can conceptualize. He does not really identify with it. It does not do anything for him, and he is not prepared to do anything for it . . . . The nationstate served a genuine purpose in Europe in the shift from traditional society to modernity. In Asia, it proved to be an invaluable instrument in

getting rid of Western colonialism. It still has an important
function in affording membership of the United Nations, the one
real hope of a supranational tomorrow. It does little or nothing to
help Asians solve their most immediate problem: that of
institutionalizing the relations of communities and groups, whom
geography has made neighbours but who possess no real feeling of
a common identity.[134]

This strikes me, it must be said, as perverse in its pessimism. A more
familiar style of the 'falling away' argument is to be found in Pandy.
As I have referred to his work on several occasions I will not do so
here. It is, however, useful to note that the style of judgment offered is
fairly widespread. In the post-Second World War period very many
nationalists, commentators, development agency personnel and
scholars had high expectations of the new nation-states. In retrospect
the optimism was, I think, misplaced, but their disappointment is
certainly real.

With the historians we have nominalist summary judgments: the
aim here is, so far as it is possible, to let the detailed facts speak for
themselves. However, historians, like every other variety of social
scientist, use theories and make judgments. The collection of essays
edited by Jeffrey, to which I have referred above, adopts the strategy
of applying labels to the various nation-states considered. These
labels are relatively undeveloped, summary judgments.

Thus in the case of the Philippines the essayist[135] speaks of
'independence without decolonization' which is a neat way of
grasping the continuing role of the USA in the Philippines economy,
society and culture, and drawing attention to the continuing
inegalitarian and underdeveloped economy. This is a judgment that
most commentators would echo. There would probably be more
dispute about the second label: here the essayist[136] characterizes
Indonesia in term of 'revolution without socialism'. That there was a
revolution of sorts, rather than simply an anti-colonial War, we can
grant. However, 'without socialism' part of the label is unhelpful. Not
only do revolutions not have to be socialist but we are not told what
did happen in Indonesia. The proximate answer is military-
bureaucratic rule. The third label[137] characterizes Malaysia as having
a 'new state and old elites' and again this would command widespread
support amongst commentators – even if it does not go very far.
Focusing on Malaysian communalism generates that label 'democracy by default'. Continuing in a similar vein we could label
Singapore an 'authoritarian city state'; Thailand, a 'bureaucratic-
patrimonial state' and, finally, Burma a 'stagnating military dictatorship'. We need not pursue these historians' judgments too far. It is
enough to note that they attempt to grasp the totalities of the

experiences of the new nation-states rather than judging in somewhat narrowly liberal democratic terms.

A more critical position is taken up by Girling[138] who focuses upon the nature of the state in Southeast Asia: he takes the state to be the key political actor (in contrast to liberal democrats and orthodox marxists) and he pursues the idea of 'bureaucratic-polities'. Girling claims that it is state bureaucracies in alliance with armies and business that, typically, rule in Southeast Asia. These styles of rule have their own particular histories, internal dynamics and 'ceilings' on chances of achieving development. Girling affirms a liberal-democratic model by arguing that the future of Southeast Asian 'bureaucratic polities' will need to see internal political liberalization and a broad commitment to development (which is presently absent).

Thailand and Indonesia are taken as prime examples of 'bureaucratic polities'. In each nation-state political life has disappeared inside the state machine (where this is a particular mix of state bureaucracy, army and security forces, and local business elites). Neither Thailand nor Indonesia offers much hope for progressive reform in the near future. Girling comments 'whether directly (as in the Thai cycle of coups), or indirectly, the result of military domination is the same: the exercise of arbitrary and excessive power, which is unaccountable to any higher authority and therefore unresponsive to the interests and needs of others, including the majority of the population.'[139] He adds that the problem, isn't diagnosis or prescription but how to bring about change.

The Philippines, Malaysia and Singapore are then discussed as variations on this basic theme. Girling speaks of the Philippines as 'transitional' – between what points is not clear.[140] Malaysia is analysed, as we might expect, in terms of the ethnic divide of Malay and Chinese. Impulses towards 'bureaucratic-polity' are identifiable within the Malay community but are thwarted by the communal divide. Again – democracy by default. Finally, Singapore is discussed in terms of the dominance of the PAP. Distinguishing, rather implausible, between authoritative and authoritarian rule, he goes on to cite Chan Heng Chee and the idea of 'de-politicization'.

I think Girling's effort is most interesting: it leads us towards the idea of corporatism and his characterizations are plausible. However, he stops short of considering the external context of nation-statehood. The Southeast Asian nation-states – excepting those of Indo-China – are firmly locked into place within the world capitalist economy. This brings me to the last of my series of characterizations of Southeast Asian nation-states: the view that they are dependent or neo-colonial. I have looked at Feith's argument above.[141] Here I will offer a note of another strategy – and there are many debates internal to the marxist tradition – presented by Berberoglu,[142] who focuses upon internal sets of class relations within peripheral capitalist regions. Against the world-system theorists the internal class forces are emphasized.

Three types of peripheral states are identified. 'These are: (1) neo-colonial dependent states; (2) national, state capitalist states; and (3) socialist states. The first of these is further divided into two sub-types: (a) comprador-capitalist and (b) semi-feudal/semi capital-ist.'[143] It is the first type that is the most familiar: they are characterized by the key role of the 'comprador bourgeoisie' in linking/integrating local economies with the world system. An earlier form of neo-colonial dependency is indicated by sub-type 2 where the continuing role of 'feudal' elements is acknowledged. The second type – national, state capital – is characterized as effecting a protected bourgeois revolution under the rhetoric of socialism. And the third type – socialist – involves the displacement of the 'feudal bourgeois' state and the constitution of a 'proletarian state'. Berberoglu offers a summary diagram – from which I have extracted the Asian cases.

State-forms in South-east Asia

Neo-colonial		National state capitalist	Socialist
Comprador-capitalist	Semi-feudal/ semi-capitalist		
South Korea	Pakistan	India	North Korea
Taiwan	Bangladesh		China
Philippines	Sri Lanka		Vietnam
Singapore*			Burma* ← (?)
Indonesia*			
Malaysia*			
Thailand*			

* my additions.

(Source: After Berberoglu)

What the table reveals is the clear judgment that all the ASEAN countries are neo-colonial comprador-capitalist. Superficial success – as witnessed in GNP data – disguises an underlying set of contradictions. This strategy of national development facilitates the transformation of the local economy into an appendage of the world capitalist system . . . the expansion of foreign capital into the local economy . . . has increasingly become a threat to the survival of national and petty bourgeois elements, giving rise to nationalist sentiments among them. But, more fundamentally . . . has more decisively given rise to the growth in size of an increasingly militant working class.[144]

In sum: what we have looked at in this section is the nature of the nationalist elite in pursuit of 'effective nation-statehood'. The discussion has presented the triune model of their concerns – for coherence, stability and development – and offered a review of a range of 'summary judgments' that have been made on their performance since independence. These 'summary judgments' enable us to place the recent examples of Southeast Asian nation-statehood within the broad history of the rise and spread of nation-statehood itself. In this way my treatment of 'Nationalism II' follows on from the material 'Nationalism I'.

However, to conclude, two things are clear, notwithstanding the benefits to our understanding of the internal dynamics of the new nation-states afforded by this analysis: firstly, the presentation of 'summary judgments' is no substitute for the detailed analyses of development in Southeast Asia; and, secondly, a review of other people's judgments is no substitute for offering one's own. I hope to be able to remedy both defects in a subsequent text.

Notes

Introduction

1 P.W. Preston (1985), *New Trends in Development Theory*.
2 H–D Evers (ed) (1980), *Sociology of Southeast Asia: Readings on Social Change and development*.
3 See Preston (1985).
4 See R.J. Anderson, J.A. Hughes and W.W. Sharrock (1985), *The Sociology Game*, who speak of 'metaphysical pictures' where I speak of 'general theories'.

Chapter 1   Rethinking development

1 My own focus will be restricted primarily to First World material and thereafter to Third World work. I will not discuss the endeavours of Second World thinkers.
2 I think that this claim would command fairly wide assent. My own intellectual route into these matters has been occasioned by a remark of Gellner's, in his *Thought and Change* (1964), to the effect that recent attempts to theorize development *both* recall the efforts of the 'founding fathers' of social science *and* demonstrate that sociology (as he understands it) is now the heir to classical political philosophy. I have pursued this theme in P.W. Preston (1985), *New Trends in Development Theory : Essays in development and social theory*. See also: Elbaki Hermassi (1980), *The Third World Reassessed*; C.A.O. Van Nieuwenhuijze (1982), *Development Begins at Home*.
3 For more extensive discussion of the themes presented here see P.W. Preston (1982), *Theories of Development*; and P.W. Preston (1985), *New Trends in Development Theory*.
4 Various dates for the 'start' of development studies (in its modern guise) could be proposed: in 1940 the UK passed the Colonial Development Act; 1941 saw the Atlantic Charter; 1945 saw the end of the war and the start of the shaping of the post-war world; or 1951 which saw the UN report of Lewis et al. Thus we have a period of anywhere between 32 and 43 years. I call this development studies in 'modern' guise because we could, fairly easily, trace debate back into the inter-war period, to the turn of the century and into the late nineteenth century.

5 Preston (1982).
6 See B. Fay (1975), *Social Theory and Political Practice*.
7 See Aidan Foster-Carter (1979), 'Marxism versus Dependency? A Polemic'.
8 United Nations (1951), *Measures for the Economic Development of Under-developed Countries*.
9 As regards the marxists, the analogous move is clear: in much recent marxian work there has been great concern to identify the core of a properly marxian analysis of development and underdevelopment.
10 I roughly follow the 'humanist marxian line'. For an interesting general review see Anthony Giddens (1979), *Central Problems in Social Theory*, essay 7.
11 Equally there is no reason to suppose that we cannot order this diversity: see P.W. Preston (1985), chapter 2.
12 This idea can be traced back to C. Wright Mills and Alvin Gouldner – subsequently the idea is broadened in the process of the rediscovery of the humanist tradition.
13 Z. Bauman (1979), *Towards a Critical Sociology*.
14 This is Giddens's term, see Giddens (1979), essay 2.
15 Now, of course, the 'naturalist-descriptive' theorists are not the wholly passive creatures I have indicated. The orthodox social scientists make sense (characterize structures) that feeds into structuration (making sense) via the policy-makers who base their 'rational decision-making' upon, *inter alia*, social scientific knowledge conceived thus. At this general sociology of sociology level, the major objection to the orthodox is that they deny their ideological role and mode of (political) engagement and, as an irritating and absurd corollary, urge that all enquiry that is 'social scientific' should either be forced into their mould or dismissed as pseudo-scientific.

    To add a general note to this: I centre my own work on the *process* of social theorizing, in contrast to: (a) the orthodox who look for theory grounded in facts; or (b) the philosophically rationalistic who look to securely base enquiry in formal theory (for myself philosophy enters social theory's agenda as a 'matter arising'); or (c) those, of various political persuasions, who centre their work upon a narrow practicality.
16 I will pursue this idea of ideology in my own fashion. I am aware that the term has been much discussed in the social scientific literature but I do not here wish to become embroiled in these debates. It will be quite clear that I am using the term in a way that relates quite directly to the humanist marxist, Frankfurt School, approach.
17 If social theorizing is diverse then theorists will be 'aiming at different targets': when commenting upon their work it seems to me that we have to begin by judging the work on its own terms and then those of the discipline: this is the narrowly academic, or technical, business of criticism. Thereafter we can go on to evaluate, according to our own criteria, the work as a whole. Technical criticism thus gives way to (political) critique.

18 See R. Bernstein (1976), *The Restructuring of Social and Political Theory*, p.114:

> Once the limiting perspective of mainstream social science has been challenged . . . new questions and problems emerge. These cluster about the interpretation and understanding of political and social reality. . . . Looming in the background is the central question of how one can rationally adjudicate among competing and conflicting interpretations.

19 Giddens (1979).
20 The obvious question to ask is how must *Third World* scholars proceed? I cannot give an answer: the creative assimilation/reworking of the intellectual legacies of 'the West' to the problems and circumstances of the 'non-Western' has – in the area of development studies work – only been accomplished once. And if that sounds pessimistic, the example I have in mind is Latin American dependency theory and no one would doubt the quality of this contribution.
21 Roy Harrod (1939), 'An Essay in Dynamic Theory', *Economic Journal*, March.
22 See H. Brookfield (1975), *Interdependent Development*, or Kevin P. Clements (1980), 'From Right to Left in Development Theory'.
23 Fay (1975).
24 *Ibid.*, p.10.
25 Brookfield (1975), p.29.
26 United Nations (1951).
27 W.A. Lewis (1955), *The Theory of Economic Growth*.
28 K. Kurihara (1968), 'The Dynamic Impact of History on Keynesian Theory', pp. 137–8.
29 See Preston (1982).
30 David Caute (1978), *The Great Fear: the Anti-Communist Purges Under Truman and Eisenhower*, p.22.
31 Dudley Seers (1963), 'The Limitations of the Special Case' in *Oxford Bulletin of Statistics*. Picking up this business of typologies, see P.W. Preston (1985), *Making Sense of Development*, where I speak of 'orthodox I and II' plus 'marxist'. The 'orthodox II' I label 'dissenting-economics' and they would include a swathe of essentially orthodox theorists who nonetheless move sharply away from neo-classicism: Veblen, Myrdal, Galbraith, Keynes, Kalecki, Robinson and the like.
32 See Preston (1982).
33 Gunner Myrdal (1970), *The Challenge of World Poverty*, p.21.
34 For a good review see P.J. O'Brien (1975), 'A Critique of Latin American Theories of Dependency' in I. Oxaal (ed.) *Beyond The Sociology of Development* (London, Routledge and Kegan Paul).
35 N. Girvan (1973), 'The Development of Dependency Economics in the Caribbean and Latin America: review and comparison' in *Social and Economic Studies vol. 22*.
36 Distinguishing elements of a thinkers work in terms of 'early' and 'late'

is a somewhat crude device: in Furtado's case the publications of 1965 and 1969 probably represent his shift from essentially orthodox to a radical thinker influenced by Marx. Whether you want to call the 'late' Furtado Marxist or not probably depends on how you retrospectively reconstruct the revival of Marxian analysis! Palma would both claim dependency as marxist and set Furtado aside as reformist!

37 See Preston (1982).
38 See, for example, B.N. Pandey (1980), *South and South-East Asia 1945–1979: Problems and Policies*.
39 C.Furtado (1965), *Diagnosis of the Brazilian Crisis*.
40 See Preston (1982).
41 See R. Sutcliffe (1973), 'Introduction' to Paul Baran, *The Political Economy of Growth* (Harmonsworth, Pelican).
42 R. Brenner (1977), 'The Origins of Capitalist Development'.
43 G. Palma (1978), 'Dependency: a formal theory of underdevelopment or a methodology for the analysis of concrete situations of underdevelopment'.
44 See Terrel Carver (1975), *Karl Marx: Texts on Method*, and F.H. Cardoso and E. Faletto (1979), *Dependency and Development in Latin America*.
45 Cardoso and Faletto (1979), p. xi.
46 Palma (1978), p.911.
47 A. Hoogvelt (1982), *The Third World in Global Development*.
48 Paul Streeton (1981), *Development Perspectives*, pp. 332–3.
49 See Aidan Foster-Carter (1979).
50 See Streeten (1981).
51 F. Clairmonte (1960), *Economic Liberalism and Underdevelopment*.
52 See Jurgen Habermas (1971), *Towards a Rational Society*.
53 One of the claims that I have been advancing in this essay is that 'development studies' now stands ready to rejoin the social scientific 'mainstream'. Here is one more, obvious, illustration: 'rationalization' of the world was a key concern of Max Weber.
54 Habermas (1971).
55 The idea of 'inertia' is built into his scheme of 'circular cumulative causation'.
56 V. Allen (1975), *Social Analysis: A Marxist Critique and Alternative*.
57 It can also be noted that there was considerable optimism in the neo-marxian line – it was *activist* in tone. I think this optimism has declined.
58 Brookfield (1975), pp. 76–7.
59 Streeten (1981), pp. 61–2.
60 Ernest Gellner (1964), *Thought and Change*.
61 B. Davidson (1978), *Africa in Modern History*.
62 By 'post-neo-marxism' I have in mind the debates which have flowed from critical discussion of the work of Baran, Frank and Wallerstein. I think Cardoso and Faletto's stress on illuminating concrete situations via political economic enquiry – where Marx is the exemplar – is correct.
63 One issue that I have not thus far satisfactorily presented, let alone

resolved, is that of the precise role of 'general theories' in social theorizing. It seems as though I must regard them as 'preliminary cashings of moral stances' – they make sense of the world in a practical fashion. Moreover, they achieve their task in this form – subsequently we can posit two stages of revision: an initial 'polishing process', which sees the removal of gross errors, provision of examples, etc; and then the business of being taken up into elaborate academic discourse. This last step seems to me to be secondary and often misconceived in the light of the 'received model' – thus 'preliminary cashings' are misunderstood as research project outlines.

Chapter 2   The rediscovery of the rationalist tradition

1 There are few exceptions to this so far as I can see: some issues have exercised development theorists, for example the anthropologists' debates on rationality surrounding Winch, and it is true that some development theorists have tackled philosophical material, for example Paul Streeten, but these are exceptions rather than the rule.
2 P.W. Preston (1982), *Theories of Development.*
3 P.W. Preston (1985), *New Trends in Development Theory.*
4 E. Gellner (1964), *Thought and Change.*
5 This claim reveals my own orientation to these debates both in the approval of this process of supersession, and in the location of my reading of this material within the realm of English language theorizing. My treatment also focuses upon the ideas advanced themselves and the historical and sociological occasions for the presentation of these ideas are not treated.
6 These debates begin with the Enlightenment and culminate, for sociology, in Compte's positive philosophy.
7 See A. Giddens (1979), *Central Problems in Social Theory*, essay 7.
8 See A.J. Ayer (1936), *Language Truth and Logic.*
9 For a review of the varieties of 'positivism' see C. Bryant (1985), *Positivism in Social Theory.*
10 Otto Neurath (1944), *Foundations of the Social Sciences.*
11 Ernest Nagel (1961), *The Structures of Science.*
12 B. Russell (1927), *An Outline of Philosophy*, p. 1.
13 Nagel (1961), p. 13.
14 Criticisms of Nagel that would begin with a flat rejection of his strategy – hermeneutics and critical theory – I will pursue not here but later. What I want to do is to present the material as a dialogue.
15 See A. Giddens (1976), *New Rules of Sociological Method*
16 See G. Hawthorn (1976), *Enlightenment and Despair* or M. Hollis (1977), *Models of Man.*
17 For a fuller review of the philosophy of science, see R.J. Anderson *et al.* (1986), *Philosophy and the Human Sciences*, ch. 10.
18 Robert Merton (1968), *Social Theory and Social Structure.*
19 C. Wright Mills (1959), *The Sociological Imagination.*
20 There is a fourth element – a metaphysics – but this is thoroughly odd

and apparently not much liked even by Popper's admirers, so I will omit any treatment of it.

21 J. Passmore (1970), *The Perfectibility of Man*.
22 See Habermas below: technocratic consciousness impinging on the life world to such an extent that progress in moral (communicative) sphere is overshadowed or even blocked.
23 Compare with Gellner's anti-democratic theory in *Thought and Change*, discussed in Preston (1985).
24 See T. McCarthy (1978), *The Critical Theory of Jurgen Habermas*.
25 See Passmore (1970).
26 M. Green (1966), *The Knower and the Known*, London, Faber.
27 Compare with Kuhn's paradigms and normal science.
28 A. Tudor (1982), *Beyond Empiricism*, p.144.
29 Greene (1966).
30 C.B. Macpherson (1973), for example, *Democratic Theory: Essays in Retrieval*.
31 See Preston (1985).
32 Giddens (1979).
33 Brian Fay (1975), *Social Theory and Political Practice*.
34 In the realm of development theory this habit of 'arguing on behalf of the planners' is utterly pervasive: see essay 5 below and A.F. Robertson (1980), *People and the State: An Anthropology of Planned Development*.
35 See also M. Hollis and E.J. Nell (1975), *Rational Economic Man*, who argue that orthodox neo-classical economics rest on a positivist epistemology which, if denied, leaves neo-classicism bereft of value: Hollis and Nell urge a rationalist classical (or political economic) approach to matters economic.
36 R. Bernstein (1976), *The Restructuring of Social and Political Thought*, p.114.
37 For a recent 'synthetic' defence of empiricism see Tudor (1982).
38 Edmund Husserl (1970), *The Crisis of European Sciences and Transcendental Phenomenology*.
39 See Z. Bauman (1976), *Towards a Critical Sociology*, pp.49–51.
40 For a discussion of Heidegger see Mary Warnock (1970), *Existentialism*.
41 *Ibid.*, pp.44–5 and ch.3.
42 Bernstein (1976), p.140.
43 An interesting application of this notion to development issues is to be found in a book edited by G. Wood, who looks at the distribution of knowledge, as a resource, in peasant societies and in development projects involving rural life.
44 Bernstein (1976), p.135.
45 A further extension of this review could be made by discussing ethnomethodology. The approach derives from a phenomenological critique of Talcot Parsons and, with Harold Garfinkel, insists that an empirical sociology must attend to the real world detail of the manufacture of meanings – of the life-world – and that sociological method must be determined by this orientation. However, the material

produced is arcane in the extreme in its 'pure' form and of no very obvious relevance to development theory work. For reviews see: P. Filmer (ed.) (1972), *New Directions in Sociological Theory* which is a 'soft' ethnomethodology; and Wes Sharrock and Bob Anderson (1986), *The Ethnomethodologists* for an 'austere' version. References to original texts can be found therein. See also Z. Bauman (1978), *Hermeneutics and Social Science*, ch.8, for a sympathetic critique of the phenomenological project as a whole.

46 For a discussion of logical atomism see Geoffrey Warnock (1969), *English Philosophy Since 1900*, ch.3.

47 The notion of 'analysis' was a key for this group of philosophers: it was understood as the means whereby the language of common sense could be broken down into its component parts. Problems were to be analysed out so as to display/dissolve them.

48 This notion of the task of philosophy goes back to John Locke.

49 Peter Winch (1958), *The Idea of a Social Science and Its Relation to Philosophy*, p.15.

50 *Ibid.*, p.41.

51 *Ibid.*, p.42.

52 *Ibid.*, p.52.

53 *Ibid.*, p.72.

54 See Giddens (1976).

55 Winch (1958), p.122.

56 *Ibid.*, p.123.

57 *Ibid.*, p.178.

58 Bernstein (1976), pp.67–74.

59 Giddens (1976), pp.44–53.

60 *Ibid.*, p.53.

61 *Ibid.*

62 See David Bloor (1983), *Wittgenstein: A Social Theory of Knowledge* for a sympathetic extension of his work. See also E. Gellner (1979), *Words and Things* for a hostile treatment.

63 A. MacIntyre (1962), 'A mistake about causality in social science' in P. Laslett and W.G. Runciman (eds), *Philosophy, Politics and Society*, Series 2. See also A. MacIntyre (1971), 'The idea of a social science' in his *Against The Self Images of the Age*.

64 MacIntyre (1962), p.52.

65 *Ibid.*, p.58.

66 *Ibid.*

67 *Ibid.*

68 *Ibid.*, p.60.

69 *Ibid.*

70 *Ibid.*, p.63.

71 *Ibid.*, p.69.

72 C. Taylor (1967), 'Neutrality in Political Science' in P. Laslett and W.G. Runciman (eds), *Philosophy, Politics and Society*, Third Series.

73 A. MacIntyre 'Is a science of comparative politics possible?' in MacIntyre (1971).

74 *Ibid.*, p.276.

75 *Ibid.*, p.278.

76 See W. Outhwaite (1975), *Understanding Social Life: The Method called Verstehen.*

77 See Bauman (1978).

78 *Ibid.*

79 C. Taylor (1971–2), 'Interpretation and the Sciences of Man', *Review of Metaphysics*, vol. 25.

80 *Ibid.*, p.45.

81 Bauman (1978), p.17.

82 A recently influential figure in hermeneutics has been H.G. Gadamer: see his *Truth and Method* (1975) and *Philosophical Hermeneutics* (1976).

83 Fay (1975).

84 Martin Jay (1973), *The Dialectical Imagination.*

85 See Phil Slater (1977), *The Origins and Significance of the Frankfurt School.* Slater argues that this detachment proved fatal to the theoretical and practical project enunciated, which quickly became irrelevant to the pursuit of social change.

86 Jay (1973), p.61.

87 See Goran Therborn (1970), 'The Frankfurt School' in *New Left Review*, vol.63 for their reaction to National Socialism. Also Slater (1977), pp.15–25.

88 See Jay (1977), p.51 et seq.

89 See D. Held (1980), *Introduction to Critical Theory: Horkheimer to Habermas*, ch.14.

90 It must be noted that what follows is very much my own version of Habermas, whose work is thoroughly difficult and not easy to present in any simple fashion. When I am relying on any particular commentator this is specified.

91 The incoherence flows from positivism's commitment to science and their view of values as irrational. Thus their own commitment to science (reason) is rationally indefensible.

92 See J. Habermas (1971), *Knowledge and Human Interests*, appendix.

93 McCarthy (1978), ch 2.2.

94 *Ibid.*, p.74.

95 On this notion of democracy see Macpherson (1966).

96 See McCarthy (1978), J.B. Thompson and D. Held (eds) (1982), *Habermas:Critical Debates*; R.J. Bernstein (ed.) (1985), *Habermas and Modernity.*

97 See Held (1980), ch.13.

98 A. MacIntyre (1970), *Marcuse.*

99 *Times Higher Education Supplement*, 22.6.84.

100 Giddens (1979), pp.238–40.

101 See Joe Bailey (1980), *Ideas and Intervention.*

102 Myrdal advances this argument as an autobiographical report on his response to the 1930s depression.

103 Giddens (1979), p.239.

104 See for example Frank Parkin.

105 This of course must be the doubt that attaches to Habermas's fully expressed project.
106 See Preston (1985).
107 Gellner (1964).
108 Giddens (1979), ch 7.
109 Preston (1985).
110 See MacIntyre (1971), 'The end of the end of ideology'.
111 See Hollis and Nell (1975).
112 See R. Higgot and R. Robison (eds) (1985), *Southeast Asia: Essays in the Political Economy of Change.*
113 See M. Friedman (1953), *Essays in Positive Economics.*
114 See Preston (1982) on Latin American dependency theory as, in one guise, interpretive-populist.
115 See M. Blomstrom and B. Heltne (1984), *Development Theory in Transition* for an attempt to recover indigenous interpretations of dependent positions for the dependency tradition generally.
116 See T. Assad (ed.), *Anthropology and the Colonial Encounter* (1973).
117 J.C. Scott (1971), 'Protest and Profanation: Revolt and the Little Tradition', *Theory and Society*, vol.4.
118 P. Worsley (1984), *The Three Worlds,*
119 C. Thorne (1986), *The Far Eastern War.*
120 B. Anderson (1983), *Imagined Communities.*
121 Preston (1982).
122 See S. Lukes (1977), *Essays in Social Theory.*
123 See H.C. Chan and H.D. Evers in P. Chen and H.D. Evers (eds) (1978), *Studies in ASEAN Sociology*, who argue that Singapore's record can be seen as modernization theory 'put into practice'. Also the labels used as chapter headings in R. Jeffrey (ed.) (1981), *Asia – the Winning of Independence.*
124 Preston (1982).
125 G. Challiand (1977), *Revolution in the Third World.*
126 P.W. Preston (1983), 'A critique of some elements of the residual common sense of development studies', *Cultures et Développement*, vol.XV, no.3.

Chapter 3 Boeke and Furnivall's 'Southeast Asian sociology'

1 This phrase I take from Evers below. See also M. Blomstrom and Bjorne Heltne (1984), *Development Theory in Transition* for a survey style discussion of the issue I raise here. On Asia (ch.6) they say dissapointingly little.
2 H. Brookfield (1975), *Interdependent Development.*
3 To pursue this, briefly see: Brookfield (1975); Meir (1970); Girvan (1973).
4 See P.W. Preston (1985), *New Trends in Development Theory*, essay 6.
5 Evers (ed.) (1980), *Sociology of South-East Asia: Readings on Social Change and Development*, p.ix.
6 *Ibid.*

7 *Ibid.*, p.2.
8 *Ibid.*
9 *Ibid.*
10 *Ibid.*
11 *Ibid.*, p.6.
12 *Ibid.*
13 *Ibid.*
14 I will focus on Boeke and Furnivall as these are the two key figures. Embree, on Evers's exegesis, is a marginal figure and Geertz, with his 'agricultural involution', offers yet another dualistic scheme which I'll set aside for ease of presentation.
15 Thus Yamada argues that Boeke's 'social system or style' is a reworking of Sombart's Wirtschaftssystem. Yamada, however, is not all that impressed and finds Boeke's usage of social system/dualism/ etc. imprecise and unclearly derived: indeed he speaks of 'the tragic shadows of two great men – Werner Sombart and Max Weber – cast upon a small man' (Evers (ed.) (1980), p.60).

   Sombart himself – dates 1863–1941 – was an economist and sociologist and was, roughly speaking, a contemporary of Max Weber. Sombart also seems to have adopted a similarly scholarship-based critical stance towards the German status quo and the capitalist system he found around him. For a review of his work see Arthur Mitzman (1973), *Sociology and Estrangement*, Part III.
16 J.H. Boeke (1953), *Economics and Economic Policy of Dual Societies*, p.3.
17 *Ibid.*
18 *Ibid.*, p.4 (his emphasis).
19 *Ibid.* Compare also with the notion of articulation of modes of production – Boeke is obviously groping towards such an idea, even if his particular role would block his achievement of such a scheme.
20 Cf. Myrdal and the influence of T. Veblen and G. Cassel.
21 H. Yamada in Evers (ed.) (1980).
22 Boeke (1953), pp.4–5.
23 *Ibid.*, p.8.
24 *Ibid.*, p.11.
25 *Ibid.*
26 *Ibid.*
27 *Ibid.*, p.12.
28 *Ibid.*, p.15.
29 *Ibid.*, p.20.
30 *Ibid.*
31 The goal of Boeke we'll return to below, when we ask if Evers is sensible in invoking a colonial administrator-scholar as a key element of Southeast Asian theory of development.
32 Myrdal is an obvious figure to associate with Boeke: in approach and background if not mechanisms and results.
33 See, for example, Hamish McDonald (1980), *Suharto's Indonesia*, which begins with Suharto's Javanese mystical beliefs. Or, again, the vulgar Weberian work of Brian May (1981), *The Third World Calamity* –

earlier work focused on Indonesia – who remarks that the pursuit of development is hopeless due to 'superstition' (p.2) and 'impenetrable psycho-cultural barriers' (p.2).

34 J.S. Furnivall (1939), *Netherlands India: A Study of a Plural Economy*, p.xv.

35 *Ibid.*, pp xv–xvi.

36 *Ibid.*, p.446.

37 *Ibid.*

38 *Ibid.*, p.447.

39 *Ibid.*

40 *Ibid.*, p.449.

41 *Ibid.*

42 Furnivall expresses this as a focus upon production (how to secure goods) not consumption (which goods and why) – the idea he has of a self-degrading market place, unrestrained by shared social values.

43 At one point (pp.452–7) Furnivall picks up the claim, associated with Boeke, that the 'natives' are not economically motivated. Furnivall disagrees: he points to positive evidence for economic motivation (in Burma) and says that in Netherlands India the Dutch have suppressed economic activity; which is not the same as saying it's not there. Again, Furnivall is offering a *different* analysis: where Boeke speaks of two forms of life, essentially traditional/modern, each with their own economic force (the one vigorous and mostly imported, the other local, weak and set aside for a religious approach to life), Furnivall speaks of one economic impulse working, but in contexts of different societies/ cultures. The final 'surface image' is the same – dualism/pluralism – but the route to the diagnosis is very different and so – as will be made clear – are the prescriptions.

44 Furnivall (1939), p.459.

45 *Ibid.*, p.462.

46 *Ibid.*, p.463.

47 *Ibid.*

48 *Ibid.*

49 *Ibid.*

50 *Ibid.*

51 *Ibid.*, p.464.

52 *Ibid.*, p.465.

53 *Ibid.*, p.467.

54 *Ibid.*, p.468.

55 *Ibid.*

56 *Ibid.*

57 *Ibid.*

58 Brookfield (1975), p.54.

59 *Ibid.*, p.57.

60 Evers (ed.) (1980), p.6.

61 See above, section 1, introduction.

62 There is another argument we could advance here. It revolves around the claims of Boeke and Furnivall (and implicit in Evers) in respect of

the *unusualness* of Southeast Asia. Both seem to claim it as an atypical case of a general phenomenon: so, again, *just how unusual* is it? If the unusualness of the diversity of Southeast Asia is a key element in the claim to status of the concepts fashioned to interpret it, then we surely need to know *how* unusual: and the only way to answer this 'how question' is by offering comparisons – between 'east' and 'west' or, in their terms, between homogeneous and dual or plural societies. But is Southeast Asia any different to *any other colonial territory*? The answer must be no: even Boeke and Furnivall would go far to agreeing with this.

In Evers's hands, and in the hands of his chosen essayist, diversity-occasioned-by-colonial-status is transformed into a 'naturally occurring' and novel diversity – a matter of passive ethnographic facts, which facts are then taken as a part of the base for the argument to a novel Southeast Asian contribution to social science. It won't do.

63 H. Yamada in Evers (ed.) (1980), p.64.
64 *Ibid.*
65 One could argue that those who fail to see that Boeke and Furnivall are offering coherent argued cases – 'package deals' – actually degrade those whom they would otherwise celebrate with their naive borrowings.

Chapter 4 Arguing on behalf of scholarship: Barrington Moore

1 See P.W. Preston (1986), *Making Sense of Development*.
2 See G. Hawthorn (1976), *Enlightenment and Despair* and A.D. Smith (1973), *The Concept of Social Change*.
3 See A.D. Smith (1976), *Social Change: Social Theory and Historical Processes*.
4 I take the phrase from A. Flew (1975), *Thinking about Thinking*.
5 Dennis Smith (1983), *Barrington Moore: Violence, Morality and Political Change*, p.6.
6 *Ibid.*, p.7. See also P.W. Preston (1982), *Theories of Development* for a note on development theory's 'intelligent modernizers'.
7 C. Wright Mills (1959), *The Sociological Imagination*, p.28.
8 Barrington Moore (1950), *Soviet Politics – The Dilemma of Power: The Role of Ideas in Social Change*; (1954), *Terror and Progress USSR: Some Sources of Change and Stability in the Soviet Dictatorship*; (1958), *Political Power and Social Theory*; (1972), *Reflections on the Causes of Human Misery and on Certain Proposals to Eliminate Them*; (1978), *Injustice: The Social Bases of Obedience and Revolt*.
9 Smith (1983), p.vii.
10 Cf. *ibid.*, p.43.
11 Barrington Moore (1967), *The Social Origins of Dictatorships and Democracy*, p.3 (The numbers in the text are mine.)
12 See Preston (1986), for a discussion of Gellner.
13 Moore (1967), p.ix.
14 *Ibid.*, p.xii.

15 *Ibid.*, pp.xii–xiii.
16 See Preston (1986).
17 Moore (1967), p.230.
18 *Ibid.*, p.234.
19 *Ibid.*
20 *Ibid.*
21 *Ibid.*, p.245.
22 *Ibid.*, pp.247–8.
23 *Ibid.*, p.249.
24 *Ibid.*, p.250.
25 *Ibid.*, p.xiii.
26 *Ibid.*
27 See, for example, Clark Kerr *et al.* (1960), *Industrialism and Industrial Man*, or, P.W. Preston (1985), *New Trends in Development Theory* on Galbraith, Gellner and Myrdal.
28 Evidently he could not ask his actors, so he is imputing motives: he should tell us how.
29 Compare this with, say, The history of E.P. Thompson or C. Hill.
30 Compare with Celso Furtado – he does a similar thing in some of his earlier work.
31 See Preston (1982).

Chapter 5 Arguing on behalf of 'the planners': Chen, Fisk and Higgins

1 This is a phrase taken from Norman O. Brown's (1959), *Life Against Death* and it is to the psychoanalytic/neo-marxist tradition of the Frankfurt School that my own thoughts on these matters trace back.
2 See P.W. Preston (1982), *Theories of Development* for a discussion of Myrdal.
3 See P.W. Preston (1985), *New Trends in Development Theory*.
4 Peter Chen (1983), 'Singapore Development Strategies: a model for rapid growth' in Chen (ed.), *Singapore Development Policies and Trends*.
5 E.K. Fisk (1982), 'Development in Malaysia' in E.K. Fisk and H. Osman-Rani (eds), *The Political Economy of Malaysia*.
6 Benjamin Higgins (1982), 'Development Planning' in Fisk and Osman-Rani (eds).
7 The aim of this critique of Chen, and those of Fisk and Higgins, is to display the structure of the argument and consider its use of the ideas of planning: these are not exercises in complaining or simple political disagreement.
8 Chan Heng Chee (1976), 'The Political System and Political Change' in Riaz Hassan (ed.), *Singapore: Society in Transition* and Noleen Heyzer (1983), 'International Production and Social Change: An analysis of the state, Employment and Trade Unions in Singapore' in Chen (ed.).
9 Chen (1983), p.4.
10 *Ibid.*
11 *Ibid.*

12 *Ibid.*
13 *Ibid.*
14 *Ibid.*, p.5.
15 Many have seen this as very problematic: see Chan and Heyzer below.
16 Chen (1983), p.12.
17 *Ibid.*, p.13.
18 Chan (1976), p.45.
19 Chen (1983), p.18.
20 *Ibid.*, p.20.
21 *Ibid.*, p.22.
22 *Ibid.*
23 *Ibid.* pp.22–3.
24 *Ibid.*
25 *Ibid.*
26 Chan (1976), p.35.
27 *Ibid.*, p.36. Indeed after the 1985 election which saw the PAP's share of the vote fall sharply senior ministers, following Lee's lead, began talking of altering the electoral system so as to 'protect Singapore' from an irresponsible electorate and irresponsible opposition figures! (See *Far Eastern Economic Review*, 10/1/85).
28 *Ibid.*, pp.38–9.
29 *Ibid.*, p.43.
30 *Ibid.*, p.45.
31 *Ibid.*
32 *Ibid.*, p.47.
33 *Ibid.*, p.48.
34 Chen (1983), p.24.
35 Chan (1976), p.49.
37 *Ibid.*
37 Heyzer (1983), p.105.
38 *Ibid.*, p.113.
39 *Ibid.*, p.116.
40 *Ibid.*
41 *Ibid.*, p.120.
42 *Ibid.*, p.121.
43 *Ibid.*, p.122.
44 *Ibid.*, pp.125–6.
45 Fisk (1982), p.1.
46 *Ibid.*, p.2.
47 *Ibid.*, p.4.
48 *Ibid.*, p.5.
49 *Ibid.*, p.7.
50 See Preston (1982).
51 Fisk (1982), p.8.
52 *Ibid.*, p.10.
53 *Ibid.*, p.14.
54 See *Far Eastern Economic Review*, January to August 1984 – discussing Singapore's Malays, Bindranwale, Sri Lanka and so on. Or *FEER*, 2/1/

86, discussing religion and politics in Malaysia (pp.24–5) following the 'Memali incident' of 19/11/85 (see *FEER* 5/12/85).
55 Fisk (1982), pp.15–16.
56 *Ibid.*, p.18.
57 *Ibid.*, p.19.
58 *Ibid.*
59 *Ibid.*
60 *Ibid.*
61 *Ibid.*, p.23
62 Higgins (1982), p.148.
63 *Ibid.*, p.152.
64 *Ibid.*, p.155.
65 *Ibid.*
66 *Ibid.*, p.156.
67 *Ibid.*, p.157.
68 *Ibid.*, p.164.
69 *Ibid.*, p.164–5.
70 Higgins adds that all these problems became compounded at the implementation stage. Here the 'real problems' (p.166) emerged!.
71 Higgins (1982), p.168.
72 *Ibid.*
73 For a brief discussion see Harold Brookfield (1975), *Interdependent Development*, ch.4.
74 Higgins (1982), pp.169–70.
75 *Ibid.*
76 *Ibid.*, p.174.
77 *Ibid.*, p.179.
78 *Ibid.*, p.180.
79 *Ibid.*, p.180.
80 *Ibid.*, p.182.
81 *Ibid.*, p.183.

Chapter 6   A.G. Frank: the mode of engagement of the 'political writer'

1 P.W. Preston (1982), *Theories of Development*; (1985), *New Trends in Development Theory:Essays in Development and Social Theory*; (1986), *Making Sense of Development*. In these texts I have usually labelled Frank as a pamphleteer. In this essay I prefer the term 'political writer'.
2 See Preston (1985).
3 R. Kilminster (1979), *Praxis and Method*.
4 See R. Williams (ed.) (1974), *George Orwell: a collection of critical essays*; S. Hynes (ed.) (1971), *Twentieth Century Interpretations of 1984*; R. Williams (1979), *Politics and Letters*; B. Crick (1980), *George Orwell*.
5 I hope to pursue this issue of social theoretic engagement in a later text.
6 See Preston (1985).
7 D. Booth (1974), 'Andre Gunder Frank: An Introduction and Appreciation' in I. Oxaal *et al.* (eds), *Beyond the Sociology of Development*.

8 D. Caute (1978), *The Great Fear: The Anti-Communist Purges under Truman and Eisenhower.*

9 At this point I had thought to further underline my claims about the existence of various modes of social theoretic engagement by citing a couple of further examples: the mode of engagement of the planner and arguing on behalf of the proletariat-in-general – but these are discussed elsewhere in this text so readers may consult them there.

10 N. Chomsky (1982), *Towards a New Cold War*, p.69. All the material cited here is from these essays plus one article from the *New Statesman*, 'The Shadow of the Great Satan', 29/7/83.

11 John Wain, 'George Orwell as a Writer of Polemic' in R. Williams (ed.) (1974).

12 *Ibid.*, p.89.

13 *Ibid.*

14 In Crick (1980), p.15.

15 *Ibid.*, p.26.

16 *Ibid.*

17 *Ibid.*

18 *Ibid.*, p.19.

19 R. Williams (1979), p.385.

20 *Ibid.*, p.388.

21 *Ibid.*, p.389.

22 Isaac Deutscher, '1984 – The Mysticism of Cruelty' in Hynes (ed.) (1971), p.29.

23 E.P. Thompson, 'Inside *which* Whale' in R. Williams (ed.) (1974), p.82.

24 Wain in Williams (1974), p.93.

25 Julie Burchill, 'A Tory Trauma', *New Society*, 18/10/85, p.114.

26 Deutscher in Hynes (1971), pp.36–7.

27 G. Orwell (1937), *The Road to Wigan Pier*, p.152.

28 *Ibid.*, p.156.

29 *Ibid.*, pp.159–60.

30 *Ibid.*, p.184.

31 *Ibid.*, p.190.

32 Germaine Greer, 'The Nanny of the Nation', *New Society*, 16/10/85.

33 *Ibid.*, p.235.

34 Preston (1982).

35 Private communication.

36 For further comment see my review in *Cultures et Développement* forthcoming.

37 See *ibid.*

38 See Preston (1986), *Making Sense of Development.*

39 For a brief autobiographical note see A.G. Frank (1976), *Economic Genocide in Chile.*

40 See Booth (1974).

41 A.G. Frank (1975), *On Capitalist Underdevelopment*, p.96.

42 A.G. Frank (1967), *Capitalism and Underdevelopment in Latin America*, p.3.

43 For an interestingly direct attempt to utilize this notion of

disengagement as a prerequisite to development see Bob Catley on Vietnam in his essay 'The Development of Underdevelopment in South East Asia' in Hans Dieter Evers (ed.) (1980), *Sociology of South East Asia*.

44 At which point I must confess that it occurs to me that I have never come across an historian commenting on Frank's work.

45 A.G. Frank (1969), *Latin America: Underdevelopment of Revolution*, p.ix.

46 *Ibid.*, p.x.

47 *Ibid.*, p.3.

48 *Ibid.*

49 *Ibid.*

50 *Ibid.*

51 *Ibid.*

52 *Ibid.*

53 *Ibid.*

54 *Ibid.*

55 *Ibid.*, p.5.

56 A.G. Frank (1972), *Lumpenbourgeoisie – Lumpendevelopment*, p.4.

57 *Ibid.*

58 *Ibid.*

59 *Ibid.*, pp.7–8.

60 *Ibid.*, p.140.

61 J.K. Galbraith (1958), *The Affluent Society*.

62 See Preston (1982) (1985).

63 *Ibid.*

64 A.G. Frank (1984), *Critique and Anti-Critique*, p.251.

65 *Ibid.*

66 *Ibid.*

67 *Ibid.*, p.252.

68 Ernesto Laclau (1971), 'Feudalism and Capitalism in Latin America', *New Left Review*, vol.67, p.22.

69 Robert Brenner (1977), 'The Origins of Capitalist Development: A critique of neo-Smithian Marxism', *New Left Review*, vol.104.

70 *Ibid.*, p.28.

71 C. Leys (1977), 'Underdevelopment and Dependency: Critical Notes *Journal of Contemporary Asia*, vol.7.

72 *Ibid.*, p.93

73 *Ibid.*

74 G. Palma (1978), 'Dependency: a formal theory of underdevelopment or a methodology for the analysis of concrete situations of underdevelopment', *World Development*, vol.6.

75 See Preston (1986), *Making Sense of Development*.

76 A.G. Frank (1978), *Dependent Accumulation and Underdevelopment*, p.xiii.

77 *Ibid.*, p.1–2.

78 *Ibid.*

79 *Ibid.*

80 *Ibid.*

81 See Preston (1985).

Chapter 7 Analysing dependent capitalist development: the Asian NICs

1 The responses of the orthodox to the effect that supply side economics have revalidated neo-classical stress on growth and been vindicated by the performance of the NICs are not treated here. The recent fashion for supply side neo-classicism is politically rather than intellectually driven and does not help us understand the NICs.

   In respect of the radical tradition we must note that there is now a diverse series of modes of enquiry and commentators relate them variously. Thus Palma (1978) subsumes the positions from ECLA through A.G. Frank to Cardoso and Faletto's political economy within the marxist tradition. Higgot and Robison (1985) distinguish marxist, dependency and modernization. For my part I prefer to speak of discrete efforts of theorizing and thus tend to speak of Latin American dependency theory, neo-marxism (including Frank and Baran) and post-neo-marxism. It is from within this last noted area that this essay is written and when I speak of marxism I will generally have in mind the debates of this area – neo-marxism and Latin American dependency I thus tend to separate out as related (often closely, but sometimes hardly at all) positions.

2 Clive Hamilton (1983), 'Capitalist Industrialization in East Asia's Four Little Tigers'.

3 Running down A.G. Frank has become something of a routine amongst development theorists in recent years. However, in direct defence of his work (rather than my 'formal' defence via 'roles'), one could say that with the recent surge of the 'New Right' Frank's position has been amply vindicated as the radical view of the Third World's situation evidently has not been fixed in place in public consciousness in the West. Again compare Frank with the polemical work of Chomsky.

4 See the review by A. Brewer (1980), *Marxist Theories of Imperialism: A Critical Survey*, ch.7.

5 The question 'why not?' can be answered variously by pointing to particular social, economic or political factors that can then be characterized as unsatisfactory in some way or other.

6 See the editors' 'Introduction' to R. Higgot and R. Robison (eds), (1985), *Southeast Asia: Essays in the Political Economy of Structual Change*.

7 M. Bienefeld (1980), 'Dependency in the Eighties', *Bulletin of the Institute of Development Studies*; 'Dependency and the Newly Industrializing Countries' in D. Seers (ed.) (1981), *Dependency Theory: A Critical Reassessment*. See also the editors' 'Introduction' in M. Bienefeld and M. Godfrey (eds) (1982), *The Struggle for Development: National Strategies in an International Context*.

8 See the chapter 5, 'Arguing on behalf of 'the planners':Chen, Fisk and Higgins'.

9 Aidan Foster-Carter (1985), 'Development Theory Revived: Friedrich List Lives!', *Inside Asia*, vol.5, pp.33–4.

10 See, for example, Benjamin Higgins, 'Dualism and dependency in

Southeast Asian Development' in G.P. Means (ed.) (1976), *Development and Underdevelopment in South East Asia*.

11 I think we can speak of delimited-formal ideologies in this general fashion but with several provisos: (i) identification is retrospective by commentators looking at the work and milieux of others; (ii) those identified as involved would, if they were modernizers, reject the strategy of interpretation I am using; (iii) those involved would have contributed unevenly and irregularly; (iv) the delimited-formal position is not a monolithically fixed or closed set of ideas but rather the interpreters' construct – a snap-shot of a 'debate in progress'; (v) the supersession of one delimited-formal position by another is likely to be long drawn out and rest on complex intra-disciplinary and group responses to real world changes. One can also note that this view is to be contrasted to the orthodox discussions about theory where better/worse will tend to be cast in terms not of process theories of truth but instead correspondence theories. The former position encourages a stress on clarity of formulation whilst the latter encourages the pursuit of finally definitive statements (again reiterative versus cumulative images of social science).

12 See P.W. Preston (1985), *New Trends in Development Theory: Essays in Development and Social Theory*, especially the debate between Girvan and Cumper.

13 *Ibid.*

14 See my discussion of Streeten in P.W. Preston (1982), *Theories of Development*.

15 Preston (1985).

16 A. Giddens (1979), *Central Problems in Social Theory*, especially ch.7.

17 See E. Hobsbawm's 'Introduction' to Karl Marx (1964), *Pre-Capitalist Economic Formations*.

18 See P.W. Preston (1986), *Making Sense of Development*.

19 Hamilton (1974).

20 See Preston (1986).

21 Bienefeld (1981).

22 *Ibid.*, p.7.

23 *Ibid.*

24 *Ibid.*, p.8.

25 Compare this with the strategy of Lim Chong Yah, 'Southeast Asia: Challenges of Economic Independence' in E.P. Wolfers (ed.), (1976), *Australia's Northern Neighbours*, pp.22–3. Or, John Wong (1979), *The Asean Economies in Perspective*.

26 Bienefeld (1981), p.86.

27 G. Lamb, 'Rapid Capitalist Development Models: A New Politics of Dependence' in D. Seers (ed.) (1981).

28 Bienefeld and Godfrey (1982), pp.1,7.

29 Foster-Carter (1985).

30 *Ibid.*, p.34.

31 *Ibid.*

32 P. Limqueco (1983), 'Contradictions of development in Asean', *Journal of Contemporary Asia*, vol.13, p.283.

33 *Ibid.*

34 *Ibid.*, p.288.

35 Again this has to be disaggregated: Philippines, Indonesia, Malaysia may have debts, the Philippines acute ones. Singapore, in contrast, has large reserves.

36 Limqueco (1983), p.297.

37 Hamilton (1974).

38 *Ibid.*, p.35.

39 *Ibid.*

40 *Ibid.*, p.36.

41 *Ibid.*

42 *Ibid.*

43 *Ibid.*, p.38.

44 *Ibid.*, p.40.

45 *Ibid.*, p.42.

46 *Ibid.*, p.43.

47 *Ibid.*, p.47.

48 *Ibid.*

49 *Ibid.*

50 Chan Heng Chee and Hans Dieter Evers, 'National Identity and Nation Building in Singapore' in P. Chen and H.D. Evers (eds) (1978), *Studies in ASEAN Sociology*.

51 Preston (1985).

52 J. Halliday (1977), 'Recession, Revolution and Metropolis Periphery Relations in East Asia With Special Reference to Japan', *Journal of Contemporary Asia*, vol.7.

53 J. Halliday (1980), 'Capitalism and Socialism in East Asia', p.3.

54 *Ibid.*, pp.4–5.

55 *Ibid.*, p.5.

56 *Ibid.*, p.11.

57 *Ibid.*, p.12.

58 *Ibid.*, p.13.

59 *Ibid.*

60 *Ibid.*, p.22.

61 *Ibid.*, p.23.

62 Philip Bowring (1985) 'Export-led Slowdown', *Far Eastern Economic Review*, 26 Sep, pp.99–100.

63 *Ibid.*, p.99.

64 See especially W. Ziemann and M. Lanzendorfer, 'The State in Peripheral Societies' in R. Milliband and J. Saville (eds) (1977), *The Socialist Register*.

65 H. Feith, 'South East Asian Neo-Colonialism' in Wolfers (ed.) (1976).

66 This is routine element of the orthodox position: see *Far Eastern Economic Review* for Fairly routine pieces claiming to spot liberalization amongst the authoritarian regimes of capitalist Asia.

67 There is a wealth of good class analysis available in, amongst other

places, the *Journal of Contemporary Asia*: however, most of it seems to deal not with the NICs but instead treats Malaysia, Philippines, Thailand, and Indonesia. See also Preston (1986), *Making Sense of Development*.

68 For a review see Leo Panitch (1980), 'Recent Theorizations of Corporatism: reflections on a growth industry', *British Journal of Sociology*, vol.13. See also J.L.S. Girling (1981), 'The Bureaucratic Polity in Modernizing Societies', *Institute of South East Asian Studies Occasional Paper* no.64.

69 See, for example, James Petras (1980), 'Neo-Fascism:Capital Accumulation and Class Struggle in the Third World', *Journal of Contemporary Asia*, vol.10.

70 See Chan Heng Chee, 'The Political System and Political Change' in Riaz Hassan (ed.) (1976), *Singapore: Society in Transition*.

Chapter 8 Constructing nation-states in Southeast Asia

1 Debate on matters of what we would now call development goes back a long time: thus in the early nineteenth century there was an extensive scholarly debate about the deleterious effects of the vast expansion of opium poppy cultivation upon established Bengal life as the British began running opium into Canton. See Brian Inglis (1976), *The Opium War*. This is additional to discussion about 'development' in the eighteenth and nineteenth centuries 'new nations'.

2 I stress this element of novelty because it is often said, quite correctly, by historians that treating 1945 as some sort of 'new beginning' is an error. Indeed for much of what now is called 'development studies' 1945 was a 'new beginning'.

3 Ernest Gellner (1964), *Thought and Change*.

4 Leonard Tivey (ed.) (1981), *The Nation State*, see Tivey's 'Introduction'.

5 The business of theory and exemplary practice is a somewhat confused tale here. The ideas of nation-statehood originated, so far as I am aware, in the work of the Scottish and French Enlightenments – broad 'schools' of rationalist thought who first presented many of the ideas current in present Western political discourse. These ideas crossed the Atlantic to be picked up and, so to say, put into practice by the North American rebellion and the later Latin American wars of independence. These events offered models, so too did the French Revolution, to add to the ideas. The resultant 'cultural package' was then used widely – spreading out from Western Europe.

6 We must distinguish: (a) the pursuit of nation-statehood; and (b) the business of withdrawal from empire. Generally (a) has come out of (b): but not in what's usually taken as paradigm case of nation-statehood, i.e. W. Europe. The paradigm case contributed (via Enlightenment) to the first but acutally came after: and then established its pre-eminence. So, curiously, the paradigm case follows after the prototype. So we have, in fact two issues here: and it's as well to keep them separate. In

this text, given my focus on Southeast Asian nation-states, I'll speak of 'withdrawal from empire' as precursor of achievement of nation-statehood: in my perspective then, the Western European paradigm becomes oddly atypical!

7 A.W. Orridge, 'Varieties of Nationalism' in L. Tivey (ed.) (1981), pp.39–40.

8 See *Far Eastern Economic Review*, 26 January, 1984.

9 Tivey (1981), p.3.

10 Hugh Seton-Watson (1977), *Nations and Nation States*, p.1.

11 Benedict Anderson (1983), *Imagined Communities*, p.14.

12 Seton-Watson makes geography the key. Of the Americas he remarks:

> There communities were bound to separate themselves from 'the metropolis' in Europe. The fundamental cause was simply geographical . . . it was impossible in the long term that men living thousands of miles . . . [away] . . . could take decisions on the colonist's behalf. Geographic distance was in fact responsible for the many conflicts of economic interest . . . and for the political controversies which broke out when doctrines first formulated in Europe were transplanted overseas (p.196).

I find this an over-statement of the role by one factor. Geographical determinism seems an implausible position to adopt.

13 In Latin America and North America those born in the colonies of parents from the colonies only ever were accorded a 'second class social status' from the citizens born in the metropolitan country. The 'colonials' were looked down on – and this aided the crystallization of their ideas of being separate and a community. In Spanish America, for example, this division gave 'creoles' and 'peninsulares'.

14 Seton-Watson (1977), p.199.

15 *Ibid.*, p.12 et seq.

16 This excludes Brazil in particular – it gained independence from Portugal relatively easily in 1822. Also excluded are a few smaller possessions of Britain, France and Holland.

17 Seton-Watson (1977), p.202.

18 See Anderson (1983), ch.4.

19 See *ibid.*

20 Thus UK and France – the paradigms of nation-states in the orthodox view – contained (each of them) a variety of disparate groupings and in the case of UK these groupings actually were separate nations. The geographical area of Scandinavia saw three nations emerge: North-West Europe produced three. German-speakers today are to be found in five nation-states in Europe. In this process the ideas of Enlightenment and the French Revolution were available, so too were the models provided by the new American Republics.

21 See Gavin Kitching (1982), *Development and Underdevelopment in Historical Perspective*, for an interesting discussion of early populism and the present institutionalized versions of it.

22 See C.B. Macpherson (1966), *The Real World of Democracy* for an

optimistic account of the political creeds of new nations.

23 B.N. Pandy (1980), *South and Southeast Asia 1945–1979: Problems and Policies*.
24 For a comparative sketch see J.M. Pluvier (1977), *South-East Asia from Colonialism to Independence*, pp. 3–21.
25 See Milton Osborne (1979), *South East Asia*.
26 Pandy (1980), pp.37–9.
27 Angus Maddison (1971), *Class Structures and Economic Growth*.
28 Salman Rushdie (1981), *Midnights Children*; (1982), *Shame*.
29 Ignacy Sachs (1976), *The Discovery of the Third World*, p.120.
30 See Pandy (1980), pp.56–61.
31 See Raymond Williams (1976), *Keywords*.
32 Tivey (1981), p.1.
33 *Ibid.*, p.3.
34 *Ibid.*
35 *Ibid.*, pp.5–6.
36 Smith, (1983), *State and Nation in the Third World* offers another way of speaking of nation-statehood. In a text which makes great play with the sub-Saharan African experience and which stresses repeatedly the issues of ethnicity and colonial territorial boundaries, Smith looks to nation-statehood as a matter of scale. Group membership runs from lineage group, to larger ethnic group, to nation. And even, with Pan-Africanism, to a supra-national community. Smith then goes on to look at problems occasioned by the pressure of 'ethnic nationalism' upon 'territorial nationalism'. Again we see the conflict that surrounds nation-statehood. See Smith, ch.4.
37 Orridge, in Tivey (1981), pp.40–41.
38 Smith (1983), p.2.
39 In doing so I am following the suggestion of Orridge.
40 Tom Nairn (1977), *The Breakup of Britain*, p.329.
41 *Ibid.*, p.339.
42 *Ibid.*, pp.339–40
43 *Ibid.*, p.359.
44 See *ibid.*, pp.342 et seq.
45 For a discussion of Gellner see P.W. Preston (1985), *New Trends in Development Theory*.
46 See Gellner (1964), p.160 et seq.
47 *Ibid.*, p.166.
48 *Ibid.*, p.168.
49 Nairn (1977), p.342.
50 Anderson (1983), pp.13–14.
51 Gellner (1964), p.169, cited in Anderson (1983), p.15; Anderson's emphasis.
52 Anderson (1983), p.16.
53 *Ibid.*, p.47.
54 *Ibid.*
55 *Ibid.*
56 The matter of changes in perceptions of time is another issue that

Anderson treats. Put simply what he says is that around the period of the Renaissance there was a very significant shift – from the experience of essentially time-less status to the now familiar progress-into-the-future.

57 For an interesting critique of orthodox political philosophical discussions of the state see A. Skillen (1977), *Ruling Illusions: Philosophy and the Social Order*.

58 Anderson (1983), p.13.

59 Smith (1983).

60 Anderson (1983), p.123.

61 *Ibid.*, p.105.

62 The following material is based on the work of: J.M. Pluvier, B.N. Pandy, M. Osborne, R. Jeffrey (ed.), S. Bedlington, H. Grimal, and others.

63 A.W. McCoy, 'The Philippines Independence without Decolonization' in R. Jeffrey (ed.) (1981), *Asia: The Winning the Independence*.

64 *Ibid.*, pp.28–42.

65 Pluvier (1977), p.305–11, 382–6.

66 Cory Aquino faces immense problems and her survival in power must be in doubt. Successful reform-from-above is one possibility but as likely are the chances of either military rule or political fragmentation.

67 A. Reid, 'Indonesia: Revolution without Socialism' in R. Jeffrey (ed.) (1981), p.129.

68 We should also note that the very name 'Indonesia' was a European coining. Anthony Reid (in R. Jeffrey (ed.) (1981), p.114) reports that the name was invented by European ethnologists in the late nineteenth century and the *idea* of 'Indonesia' is twentieth century – see Reid, and Anderson (1983), p.19. n.4.

69 Reid in Jeffrey (1981), p.131.

70 *Ibid.*, p.134.

71 *Ibid.*, pp.154–5.

72 S.S. Bedlington (1978), *Malaysia and Singapore: The building of new nation states*, p.37.

73 *Ibid.*

74 *Ibid.*, pp.61–5.

75 Lee Kam Hing, 'New state, old elites' in R. Jeffrey (ed.) (1981), p.227.

76 See Pluvier (1977), pp.467–75.

77 See Leon Comber (1983), *13 May 1969*.

78 See Pang Keng Fong (1984), 'The Malay Royals', *Academic Exercise Department of Sociology, National University of Singapore*.

79 Bedlington (1978), p.210.

80 For the detail see T.J.S. George, *Lee Kuan Yew's Singapore* (1973).

81 See G. Benjamin, 'The Cultural Logic of Singapore's Multiracialism' in Riaz Hassan (ed.) *Singapore: Society in Transition* (1976). See also: Chua Beng Huat, 'Re-opening ideological discussion in Singapore: A new theoretical direction' in *Southeast Asian Journal of Social Science* vol.11 (1983); John Clammer, 'Modernization and cultural values: the

paradoxes of transition in Singapore' in R.E. Vente et al., (eds) *Cultural Heritage versus Technological Development* (1981).

82 Pluvier *op cit.* pp.90–91.
83 *Ibid.* p.90.
84 Pandy *op cit* p.14.
85 Pluvier *op cit* p.125.
86 *Ibid.*
87 By way of an 'instant-autocritique' one could ask whether or not this last section has actually tackled the issue raised: I asked about the nationalist movements in Southeast Asia – and having discussed the idea of nation-statehood as a cultural artefact (Anderson) – a set of ideas to interpret and move people to action in the world; I have gone on to tackle nationalist movements in (generally) an orthodox external-descriptive fashion. Reports on how they achieved success – rather than interpretive studies of how they saw/interpreted things. I think this is a failing but there are two points to offer in my defence: (a) such interpretations would come best from a nationalist; (b) the above approach lets me approach the matter quickly and in a familiar fashion.
88 And by order I mean just that – organise enquiry. Given the pervasive habit of adopting a planners-view current in development studies we should beware of supposing this is the obvious, or natural or only stance to take on the matter. Doing so involves, necessarily, regarding 'social problems' as problems-from-the-point-of-view--of-the-planners. A bad habit – typical of Singapore.
89 Jurgen Habermas (1971), *Towards a Rational Society*, essays 4, 5 and 6.
90 Smith (1983).
91 H. Feith, 'South-East Asia and Neo-Colonialism' in E.P. Wolfers (ed.) (1976), *Australia's Northern Neighbours*.
92 Smith (1983), pp.80–1.
93 *Ibid.*, p.81.
94 *Ibid.*, pp.81–2.
95 *Ibid.*, p.83.
96 See Peter Hamilton (1974), *Knowledge and Social Structure*, ch.8.
97 Feith in Wolfers (1976).
98 *Ibid.*, p.29.
99 *Ibid.*, p.30.
100 *Ibid.*, p.31.
101 *Ibid.*, p.34.
102 *Ibid.*
103 *Ibid.*
104 *Ibid.*, p.36.
105 See Bob Catley, 'The Development of Underdevelopment in South-East Asia', *Journal of Contemporary Asia*, 6/1/1976 reprinted in H.D. Evers (ed.) (1980), *Sociology of South-East Asia*.
106 Feith in Wolfers (1976), p.37.
107 *Ibid.*
108 *Ibid.*, p.39.

109 Chan Heng-Chee and Hans-Dieter Evers, 'National Identity and Nation Building in Singapore' in P. Chen and H.D. Evers (eds) (1978), *Studies in ASEAN Sociology.*

110 *Ibid.*, p.118.

111 *Ibid.*

112 *Ibid.*

113 *Ibid.*, p.119.

114 Singapore had to *avoid* presenting itself as a 'Third China'.

115 Chan and Evers in Chen and Evers (1978), p.119. See also Chan Heng Chee and Noleen Heyzer – discussed in chapter 5 above. See also note 81.

116 *Ibid.*, p.122.

117 See G. Benjamin, 'The Cultural Logic of Singapore's Multiracialism' in Riaz Hassan (ed.) (1976), *Singapore: Society in Transition.*

118 Chan and Evers in Chen and Evers (eds.) (1978), p.125.

119 *Ibid.*, p.129.

120 See P.W. Preston (1985), *New Trends in Development Theory.* See also Leo Panitch (1980), 'Recent Theorizations of Corporation: reflections on a growth industry', *British Journal of Sociology,* vol.31.

121 It is roughly the line Smith was pursuing.

122 Habermas (1971).

123 See, for example, Clive Hamilton (1983), 'Capitalist Industrialization in East Asia's Four Little Tigers', *Journal of Contemporary Asia,* 13.

124 See H.D. Evers, 'Group Conflict and Class Formation in South-East Asia' in H.D. Evers (ed.) (1980).

125 See Pandy (1980), pp.138–50.

126 Smith (1983), pp.128–30.

127 See also Ian Roxborough (1979), *Theories of Underdevelopment,* ch.8.

128 Hugh Tinker, 'The Nation-State in Asia' in Tivey (ed.) (1981). See also Lucian Pye (1967), *Southeast Asia's Political System,* p.37.

129 Pandy (1980), pp.114–26.

130 *Ibid.*, p.128.

131 See *ibid.*

132 See *ibid.*, ch.5.

133 Tinker in Tivey (ed.) (1981).

134 *Ibid.*, p.119.

135 A. McCoy in R. Jeffrey (ed.) (1981).

136 A. Reid in R. Jeffrey (ed.) (1981).

137 Lee Kam Hing in R. Jeffrey (ed.) (1981).

138 J.L.S. Girling (1981), 'The Bureaucratic Polity in Modernizing Societies', *Institute of South East Asian Studies Occasional Paper,* no.64.

139 *Ibid.*, p.39.

140 See also Michael Walter (1976), 'On Transitional Society', *National University of Singapore Sociology Working Paper,* no.53.

141 Feith in Wolfers (1976).

142 Berch Berberoglu (1983), 'The Class Nature of the State in Peripheral Social Formations', *Journal of Contemporary Asia* 13. (This is one of many interesting essays on class published in JCA.)

143 *Ibid.*, p.325.
144 *Ibid.*, p.330.

Bibliography

Allen, V. (1975), *Social Analysis: A Marxist Critique and Alternative*, London, Longmans.

Anderson, B. (1983), *Imagined Communities*, London, Verso.

Anderson, R.J. *et al.* (1985), *The Sociology Game*, London, Longmans.

Assad, T. (ed.) (1973), *Anthropology and the Colonial Encounter*, London.

Ayer, A.J. (1936), *Language, Truth and Logic*, London, Gollancz.

Bailey, Joe (1980), *Ideas and Intervention*, London, Routledge & Kegan Paul.

Baran, P. (1973), *The Political Economy of Growth*, Harmondsworth, Pelican.

Bauman, Z. (1976), *Towards a Critical Sociology*, London, Routledge & Kegan Paul.

Bauman, Z. (1978), *Hermeneutics and Social Science*, London, Hutchinson.

Bedlington, S.S. (1978), *Malaysia and Singapore: The Building of New Nation States*, Ithaca, Cornell U.P.

Bernstein, R. (1976), *The Restructuring of Social and Political Theory*, Oxford, Blackwell.

Bernstein, R. (1985), *Habermas and Modernity*, London, Polity.

Bienefeld, M. (1980), 'Dependency in the Eighties', *Bulletin of the Institute of Development Studies*, 12.

Bienefeld, M. and Godfrey M. (eds) (1982), *The Struggle for Development: National Strategies in an International Context*, London, John Wiley.

Blomstrom, M. and Heltne, Bjorne (1984), *Development Theory in Transition*, London, Zed.

Bloor, D. (1983), *Wittgenstein: A Social Theory of Knowledge*, London, Macmillan.

Boeke, J. (1953), *Economics and Economic Policy of Dual Societies*, New York, Institute of Pacific Relations.

Brenner, R. (1977), 'The Origins of Capitalist Development: a critique of neo-Smithian Marxism', *New Left Review*, vol.104.

Brewer, A. (1980), *Marxist Theories of Imperialism: A Critical Survey*, London, Routledge & Kegan Paul.

Brookfield, H. (1975), *International Development*, London, Methuen.

Brown, Norman O. (1959), *Life Against Death*, New York.

Bryant, C. (1985), *Positivism in Social Theory and Research*, London, Macmillan.

Cardoso, F.H. and Faletto E. (1979), *Dependency and Development in Latin America*, Berkeley and Los Angeles, California U.P.

Carroll, John (1980), *Sceptical Sociology*, London, Routledge & Kegan Paul.

Carver, T. (1975), *Karl Marx: Texts on Method*, Oxford, Blackwell.

Caute, D. (1978), *The Great Fear: The Anti-Communist Purges under Truman and Eisenhower*, London, Secker & Warburg.

Challiand, G. (1977), *Revolution in the Third World*, Hassocks, Harvester.

Chen, P. (ed.) (1983), *Singapore Development Policies and Trends*, Oxford U.P.

Chen, P. and Evers H.D. (eds) (1978), *Studies in ASEAN Sociology*, Singapore, Chopmen.

Chomsky, N. (1982), *Towards a New Cold War*, London, Sinclaire Browne.

Chua Beng Huat (1983), 'Reopening Ideological Discussion in Singapore', *Southeast Asian Journal of Social Sciences*, vol.11.

Clairmonte, F. (1960), *Economic Liberalism and Underdevelopment*, Bombay, Asia Publishing House.

Clammer, J. (1976), 'Wittgensteinianism in Social Science', *Sociological Review*.

Clammer, J. (1981), 'Modernization and Cultural Values: the paradoxes of transition in Singapore', in R. Vente *et al.* (eds), *Cultural Heritage versus Technological Development*, Singapore, McGraw-Hill.

Clements, K. P. (1980). 'From Right to Left in Development Theory', *Singapore Institute of Southeast Asian Studies*, Occasional Paper 61.

Comber, Leon (1983), *13 May 1969*, Kuala Lumpur, Heinemann.

Crick, B. (1980), *George Orwell*, Harmondsworth, Penguin.

Davidson, B. (1978), *Africa in Modern History*, London, Allen Lane.

Evers, H.D. (ed.) (1980), *Sociology of Southeast Asia: Readings on Social Change and Development*, Oxford U.P.

Fay, B. (1975), *Sociology Theory and Political Practice*, London, Allen & Unwin.

Filmer, P. *et al.* (eds) (1972), *New Directions in Sociological Theory*, London, Collier MacMillan.

Fisk, E.K. and Osman-Rani, H. (eds) (1982), *The Political Economy of Malaysia*, Kuala Lumpur, Oxford U.P.

Flew, A. (1975), *Thinking about Thinking*, London, Fontana.

Foster-Carter, A. (1979), 'Marxism versus Dependency? A Polemic', *Leeds Occasional Papers in Sociology*, no.8.

Foster-Carter, A. (1985), 'Development Theory Revived: Friedrich List Lives', *Inside Asia*, vol.5.

Frank, A.G. (1967), *Capitalism and Underdevelopment in Latin America*, New York, Monthly Review Press.

Frank, A.G. (1969), *Latin America: Underdevelopment or Revolution*, New York, Monthly Review Press.

Frank, A.G. (1972), *Lumpenbourgeoisie – Lumpendevelopment*, New York, Monthly Review Press.

Frank, A.G. (1975), *On Capitalist Underdevelopment*, Bombay, Oxford U.P.

Frank, A.G. (1976), *Economic Genocide in Chile*, Nottingham, Spokesman.

Frank, A.G. (1978), *Dependent Accumulation and Underdevelopment*, London, Macmillan.

Frank, A.G. (1984), *Critique and Anti-Critique*, London, Macmillan.

Furnivall, J.S.(1939), *Netherlands India: A Study of Plural Economy*, Cambridge U.P.

Furtado, C. (1965), *Diagnoses of the Brazilian Crisis*, Berkeley and Los Angeles, California U.P.

Gadamer, H.G. (1975), *Truth and Method*, London, Sheed & Ward.

Gadamer, H.G. (1976), *Philosophical Hermeneutics*, Berkeley, California University Press.

Galbraith, J.K. (1958), *The Affluent Society*, London, Hamish Hamilton.

Gellner, E. (1964), *Thought and Change*, London, Weidenfeld & Nicolson.

Gellner, R. (1979), *Words and Things*, London, Routledge & Kegan Paul.

George, T.L.S. (1973), *Lee Kuan Yew's Singapore*, London, Andre Deutsch.

Giddens, A. (1976), *New Rules of Sociological Method*, London, Hutchinson.

Giddens, A. (1979), *Central Problems in Social Theory*, London, Macmillan.

Giddens, A. (1982), *Profiles and Critiques in Social Theory*, London, Macmillan.

Girling, J.L.S. (1981), 'The Bureaucratic Polity in Modernizing Societies', *Singapore Institute of Southeast Asian Studies*, Occasional Paper, no.64.

Girvan, N. (1973), 'The Development of Dependency Economics in the Caribbean and Latin America: review and comparison', *Social and Economic Studies*, vol.22.

Habermass, J. (1971a), *Knowledge and Human Interests*, Boston, Beacon Press.

Habermas, J. (1971b), *Towards a Rational Society*, London, Heinemann.

Hall, J. (1981), *Diagnosis of Our Time*, London, Heinemann.

Halliday, J. (1977), 'Recession, Revolution and Metropolis Periphery Relations in East Asia with specific reference to Japan', *Journal of Contemporary Asia*, vol.7.

Halliday, J. (1980), 'Capitalism and Socialism in East Asia', *New Left Review*, vol.124.

Hamilton, C. (1983), 'Capitalist Industrialization in East Asia's Four Little Tigers', *Journal of Contemporary Asia*, vol.13.

Hamilton, P. (1974), *Knowledge and Social Structure*, London, Routledge & Kegan Paul.

Hassan, Riaz (ed.) (1976), *Singapore: Society in Transition*, Oxford U.P.

Hawthorn, G. (1976), *Enlightenment and Despair*, Cambridge University Press.

Held, D. (1980), *Introduction to Critical Theory*, London, Hutchinson.

Hermassi, Elbaki (1980), *The Third World Reassessed*, Berkeley, University of California Press.

Heyzer, Noleen (1983), 'International Production and Social Change', in Chen (ed.).

Higgot, R. and Robison, R. (eds) (1985), *Southeast Asia: Essays in the Political Economy of Structural Change*, London, Routledge & Kegan Paul.

Hollis, M. (1977), *Models of Man*, Cambridge University Press.

Hollis, M. and Nell, E.J. (1975), *Rational Economic Man*, Cambridge University Press.

Hoogvelt, Ankie (1982), *The Third World in Global Development*, London, Macmillan.

Husserl, Edmund (1970), *The Crisis of European Sciences and Transcendental Phenomenology*, Evanston III., Northwestern U.P.

Hynes, S. (ed.) (1971), *Twentieth Century Interpretations of 1984*, Englewood Cliffs, Prentice Hall.

Inglis, Brian (1976), *The Opium Wars*, London, Coronet.

Jay, Martin (1973), *The Dialectical Imagination*, Boston, Little Brown.

Jeffrey, R. (ed.) (1981), *Asia: The Winning of Independence*, London, Macmillan.

Kerr, Clark et al. (1960), *Industrialism and Industrial Man*, Harmondsworth, Penguin.

Kilminster, R. (1975), 'On the structure of critical thinking', *Leeds Occasional Papers in Sociology*, no.2.

Kilminster, R. (1979), *Praxis and Method*, London, Routledge & Kegan Paul.

Kitching, G. (1982), *Development and Underdevelopment in Historical Perspective*, London, Methuen.

Kurihara, K. (1968), 'The Dynamic Impact of History on Keynesian Theory', in V. Eagly (ed.), *Events, Ideology and Economic Theory*, Detroit, Wayne State U.P.

Laclau, E. (1971), 'Feudalism and Capitalism in Latin America', *New Left Review*, vol.67.

Laslett, P. and Runciman, W.G. (eds) (1962), *Politics, Philosophy and Society*, Series 2, Oxford, Blackwell.

Laslett, P. and Runciman, W.G. (eds) (1967), *Politics, Philosophy and Society*, Series 3, Oxford, Blackwell.

Lewis, A. (1955), *The Theory of Economic Growth*, London, Allen & Unwin.

Leys, C. (1977), 'Underdevelopment and Dependency: Critical Notes', *Journal of Contemporary Asia*, vol. 7.

Limqueco, P. (1983), 'Contradictions of Development in ASEAN', *Journal of Contemporary Asia*, vol.13.

Lukes, S. (1977), *Essays in Social Theory*, London, Macmillan.

McCarthy, T. (1978), *The Critical Theory of Jugen Habermas*, London, MIT Press.

McDonald, H. (1980), *Suharto's Indonesia*, London, Fontana.

MacIntyre, A. (1970), *Marcuse*, London, Fontana.

MacIntyre, A. (1971), *Against the Self Images of the Age*, London, Duckworth.

Macpherson, C.B. (1966), *The Real World of Democracy*, Oxford University Press.

Macpherson, C.B. (1973), *Democratic Theory: Essays in Retrieval*, Oxford University Press.

Maddison, A. (1971), *Class Structure and Economic Growth*, New York, Norton.

Marx, K. (1964), *Pre-Capitalist Economic Formations*, London, Lawrence & Wishart.

May, B. (1981), *The Third World Calamity*, London, Routledge & Kegan Paul.

Means, G.P. (ed.) (1976), *Development and Underdevelopment in Southeast Asia*, Canadian Council for South East Asian Studies.

Merton, R. (1968), *Social Theory and Social Structure*, Chicago, Free Press.

Milliband, R. and Saville, J. (eds) (1977), *The Socialist Register*, London, Merlin.

Mills, Wright, C. (1959), *The Sociological Imagination*, New York, Oxford U.P.

Mitzman, A. (1973), *Sociology and Estrangement*, New York, Knopf.

Moore, Barrington (1950), *Soviet Politics – The Dilemma of Power: The Role of Ideas in Social Change*, Cambridge, Mass., Harvard University Press.

Moore, Barrington (1954), *Terror and Progress USSR: Some Sources of Change and Stability in The Soviet Dictatorship*, Cambridge, Mass., Harvard University Press.

Moore, Barrington (1958), *Political Power and Social Theory*, Cambridge, Mass., Harvard University Press.

Moore, Barrington (1967), *The Social Origins of Dictatorship and Democracy*, Harmondsworth, Penguin.

Moore, Barrington, (1972), *Reflections on the Cases of Human Misery and on Certain Proposals to Eliminate Them*, Harmondsworth, Penguin.

Moore, Barrington, (1978) *Injustice: The Social Bases of Obedience and Revolt*, London, Macmillan.

Moore, Barrington, Jnr (1967), *The Social Origins of Dictatorship and Democracy*, London, Allen Lane.

Myrdal, G. (1970), *The Challenge of World Poverty*, London, Allen Lane.

Nagel, Ernest (1961), *The Structure of Science*, New York, Harcourt Brace Jovanovich.

Nairn, Tom (1977), *The Breakup of Britain*, London, New Left Books.

Neurath, Otto (1944), *Foundations of the Social Sciences*, University of Chicago Press.

O'Neill, John (1972), *Sociology as Skin Trade*, London, Heinemann.

Orwell, George (1937), *The Road to Wigan Pier*, Victor Gollancz.

Osborne, Milton (1979), *South East Asia*, London, Unwin.

Outhwaite, W. (1975), *Understanding Social Life: The Method Called Verstehen*, London, Allen & Unwin.

Oxaal, I. *et al.* (eds) (1975), *Beyond the Sociology of Development*, London, Routledge & Kegan Paul.

Palma, G. (1978), 'Dependency: a formal theory of underdevelopment or a methodology for the analysis of concrete situations of underdevelopment', *World Development*, vol.6.

Pandy, B.N. (1980), *South and South-East Asia 1945–79: Problems and Policies*, London, Macmillan.

Pang Keng Fong (1984), 'The Malay Royals', unpublished Academic Exercise, Department of Sociology, National University of Singapore.

Panitch, Leo (1980), 'Recent Theorizations of Corporatism', *British Journal of Sociology*, vol.13.

Parkin, F. (1979), *Marxism and Class Theory: A Bourgeois Critique*, London, Tavistock.

Passmore, J. (1970), *The Perfectibility of Man*, London, Duckworth.

Petras, James (1980), 'Neo-Fascism: Capital Accumulation and Class Struggle in the Third World', *Journal of Contemporary Asia*, vol.10.

Pluvier, J.M. (1977), *South East Asia Colonialism to Independence*, Oxford U.P.

Popper, K. (1945), *The Open Society and its Enemies*, London, Routledge & Kegan Paul.

Popper, K. (1957), *The Poverty of Historicism*, London, Routledge & Kegan Paul.

Popper, K. (1959), *The Logic of Scientific Discovery*, London, Hutchinson.

Popper, K. (1963), *Conjectures and Refutations*, London, Routledge & Kegan Paul.

Preston, P.W. (1982), *Theories of Development*, London, Routledge & Kegan Paul.

Preston, P.W. (1983), 'A Critique of Some Elements of the Residual Common Sense of Development Studies', *Cultures et Développement*, vol.xv, no.3.

Preston, P.W. (1985), *New Trends in Development Theory*, London, Routledge & Kegan Paul.

Preston, P.W. (1986), *Making Sense of Development*, London, Routledge & Kegan Paul.

Pye, Lucien (1967), *Southeast Asia's Political Systems*, Englewood Cliffs, Prentice Hall.

Robertson, A.F. (1980), *People and the State: An Anthropology of Planned Development*, Cambridge University Press.

Roxborough, Ian (1979), *Theories of Underdevelopment*, London, Macmillan.

Rushdie, Salman (1981), *Midnight's Children*, London, Picador.

Rushdie, Salman (1982), *Shame*, London, Picador.

Russell, Bertrand (1927), *An Outline of Philosophy*, London.

Sachs, Ignacy (1976), *The Discovery of the Third World*, London, MIT Press.

Seers, D. (1963), 'The Limitations of the Special Case', *Oxford Bulletin of Statistics*.

Seers, D. (ed) (1981), *Dependency Theory: A Critical Reassessment*, London, Frances Pinter.

Seton-Watson, H. (1977), *Nations and Nation States*, London, Methuen.

Skillen, A. (1977), *Ruling Illusions: Philosophy and the Social Order*, Hassocks, Harvester.

Slater, P. (1977), *The Origins and Significance of the Frankfurt School*, London, Routledge & Kegan Paul.

Smith, A.D. (1973), *The Concept of Social Change*, London, Routledge & Kegan Paul.

Smith, A.D. (1976), *Social Change: Social Theory and Historical Processes*, London, Routledge & Kegan Paul.

Smith, A.D. (1983), *State and Nation in the Third World*, Brighton, Wheatsheaf.

Smith, Dennis (1985), *Barrington Moore: Violence, Morality and Political Change*, London, Macmillan.

Streeten, P. (1981), *Development Perspectives*, London, Macmillan.

Taylor, C. (1971), 'Interpretation and the Sciences of Man', *Review of Metaphysics*, vol.25.

Therborne, G. (1970), 'The Frankfurt School', *New Left Review*, vol. 63.

Thompson, J.B. and Held, D. (eds) (1982), *Habermas: Critical Debates*, London, Macmillan.

Thorne, C. (1986), *The Far Eastern War*, London, Counterpoint.

Tivey, L. (ed.) (1981), *The Nation State*, Oxford, Martin Robertson.

Tudor, A. (1982), *Beyond Empiricism*, London, Routledge & Kegan Paul.

United Nations (1951), *Measures for the Economic Development of Underdeveloped Countries*.

VanNieuwenhuijze, C.A.O. (1982), *Development Begins at Home*, Oxford, Pergamon.

Walter, Michael (1976), 'On Transitional Society', *National University of Singapore Sociology Working Paper*, no.53.

Warnock, Geoffrey (1969), *English Philosophy Since 1900*, Oxford U.P.

Warnock, Mary (1970), *Existentialism*, Oxford U.P.

Williams, R. (ed.) (1974), *George Orwell: a collection of critical essays*, Englewood Cliffs, Prentice Hall.

Williams, R. (1976), *Keywords*, London, Fontana.

Williams, R. (1979), *Politics and Letters*, London, New Left Books.

Winch, Peter, (1958), *The Idea of a Social Science and Its Relation to Philosophy*, London, Routledge & Kegan Paul.

Wittgenstein, L. (1961), *Tractatus Logico-Philosophicus*, London, Routledge & Kegan Paul.

Wittgenstein, L. (1974), *Philosophical Investigations*, Oxford, Blackwell.

Wolfers, E.P. (ed.) (1976), *Australia's Northern Neighbours*, The Australian Institute of International Affairs and Hawaii University Press.

Wong, J. (1979), *The ASEAN Economies in Perspectives*, London, Macmillan.

Worsley, P. (1984), *The Three Worlds: Culture and World Development*, London, Weidenfeld & Nicolson.

Index

Adorno, 67, 68
Africa, 12, 26, 84, 179, 209
Allen, 24
Allende, 25
Althusser, 48
Anderson, 78, 182, 183, 189, 191–9
Aquino, 186
Asia, 84
Australia, 88

Baran, 16-20, 143–54
Bauman, 5, 61
Bedlington, 203–5
Begin, 25
Beiner, 75
Bendix, 109
Berberoglu, 223
Berger, 48
Bergson, 66
Berkley, 32
Bernstein, 44, 47, 48, 55, 71, 72
Bienefeld, 156, 159, 162–5, 172, 174, 176–7
Blair, 137
Boeke, xi, 77, 82, 83–91, 95–8, 178
Booth, 133, 143
Bowring, 173–4
Brenner, 17, 18, 151–3
Brookfield, 9, 25, 95
Brunei, 181
Burchill, 138
Burma, 186–7, 199, 206, 217

Cardoso, 18, 19, 158, 162
Castro, 130
Catley, 211
Chan, 113–19, 169, 212, 214
Chen, xiii, 111–21
Chicago, 149
China, 83, 105–6, 170, 172, 216
Chomsky, xiii, 48–9, 136

Clairmonte, 21
Cooley, 48
Crick, 136–8
critical rationalism, 39, 41–2
critical theory, 31, 65, 71–4, 80–1
Cuba, 149

Davidaon, 26
Descartes, 45
Deutscher, 137–8
development theory, ix, x, xi, xv, 1, 2, 5, 11, 12, 27–8, 42–3, 76–8, 81
Dilthey, 61, 66
Domar, 9
dual society, 82, 84–6, 88
Durkheim, x
Dutch East Indies, 85–6

Embree, 83, 97
empiricism, 31–2, 39, 102
England, 103
Enlightenment, 68–9, 70, 102, 182, 194
Evers, xi, 83–99, 169, 212, 214, 216

Faletto, 19
Fay, 9, 43, 63–5
Feith, 174, 208, 210–12, 222
Fisk, 111, 122–4
France, 104
Frank, xiii, 17–20, 129, 131, 140–55, 161
Friedman, 77
Foster-Carter, 140, 164
Furnivall, xi, 77, 82–3, 85, 91–8, 178
Furtado, 2, 14–15, 149, 158, 163

Galbraith, 148, 213–14
Gandhi, 87, 91
Geertz, 82–3, 97
Gellner, 3, 26, 31, 42, 103, 109, 179, 191–4, 196, 208–9, 213–14

Germany, 24, 66, 104–5
Giddens, 36, 42, 54–6, 75–6, 160
Girling, 222
Girvan, 14
Godfrey, 164
Greene, 41–2
Greer, 138–9
Grunberg, 66

Habermas, 7, 21–3, 41, 51, 65, 67–75,
  81, 102, 129, 208, 214
Halliday, 171–6
Hamilton, 165–76
Harrod, 9, 11
Hayek, 130
Hegel, 52, 65
Heidegger, 46
Held, 73
Heng Samarin, 25
hermeneutics, 36, 45, 60–3, 80
Heyzer, 113, 115, 117, 119, 120–1
Higgins, 96, 11–12, 124–8
Higgot, 155
Hitler, 130
Hong Kong, 168–72
Hoogvelt, 19
Horkheimer, 66–8
Huks, 201
Hume, 32, 42
Hungary, 66
Husserl, 45–7, 52, 78

ideology, xiv, 1, 4, 6–8, 15, 18, 23, 25–6,
  43, 55–9, 70, 72, 76–7, 82, 129, 158,
  160–1, 178–9
India, 83, 87, 106–7, 184, 205
Indonesia, 87, 90, 186–7, 199, 201–3,
  211, 217–19, 221–3

Japan, 83, 104–5, 167, 176
Jay, 66
Jeffrey, 221

Kant, 51, 65
Kenyatta, 25
Keynes, 19, 21
Khomeini, 130
Kilminster, 130
KMT, 106, 168
Koentjaraningrat, 96
Korea, 167
Kurihara, 10

Laclau, 151–2
Lamb, 164
Latin America, xiii, 14–15, 77, 84, 98,
  133, 143–9, 179
Lenin, 130
Levi-Strauss, 48
Lewis, 10
Limqueco, 165–6, 172
logical positivism, 32–3, 40, 44, 50–1,
  61, 69

McCoy, 48
McCarthy, 41, 69
MacIntyre, 56–63, 73, 78
Malaysia, 112, 121, 123–7, 186–7, 199,
  203–5, 217–19, 222–3
Malinowski, 97
Mao, 130
Marcos, 186
Marcuse, 67–8, 73, 80, 101
Marx, 17–19, 25, 40, 49, 65, 67–8, 73,
  80–1, 101, 129–30, 140, 151, 153,
  157, 161, 214
Mead, 48
Meir, 25
Merton, 37–8, 75
Mill, J. S., 10, 130
Mills, 37, 101–2
Moore, xi, 100–10
Myrdal, 12, 13, 24, 97, 122, 212

Nagel, 33–8, 46, 75
Nairn, 191–4, 197–8
nation, 106, 141, 179, 188–9, 194–5
nationstate, 79, 167, 180–4, 190–1, 193,
  196, 198–9, 200, 207, 210, 212, 214–
  15, 218, 220, 224
Neurath, 33, 38
NIC, xiv, 155–9, 162–3, 166–7, 170–1,
  174, 176–7
Nietzsche, 66
North America, 88
Nyrere, 25

Orwell, xiii, 130, 136–40, 144, 146, 149
Orridge, 181, 190, 193, 209
Osborne, 185

Pakistan, 186
Palma, 18–19, 151, 153, 162
Pandy, 185, 220–1
PAP, xiii, 112–15, 117–21, 205–6, 222
phenomenology, 44–7, 56

Philippines, 185, 199, 205, 211, 216–19, 221–3
physicalism, 33
Pinochet, 25
Plato, 40
plural society, 82, 85, 91–4
Pluvier, 185
political writer, xiii, 129, 131, 134, 136, 142–3, 147, 152, 154
Pol Pot, 25, 216
Popper, 38–42, 130
pragmatism, 69
Prebisch, 14
psychoanalysis, 67, 71, 74

Reagan, 134
Reid, 201–2, 208
Rex, 97, 109
Ricardo, 130
Robison, 155
Roosevelt, 13
Rostow, 9, 100, 158
Rushdie, 186
Russell, 32, 34, 49
Russia, 105–6

Saussure, 49
Schutz, 46–8, 63, 78
Scott, 78
Seers, 12
Seton-Watson, 181–3, 190, 197
Singapore, 112–21, 167–71, 174, 186, 199, 204–6, 211–13, 217–18, 222–3
Smith, A., 17, 153
Smith, A. D., 189, 190, 198, 208–16
Smith, D., 102
South Africa, 91
South Korea, 168–74, 211, 217–18, 222–3
Southeast Asia, ix–xiv, 30, 77–8, 83–4, 87–8, 95–8, 112, 156, 165, 179, 184–5, 188, 193, 199, 205, 207, 210–19, 224
Spencer, 130

Stalin, 59
state, 13, 15, 21–2, 135, 141, 156–7, 163, 174, 179, 189, 210
Streeten, 12, 20–1, 25
structuralism, 48

Taiwan, 167–9, 172–4, 217–18, 222–3
Taylor, 59–63, 71
terminological empiricism, 33
Thailand, 188, 199, 206, 211, 217–18, 222–3
Thatcher, 139
Thompson, 138
Thorne, 78
Tinker, 217–18, 220
Tivey, 179, 181, 189

UK, xii, 24, 103–4, 109–10, 181
USA, 8, 11, 24, 47, 67, 91, 101, 103–4, 133–5, 143, 168, 178, 181–2, 188, 199, 201, 221
USSR, 11, 24, 134, 139

Veblen, 13
verstehen, 46–7, 56
Vienna Circle, 32–3
Vietnam, 135, 170–1, 217

Wain, 136, 138, 150
Wallerstein, 17–18, 20–1, 143
Warren, 151, 156, 161
Weber, x, 45–6, 49, 57–8, 61, 75, 86, 104
Weil, 65
Weimar Germany, 65–6
Wertheim, 97
Western Europe, 8, 129, 176, 178–9
Williams, 137
Winch, 48, 52–7, 62–3, 79
Wittgenstein, 49–53, 56–7, 78, 144
Worsley, xiii, 78, 132, 140–2

Yamada, 86, 96